A HOLE WHERE MY HEART SHOULD BE

A HOLE WHERE MY HEART SHOULD BE

Lifting the Curse of Intergenerational Trauma: A Memoir

MICHELE LEEMBRUGGEN

Melbourne, Victoria
2024

A HOLE WHERE MY HEART SHOULD BE
Lifting the Curse of Intergenerational Trauma
A Memoir

Copyright © 2024 by Michele Leembruggen

All rights reserved. Apart from any fair dealing for the purposes of private study, research, criticism or review permitted under the Copyright Act 1968, no part may be stored or reproduced by any process without express written permission of the copyright owner. For more information contact the author: michleem@bigpond.com

The information in this book is intended to be educational and not for diagnosis, prescription, or treatment of any health disorder whatsoever. This information should not replace consultation with a competent healthcare provider. The author is no way liable for any misuse of the material.

All names and identifying details have been changed to protect the privacy of the individuals quoted in this book.

First edition published July 2024

Design by Marina Drukman
Edited by Michael Benge

ISBN 978-0-9756136-1-0 paperback
ISBN 978-0-9756136-0-3 e-book

For Carmel and Mary

TABLE OF CONTENTS

Introduction 9

Part I

Chapter 1 — Falling Apart 15
Chapter 2 — Tuala 19
Chapter 3 — Rain in February 25
Chapter 4 — The Ski Shack 29
Chapter 5 — War Zone 35
Chapter 6 — Mac 43
Chapter 7 — Maria Callas 51
Chapter 8 — Green-eyed Monster 55
Chapter 9 — Little Dance 59
Chapter 10 — The Staircase Spur 63
Chapter 11 — Meetings and Scissors 69
Chapter 12 — The Bee 73
Chapter 13 - Marbles 79
Chapter 14 — The Jacaranda Tree 83
Chapter 15 — The Imp 89
Chapter 16 — Soft-boiled Eggs 93
Chapter 17 — Black and White 99
Chapter 18 — The Fox Cubs 103
Chapter 19 — Lolita 111
Chapter 20 — Teachers 115
Chapter 21 — The Bus 119
Chapter 22 — The Tennis Match 125
Chapter 23 — Music Therapy 129
Chapter 24 — Black Cherries and Champagne 137
Chapter 25 — Music Camp 141

Chapter 26 — The Rocks 147
Chapter 27 — Rivals 151
Chapter 28 — The Storm 155
Chapter 29 — Tug of War 163
Chapter 30 — The Sergeant Major 167
Chapter 31 — The Psychiatrist 175
Chapter 32 — The Scream 179

Part II

Chapter 33 — The 'Wild West' 187
Chapter 34 — Instant Family 191
Chapter 35 — Old Ivory 197
Chapter 36 — Big Sister 203
Chapter 37 — The Red Sea 207
Chapter 38 — Borderland 213
Chapter 39 — Matilda 217
Chapter 40 — The Distant Shore 225
Chapter 41 — The School of Life 229
Chapter 42 — Mount Sugarloaf 235
Chapter 43 — The Pier 239
Chapter 44 — Guilty 245
Chapter 45 — The Happy Nun 249
Chapter 46 — The Puppy Farm 257
Chapter 47 — The Shopping Plaza 261
Chapter 48 — The Hermit 267
Chapter 49 — Survivor Guilt 271
Chapter 50 — The Chameleon 275
Chapter 51 — On the Street Where You Live 281
Chapter 52 — The Curse 287
Chapter 53 — Play School 289
Chapter 54 — The Jailor 295

Chapter 55 — The Tea Party........................ 299
Chapter 56 — Brian................................ 303
Chapter 57 — Surrender............................ 307
Chapter 58 — Venus Again......................... 315
Chapter 59 — Dear Micheles....................... 325

Epilogue.. 329
References and resources.......................... 335

INTRODUCTION

This is my message in a bottle, my SOS.

She didn't even spell my name correctly, although it's an easy mistake to make—Mum and Dad had omitted the second 'L' in Michelle.

During the time I was seeing Ronnie the therapist, she had got it right. Her bright greetings—"Hi Michele"—had always twinkled reassuringly from the screen and I could almost hear her speaking my name in warm, honey-coloured tones and see her eyes smiling encouragingly into mine.

But in this, her last email, she had begun *Dear Michelle* and signed off, *Kind regards*, so polite, so impersonal. I remembered back to the very first email she had sent 18 months before, when she hadn't known me, known 'us' from Adam. I hadn't appreciated then that the dawn was about to break but now we were strangers again, worse than strangers, and the curse remained unbroken.

If I could count myself a real, true 'borderline', I would have been speeding recklessly up the highway to her house, 200 kilometres away. I would have been chucking a brick through her bedroom window by 11pm, screaming her name over and over, until she finally stepped into the night and offered to take me back.

The scene played itself out on the small stage behind my eyes as I lay on my bed, crying desperately and clutching at my chest, grabbing where my heart should be. As I jumped up to grab the car keys, fear paralysed my legs and unable to move forward, I threw myself back onto the bed. A voice in my head told me I was being pathetic as it watched the tug of war from somewhere deep inside. I could feel its eyes rolling.

The scene in my head continued. Cops were suddenly dragging me away. I'd torn her dark purple blouse and white buttons littered the porch step like small, hard hail stones. "Please don't send me away, I'll die. I love you," I would throw over my shoulder.

"OK then fuck off, I hate you, you bitch," I would cry when she failed to intervene. "Get OFF me you cow," I would scream at the faceless policewoman as she hurled me into the divvy van. "Ronnie," I would sob.

I didn't act out. For as long as I can remember I had pushed my emotions away, stuffed them down to writhe and fester because they displeased my mother. One day, when in her late 40s and crazy with rage, Mum had climbed the drainpipe to the first-floor balcony of her boyfriend's flat because he had refused to let her in. Even as an adult, Mum's 'crazy' behaviour had the power to shock and shame and I renewed my personal pact to be chalk to her cheese.

For many years I believed I had succeeded—I didn't act the hysterical teenager, even when I was one. My dysfunction, the trauma she had invested in me, was locked away in the many-roomed house of my mind, faint screams and groans ignored and then forgotten. That is, until Ronnie came.

As the night crawled toward the dawn, the fantasy of confronting Ronnie played out in my head, like a silent film stuck on an endless loop. I read and re-read her email, and each time I saw the two 'Ls', rage and grief washed me into ever deeper despair. The 'kind regards' laughed cynically at my suffering. God, what a naïve idiot I had been.

After all the black nights and empty days since Ronnie abandoned me, I still can't believe she has gone. Parts of me are still in shock and grieving. They can't believe she left after all her reassurances she would be there for me, for them, for us, for as long as we needed.

PART I

1

FALLING APART

When I started trauma therapy with Ronnie in February 2020, I was 56 years of age and it had been six years since I had begun to fall apart. I had managed to hold it together for another three, but was then forced to quit my job as a senior sustainability officer, too anxious and exhausted to continue. According to one internet expert, all sufferers of quiet borderline personality disorder (Q-BPD) break down sooner or later. When I first heard about it though, I had no idea what borderline personality disorder (BPD) was or that I suffered the quiet/discouraged/high-functioning version.

The falling apart began in 2014 with my last period. The steady flow of oestrogen, the elixir of youth, stopped, and its lack caused crippling anxiety that added its weight to years of chronic depression, causing the carefully constructed façade that read 'Move on, nothing to see here' to crumble.

The menopause caused my physical health to decline too, and in 2015 I was diagnosed with Hashimoto Thyroiditis, an autoimmune disease that causes one's own immune system to destroy the thyroid gland. Western medicine offers no 'cure' and so I researched natural ways to heal and found that addressing the 'root cause' sometimes induced remission. I followed the advice of the Thyroid Pharmacist, Izabella Wentz, who had developed Hashimoto as a young adult after being exposed as a child to radioactive fallout from the Chernobyl nuclear disaster.

The protocol involved giving up gluten and dairy and eliminating 19 foods from my diet that a sensitivity test identified. I found a GP who practiced functional/complimentary medicine and she ordered poo, wee, blood and saliva tests to identify potential root causes, such as candida, mould, the Epstein Bar virus, the MTHFR gene, which she referred to as 'the mother fucker gene', and mineral imbalances and deficiencies. I also undertook a sleep test that confirmed I suffer from sleep apnoea, and so started using a CPAP machine. One root cause I didn't care to acknowledge was chronic stress. I was not ready to 'go there', and so I chose instead to work through the more tangible, physical causes. I was afraid to stop running.

One blustery April afternoon of the following year, 2016, the slide intensified with the arrival of my first horse, a beautiful chestnut mare. Owning her was the fulfillment of a cherished childhood dream. But she was my undoing, the proverbial straw. She was also an instrument of my resurrection.

I limped along feeling more and more drained until the following year, 2017, when I woke one morning to find I could no longer bully myself out of bed. I didn't have the heart to face another minute at the place I worked, with its unhealthy, bureaucratic, fear-driven work culture. I called in sick, intending to take a few days off but never returned. I became dependent on my partner Matilda and felt vulnerable. What if she left me or died? Homelessness was my greatest fear and it was the next stop, the end of the line.

Living with the effects of undiagnosed childhood trauma had inexorably worn me down. All my adult life I had maintained a façade of competence, had completed university degrees and landed respectable jobs but these shows of normality had only been possible by suppressing my internal dysfunction using a combination of social avoidance, alcohol and dissociation.

These unhealthy survival strategies were unconscious, and I was not even aware I was mentally ill. To the outside world I appeared functional but inside was perpetual emptiness and chaos. Without a foundation of healthy relational skills, navigating personal and professional relationships was perplexing, exhausting, and sometimes frightening. It took a lot of energy and nerve to survive in the world with an emotional deficit. Eventually I ran out of both.

After 11 months of not working, I felt well enough to return but in a lesser role in a different organisation and the thrill of creating solutions to complex, environmental problems gave way to the tedium of administrative work, which is not my forte. The culture at the new workplace was healthier though, so I told myself I could stick at it until retirement.

Despite all the physiological changes and healthier working conditions, my anxiety levels began to escalate again. The lack of oestrogen left me feeling insubstantial and porous, like my body was inexorably evaporating. Ordinary sounds, like a car door shutting caused me to startle. Constantly on edge, the barrage of everyday noises increased the intensity of my distress, and I felt I was under perpetual attack, about to die at any second. My grip on the tenuous shore of everyday life was slipping again. And that is when I discovered Ronnie and trauma therapy.

2

TUALA

As a child, I had only ever been on the occasional trail ride but had fallen deeply in love with horses, as some girls inexplicably do. I had poured over big picture books of horse breeds and tack, read the *Silver Brumby* and *Flicka* series and played *National Velvet* with my equally enamoured twin girlfriends.

One day, after years of psychotherapy, feeling disillusioned and impatient, I had decided to quit and spend 'therapy' money instead on learning to ride horses, before I grew too old. Horses would now be my 'therapy', as it was time to put fun before 'work', so in 2012, at the age of 48, I started weekly dressage lessons at a riding school in the Yarra Valley. Four years later, brimming with confidence and excitement and with proffered support from Gene, a work colleague who had evented as a teen in Belgium and months of obsessive searching, I bought my very own horse.

Her pedigree name is appropriately, Tullow's Turn Back Time. Her everyday name is Tuala, which means 'the people's princess' in gallic. The 'princess' was a nine-year-old Irish Sport Horse mare, bred for eventing, a mix of three-quarters thoroughbred with one-quarter Irish draught horse, endowing her with a deep chest and beautiful, muscular curves.

There is a saying among horse owners, 'chestnut mare beware'. The day after Tuala arrived at her new home after an eight-hour truck journey from Gippsland, I knew something wasn't right with her although I dismissed my intuitive warning system. She had seemed calm, gentle and engaged when I'd groomed, tacked her up and ridden her before buying her, but now Gene and I stood side by side open-mouthed, our bemusement turning to concern and then fear as Tuala frantically galloped around us, attached to the lunge rope, bucking and screaming her lungs out. We couldn't work out how to make her stop. Her frantic behaviour went on for 10 minutes until, sweating and heaving, she finally slowed to a distracted walk. A couple of days later, Gene mounted her and she reared. Wide-eyed Gene jumped off, explaining a couple of horses she'd once trained had reared and fallen over backward—one of them, she was convinced, trying to crush her.

As the days passed, my confidence ebbed away, until the idea I would ever mount and ride Tuala seemed ridiculous. My dream was galloping away and I was stuck with a 'crazy' horse I didn't have the skill or guts to ride and paying a fortune for the privilege. I was advised to send her back but couldn't bring myself to do it as she was ultimately my mistake and my responsibility, but I also felt overwhelmed at the thought of keeping her.

A week later, I found a trainer who specialised in 'problem horses'. Tuala's intractable metal shoes were removed and she was rested for a year. The rich Gippsland pasture had caused a bout of laminitis, a dreaded, extremely painful hoof condition caused by too much sugar in grass designed to fatten dairy cattle.

Over the ensuing years I would pay for yet more riding lessons on school horses, which added to my anxiety rather than re-building my confidence, subscribe to a plethora of online training courses and obsessively research and try numerous calming supplements. Nothing soothed Tuala though and my anxiety became worse and worse until the thought of even taking her out of her paddock was overwhelming.

I knew horses picked up on anxiety—enough horsey people had helpfully pointed this out. If only I thought, I could rationalise away the fear but it lives in the ancient part of our brain, the amygdala not the pre-frontal cortex and rather than calming her down, I was a tuning fork for her anxiety and she mine. We were too alike, sharing the same 'feminine energy' as one horse 'therapist' put it—insecure, needy and clingy, yet intelligent, independent and adaptive, and empathic, gentle and sensitive.

Looking back to those early years with Tuala, I now appreciate I was doing a lot that was right. Today in 2023 after three years of trauma therapy we have built a stronger connection as I am more confident, however there is still something 'wrong' with her and I recently discovered the cause. Radiographs identified a congenital abnormality of the sixth cervical vertebra, called equine complex vertebral malformation (ECVM) and severe kissing spine. The abnormality and degeneration of her spine cause her pain and an understandable aversion to being saddled and ridden. The vet surmised she was already damaged when I bought her and recommended she be retired. Three weeks ago, in October 2023, she moved to a beautiful property, where she will live out her days as a horse in a herd of mares like her—roaming and grazing, sleeping under the starry sky with her 'people', living the life she was designed to live.

It was during the days of struggle with Tuala that one day in early January 2020, when I was on annual leave from my admin role, I ran into a fellow horse owner who I had met at a natural horsemanship clinic the previous year. I had taken Tuala for groundwork lessons, hoping to find her 'inner horse' there, and had met Lisa. We had much in common, including autoimmune diseases and a history of childhood trauma. After the clinic ended however, I had not given our encounter any more thought until we serendipitously ran into each other again, on that warm January morning.

We chatted in the pleasantly cool stable as Lisa brushed the black, silky tail of her bay pony and I told her of my continuing struggle with anxiety. Since I had seen Lisa at the clinic, she had suffered a serious health crisis and discovered a new trauma therapy, which she recommended in glowing terms, confident it would cure my anxiety—and in only three sessions. Lisa had gained an enormous sense of relief and had made a complete recovery. The method sounded almost too good to be true.

The next morning, I undertook a Google search and found a list of practitioners. I paid as much attention to the photos as to their qualifications and experience, letting my intuition evaluate their suitability—did they look kind or cold, trustworthy or full of themselves, judgemental or empathetic? My chest tightened when I viewed the photos of men, but I stopped scrolling at the photo of a middle-aged woman with black hair, cut in a pixie style. The photo showed clear grey eyes and a warm if tentative smile. I continued scrolling but finding no one else who piqued my interest, returned to her entry.

The notes accompanying her photo said she also practiced the Emotional Freedom Technique (EFT), otherwise known as 'tapping', and Havening. I'd had no experience of EFT—in fact I'd never even heard of it—but I'd had a few sessions of

Havening a couple of years before and found it very effective. I had thought it advantageous that she had multiple strings to her therapy bow and so I scrutinised her photo again.

I could tell she was empathetic. There was uncertainty too, in the slight parting of her lips, and I wondered if she had it all together. There was vulnerability in the crumpled collar of her white linen shirt, and while she was mature in years, she also exuded an air of something I couldn't quite put my finger on: innocence perhaps, or candour?

It was a few days after my conversation with Lisa and I was in bed, perusing on my computer the list of potential practitioners, a cup of Earl Grey tea steaming fragrantly on the bedside table. Maisie, our little calico rescue cat was pressed snuggly against my side, purring gently, and Pepper, our big Maine coon, was hanging off the end of the bed snoring quietly, like a leopard on a branch.

I dialled Ronnie's number and after three rings a warm, receptive voice said, "Hello". I told her about my conversation with Lisa and that I was interested in trauma therapy. Ronnie sounded open to the idea and asked if I wouldn't mind telling her a little of my story. I rattled off a list of childhood traumas and she commented sounding impressed, that I seemed 'integrated'. I laughed self-consciously at her praise, saying dismissively, "I've done a lot of therapy over the years," but had no idea what she meant.

Ronnie was on her annual holiday, so we scheduled the first session for mid-February. Before then she advised, it would be useful to see her Feldenkrais practitioner friend because it would help my "hippocampus to switch on". I had no idea what that meant either but intrigued, I agreed to make an appointment. For the first time in years, I felt hope flutter like a soft-winged bird in my chest.

I got up, dressed in my horsey gear of comfy riding tights,

old tee shirt and battered leather riding boots, and headed out to Arthurs Creek in Melbourne's outer northeast, 50 minutes from home, to Tuala. I made the trip a couple of times a week and looked forward to leaving the inner city for the green rolling hills, fresh country air and sound of magpies and rosellas living their best lives.

I've heard it said, 'you get the horse you need, not the horse you want', and the stress and strain of learning to manage Tuala finally led me to the therapy I so desperately needed to heal.

3

RAIN IN FEBRUARY

The day of my first session with Ronnie was rainy and humid. I drove the two kilometres to the neighbouring suburb of North Fitzroy, made a sprint from the car and pressed the buzzer by the front door of the old house, made ugly by its dirty, dark grey façade.

A balding man in smart trousers and open-necked checked shirt frowned as he let me in before quickly disappearing. I walked down the hall to a small, open waiting room and sat in an old, slightly shabby armchair. Defensively I grabbed a magazine, opened it at random and then peered over the top, to take in the dim lighting, the kitchenette to my left and a consulting room opposite. I could hear the quiet murmur of voices and strained to discern what was being said. The man who'd let me in had mysteriously vanished, I assumed into another consulting room.

Suddenly there was the rattle of a key in the front door and a figure shrouded in a translucent raincoat and grasping the handle of a dripping umbrella entered the dim hallway.

She shook and shut the umbrella as she turned and bustled down the hall toward me.

Instinctively, I knew it was her, Ronnie, but had a sudden misgiving. She looked older and more confident than the woman in the photo I had so carefully scrutinised. I felt a fleeting sense of foreboding, a momentary panic and made a silent plea, "Don't let it be her, please don't let it be her". She strode toward me, looking expectant, "Are you Michele?" she asked. I nodded mutely. "Hi, I'm Ronnie," she said smiling. She seemed quite tall and would have been imposing but for her demeanour. There was something fluid and candid, open and inclusive in the way she stood, leaning slightly toward me and my doubts melted away.

"I usually have the front room but there's someone in there," she said, frowning as she rummaged in her holdall, finally pulling out a laptop. "Sorry about this, just give me a sec to check." She opened her computer and balanced it awkwardly on one hand while navigating with the index finger of her other. "Oh, come on," she told it. "I caught the train from Beechworth," she said brightly, while continuing to navigate her recalcitrant laptop.

"Uh, here it is yes, the front room." She snapped her computer shut as she headed back up the hall, throwing over her shoulder, "Well, come on!"

I extricated myself awkwardly from the low seat, quickly grabbed my bag and umbrella and came up behind Ronnie as she knocked imperiously on the door. The sound reverberated loudly and I winced and shrank back a little.

After a few seconds, the door opened a crack. "This room has been booked," Ronnie stated authoritatively to the crack and the door closed again. "There's someone standing on a chair," she told me quizzically, raising an eyebrow. The door opened again and a line of awkward women filed past, as though from the Tardis.

Ronnie stood back and gestured me inside. The room contained a desk beside the door, with two big office chairs in front of it. There were also two armchairs facing a black 'leather', three-seater sofa at the back of the room, and a round glass coffee table between it and the chairs.

With a gesture to sit anywhere, I made for one of the armchairs but changed my mind and sat on the end of the sofa, the low glass table a solid barrier between me and whatever Ronnie had in store.

With a final glance at the notes on her computer, Ronnie turned from the desk and removed her raincoat. With a warm, reassuring smile we began, and Ronnie explained that she wanted to take some time to understand how my nervous system was configured. Only the word 'nervous' registered and I took it as a prompt to download about Tuala and the panic she instilled in me, of how I had just stopped going to work one day because I couldn't go on, and how anything I was vaguely excited about or looking forward to turned to shit.

She flopped down into an armchair opposite and started to tap on the side of her hand above her little finger. She indicated I do the same.

"Just repeat what I say..." she told me, "...and tap where I tap." This was my first experience of EFT and we tapped for a few rounds, Ronnie checking in periodically to adjust the 'script'.

"How does that feel?" she asked, looking keenly at me.

"OK," I replied tentatively. I wasn't sure if I was supposed to now be cured of my horse-related anxiety, or that nothing would ever again 'turn to shit'.

After the tapping, the session flew by as Ronnie talked about the nature of trauma, its effects on the developing brain and on relationships. I told her that the violent and sadistic behaviour of my step-father, Uncle Arthur, had instilled in me a deep fear of life, which I had carried inside for 45 years.

"You are amazing to have survived your traumatic childhood," she told me and I blushed, feeling confused and overwhelmed by the praise, which I considered a little over the top. "Your inner children have survived a lot," she said.

"What do you mean?" I exclaimed. "You mean there's more than one?"

"Oh, yes," she replied, as I continued to goggle.

"But they've never been seen before," I told her in a quiet voice. For the briefest moment, Ronnie looked piercingly into my eyes, but then turned away to grab her diary so we could schedule our next appointment.

As I got up to leave, she told me, "Enjoy your week. Next time, we tackle Uncle Arthur. Tell the children we are coming for them." I knew what she meant but still, it sounded ominous.

Later that night, as I lay down to sleep, a feeling of panic erupted in my gut. I hadn't realised until I had stopped doing things how deeply unsettled I felt. A great calamity was approaching like a hurricane bent on destruction. I lay sleepless waiting, until finally I fell into a shallow sleep and dreamed of roses and choking earth.

4

THE SKI SHACK

It was Christmas 1973 and Dad's uncle, my great Uncle Arthur, a widower who lived in Melbourne, came to spend the festive season with us in Sydney. I was nearly nine years old and my brother Luke, two and a half.

Uncle Arthur gave me a travelling chess set for Christmas and seemed innocuous enough as he taught me the names of the pieces and how they moved. Apart from the daily lessons, I didn't pay him much attention, except to watch him squish his strawberries and vanilla ice cream in his parfait glass at Christmas lunch. Mum always trotted out her best crockery and glassware when we had visitors, and Uncle Arthur was using the long, fine spoon to macerate the fat, juicy, red fruit and it looked like a tiny toy in his meaty hand. If I'd turned my dessert into a pink Mr Whippy, I'd have been told to "stop playing with your food Michele." While the adults talked, I sat enthralled, watching as each mini snowcapped mountain floated toward his mouth, wishing I still had some left to squish.

One morning a few days after Dad had returned to work, I'd been searching for Mum when I heard the dim murmur of voices coming from the lounge room. Uncle Arthur was camped on the floor behind the sofa to afford him some privacy. I bounced into the room and addressed the back of the couch, "Mum, can I have some cordial?" Mum's head popped up and she replied lightly, "Off you go, I'll be out in a minute Michele, I'm just rubbing some cream on Uncle Arthur's sunburn."

She told me many years later that Uncle Arthur had suggested we could live with him, "If you ever need to get away," he'd said. He made it sound as if my Dad was a wife beater, rather than the introverted, unconfident, critical, self-absorbed man I adored.

Mum made her secret move three months later, packing our belongings while Dad was away on one of his frequent business trips and we disappeared without warning one perfect April morning. She left a note for Dad and told no one, including her parents who lived next door, that she was running away to Melbourne with Luke and me.

A couple of days after the first session with Ronnie I sat on the lounge room sofa, remembering the torture of living with Uncle Arthur for five gruelling years. Looking back, I can't fathom how I survived his cruelty and sadism and propensity for rage. Uncle Arthur carried his own unresolved trauma, regularly beaten by his austere, yet violent father, my great grandfather. Despite my very best efforts, nothing I ever did was right or acceptable and my feelings for him oscillated between love, resentment and fear, and my behaviour reflected a topsy-turvy mix of meek subservience and passive defiance.

As I sat on the sofa, staring unseeing through the window at the next-door neighbour's Japanese Maple, a cold draft of air squeezed through a gap between window and ledge and I fell suddenly into the winter of 1975. We'd been living with Uncle Arthur for just over two years and I was 11 years old. I had taken an Ansett flight from Melbourne to Sydney airport, where Dad picked me up and drove us directly to a bus terminal, where we boarded a coach bound for the New South Wales ski resort of Perisher Valley with a group of Dad's work colleagues.

I had found it difficult to sleep on the bus and the next morning I had had a panic attack in the queue for the ski gear hire. The diesel-tinged air of ski hire shack made me feel ill and I stopped breathing in an unconscious attempt to hold inside the rising tide of panic and nausea. Losing my spot in the queue, I ran outside fearing I might be sick. That was the last thing I remember about that distressing holiday.

My next recollection is of the shuddering jolt as the plane's wheels hit the slick tarmac of Melbourne airport and then the jerk as the engines were thrust into reverse. Mum usually collected me from the airport after school holiday visits to Sydney but as I stumbled into the airport lobby, I spied with dismay the hulking figure of Uncle Arthur.

Assuming he was angry with me, I hurriedly wove around the other disembarking passengers, some of whom were smiling and waving at friendly faces in the crowd. He turned and started toward the exit.

"Uncle Arthur, where is Mum?" I spoke to his back as I ran to catch him up.

"Mum and Luke are at home, sick."

"Oh," I said, knowing this would somehow be my fault.

The giant strides slowed to a stop, and he turned back to glare, "... and what the hell is the meaning of this?" I watched his chin as he spoke because he'd once cracked his huge hand across my face when I'd held his gaze in what he considered an 'insolent' stare. It had been during one of his lectures on how I could do whatever I was doing better.

"Your father told Mummy you would be home tomorrow," he snarled, then muttered, "Bloody hopeless," as he strode off again. When we'd reached the baggage carousel, I darted away to drag my case off before it could make another round.

Outside the terminal the night air was freezing and the vinyl seat of his car as frigid as a block of ice. I sat shivering, as much from fear as from the cold, as he pulled out of the car park and drove down the freeway in thick, brooding silence. My eyes darted to his profile, the weathered granite as dark and cold as the night. Below the inverted sickle of his mouth and jutting chin, his huge arthritic hands gripped the steering wheel, fingers sticking every which way like the gnarled, twisted branches of a dead tree.

Tears began leaking from my eyes. He got angry when I cried or he sneered, 'crocodile tears'. Slowly I turned my head to stare unseeing out of the window, hoping he wouldn't notice. I searched out the rhythmic back and forth, the squeak and thud of the wipers, but the harder I tried not to cry the more I did, big tears splashing like rain onto the front of my jumper.

There was no escaping the scrutiny of this ex-Deputy Inspector General of the Ceylon police force and when the car slid to a stop, he turned his gaze on me, the red of the traffic light reflecting demonically in the black pupils of his eyes. The slit opened, "If you upset your mother, by Christ, I will kill you".

Finally, we arrived 'home', and with enormous relief I went straight to Mum's room. She was awake, sitting up in bed. "Hello," she said coolly, "Dad told us you were coming back tomorrow."

The next morning, I skipped up the driveway, which skirted the side of the 1930s brick house, past the front garden to the street. The air was still and damp and smelled earthy. The first of the daffodils had opened and glowed brightly, although the sun projected an insipid glare.

Exotic and lovely, a row of azalea bushes festooned the front façade of the house, their blushing flowers thriving in dankness. Beyond the azaleas and the dark twinkle of the diamond-shaped lead-light windows, an emerald carpet stretched to the low front fence, like a long handkerchief. In the centre of the lawn there was a dark gash I had not seen before. It was surrounded by a border of red bricks, which gave it the appearance of a newly dug grave. I stood considering it for a long time, wondering if he would be able to fit me in in one piece. Perhaps he would need to chop me up? Inexplicably drawn to the idea, I lay down alongside it on the wet grass to see.

5

WAR ZONE

Ronnie wrote mid-week to check in after our first session and to let me know I could email her between sessions with any questions or concerns I might have. I wrote back, telling her I was feeling unsettled and had suddenly remembered the 'snow trip'.

Ronnie responded reassuringly with an email:

. . . Basically, the inner children don't know they've grown up. They have no idea that the abuser is dead or old and have no idea that they got themselves together enough to come to therapy—that there is such a thing as therapy. They are stuck in their trauma, reliving it daily.

I took comfort from Ronnie's insights and suddenly wanted to see her quite badly. I arrived early for the second appointment and as I lifted my hand to the bell, noticed a bold sign next to the door telling clients to wait until the appointed hour before ringing. This explained the annoyance of the bald man who had let me in the previous week.

As there was nowhere to sit on the narrow concrete porch, which was anyway unpleasantly dusty and noisy due to the relentless ebb and surge of traffic on Brunswick Street, I went back to wait in my car. I scrolled impatiently through emails and then returned to the dirty porch ten minutes before the hour, reflexively checking my watch every 30 seconds.

Four o'clock arrived but I forced myself to wait another minute, suddenly nervous, not wanting to appear too eager. When I finally knocked, Ronnie immediately swept the door open and greeted me with a warm, embracing smile. Relief swelled like a happy balloon in my chest as she stepped aside and I ducked straight into the front room and made directly for the far sofa. The room felt like a blessed sanctuary.

"So, the children were triggered last session," Ronnie confirmed solicitously.

I nodded.

"I thought we might try some Havening this week," she suggested.

I had experienced Havening a couple of years back when the next-door neighbour's thumping stereo had incessantly triggered my nervous system into hyperarousal. It had evoked in my body, memories of slammed cupboards and doors, swearing and vicious rebukes but the Havening had worked its magic and that particular trigger had been de-activated. Havening is a relatively new psychosensory therapy that uses touch to stimulate the brain to produce soothing delta waves. When a distressing feeling is experienced while the person is receiving Havening Touch, the activation of delta waves can resolve long-standing and intractable traumatic stress.

Ronnie wanted me to describe the 'landscape' of my childhood, that is, to encapsulate an entire childhood in a 'picture'. At a loss, I sat mutely until Ronnie suggested many people with dysfunctional childhoods describe the landscape as a 'war zone'. Immediately, pictures of the desolate fields of France during WWI came to mind, and I thought I could discern the echo of artillery reverberating down the decades to the present. Ronnie started to Haven herself and indicated I do the same. Although the Havening Touch can be applied by the self (Self Havening), I had assumed she would Haven me, and felt a rush of disappointment and shame, although I said nothing.

With guidance from Ronnie, I started to imagine the war zone scene gradually transforming, as I alternatively stroked my arms, face and hands, activating soothing delta brain waves. My mind wandered automatically to the beautiful farm and surrounds where Tuala is agisted, with its lush grass, swooping swallows and the mysterious peak of Mt Sugarloaf on the northern horizon.

With the image already complete and perfect, my mind began to wander, but I dutifully continued to stroke. My arms were a little sunburned and the repeated touch of hand on bare forearm began to feel irritating and I became distracted by thoughts that perhaps I was incurable. "Yes, you know you are," agreed a little voice in my head.

As soon as I arrived back home, I took my laptop and a gin and tonic out into the warm evening and sat on the banana lounge under the lemon verbena. I was intrigued to find out more about Ronnie and began by reading the blurb on her professional website before moving to Facebook. I discovered that Ronnie had taught fine arts and created installations representing trauma and child abuse. Deeply impressed, I continued 'researching', even more intrigued. I was determined to read every entry and all comments associated with ten years' worth of posts.

The next day after a better night's sleep, I eagerly resumed the search. Was Ronnie married? Did she have children? After some more scrolling, I came across an oblique reference to a man that may have been a son. At that point, Matilda my partner of 22 years, found me propped up in bed and suggested we head out to a café for Sunday brunch. "No thanks, it'll be too busy, we'd never get a table," I told her, looking back to the screen in silent dismissal. As soon as she'd gone, on a hunch, I Googled the man's first name with Ronnie's last and there he was, her son. But why didn't he have his father's name? In the very first session, I'd noticed Ronnie wore a wedding ring too.

From the moment we had met, I had become deeply fascinated with Ronnie and wished she was my mother, a proper one, not the one for whom I felt nothing and who was now dead. Even after only two sessions, I yearned to spend every minute with lovely Ronnie, and was deeply enamoured of her. The parts of me longing for wholeness and connection set about collecting little facts and memories, like blue trinkets in a bower bird's nest. I had felt this way about another female therapist who I had seen for five years, although not as intensely. Even at this early stage of our therapeutic relationship, I recognised I was falling into a deep hole but I didn't care—the mere thought of Ronnie was utterly intoxicating.

The treasure trove of personal and professional information to be found so easily on social media made my growing obsession so much worse, so much more intense. Over the coming months I would spend hours scrutinising photos of her, staring hungrily at pictures of people I assumed to be her friends. I felt an agonising sense of abandonment as my imagination peered through a dirty window into the cosy parlour of her life, as if from a cold Dickensian street. It seemed ludicrous that only weeks before I had not even known Ronnie existed, whereas now, I felt I couldn't live without her.

As the third session approached, I wondered how I could get Ronnie to Haven me. Aside from asking, which I felt would be too embarrassing, I decided I would just have to wait for the right opportunity to present itself, which it did as we were discussing the best way to approach the memory of a particularly traumatic event. "Would you prefer to use tapping or Havening to process it?" Ronnie asked. "Let's Haven; can't you Haven me? Lucy did," I blurted out. Lucy was the Havening practitioner I had seen about the intrusive stereo a couple of years before.

"Of course," Ronnie replied easily and rose from her armchair, saying, "We'll have to sit up here on the office chairs." Immediately, I jumped up and made for one of them. Ronnie came and sat opposite and there was some shifting around as we positioned ourselves to allow her the proximity she needed. "Now close your eyes," Ronnie said smiling and began to stroke my face with the tips of her fingers. I focused on the feel of her skin on mine with the intensity of a starving child given a crust of stale bread.

As she Havened, Ronnie told me about the technique, that the delta receptors were most concentrated on the places she was stroking. She changed again, from upper arms to upturned hands, which felt particularly intimate. All was mellow and soft. The setting sun through the veil of my eyelids was red like the womb.

After a time, she stopped and I opened my eyes a little, recognising the opportunity to satisfy my curiosity, willing myself to ask her about the wedding ring on her finger. Ronnie told me she was married and determined to make it through my list, she confirmed my detective work, "Yes, I have a son," she said, and I immediately felt devastated because I have no children. Finally, I asked, "Have you any personal experience of mental illness?"

"Oh yes," she replied easily. I already knew she had been prescribed lithium at some stage, again from an oblique comment to a friend on Facebook from years before and so I assumed she suffered or had suffered from bipolar disorder. "I had my first breakdown when I was 21." Instinctively, I reached out my hands to cup her lower arms. Gently, she disengaged herself so it didn't feel like a rebuff and instead took each of mine in hers.

There we sat, close together holding hands as she talked and I listened, feeling deeply connected, warmly and utterly 'held'. This must be what it feels like to have a mother who loves you, little parts of me thought.

"I had bipolar and borderline personality disorder," she continued, almost swallowing the word 'borderline', "and 12 years ago, I had been given one year to live, due to severe heart failure." It had been her discovery of Emotional Freedom Techniques (EFT) that had cured her heart and over the course of ten years, her mental illness too, so that she no longer met the diagnostic criterial for bipolar or borderline and her heart was healthy.

What a story, I goggled. I'd heard of borderline personality disorder (BPD) but didn't know anything about it. I'll have to look it up when I get home, I thought excitedly, happy to have a new topic to research and to find a deeper connection with Ronnie.

We ended the session and I floated out into the noisy street, for once not noticing the traffic fumes and oppressive late-summer heat. I didn't drive away immediately but sat sweating in the car, eyes closed as I sought to contain the heady feelings of connection and wholeness before they could leach away. The little inner kids felt blissfully replete.

I went home and immediately Googled borderline personality disorder and spent a couple of hours reading all I could find about the severe mood swings, terror of abandonment and the propensity to attempt suicide. My heart squeezed in anguish at the thought of Ronnie suffering so dreadfully. It was now late but I felt compelled to do some more research into Ronnie's son, probably to avoid turning out the light. Contemplating his existence filled me with feelings of shame and inadequacy and jealousy.

An hour later, I lay down and turned off the bedside lamp but rather than drifting off, I lay in an agony of grief at the loss of my baby all those years before. I had aborted him, while Ronnie had kept hers despite her own severe mental illness, which must have been so much worse than mine. I felt such a failure, and the crushing sense of shame overtopped the dam of tears that had finally begun to flow.

I imagined Ronnie giving birth to her beautiful son, holding him. I wished she would hold me, love me with the intensity of a mother, an intensity I would never feel, either as child or mother. I wanted to hold my baby, to remember him on his first day of school, of tucking him into bed, soothing his small hurts and smiling into his eyes.

Finally, sleep took me and dreamed I was staying at a guest house in Katoomba, in the Blue Mountains where Mum, Dad and I had stayed for a weekend when I was four years old. I was walking down a long corridor with countless rooms on either side. All the doors were shut except one. I peered inside to see a ten-year-old boy with black hair and grey eyes standing while his mother Ronnie, knelt in front of him, smiling into his eyes. As she brushed his hair, her caresses fell around his face like warm snowflakes. I kept walking but was quickly drawn back. I pushed the door open and entered. A big, dark tallboy dominated the room. I pulled out one of the heavy draws and peered inside. It was empty. They had already gone.

6

MAC

Later that week, in the lead up to our fourth appointment, Ronnie contacted me to say that due to the worsening COVID situation, she thought it would be safer to continue our sessions via Zoom. The idea threw me into a state of utter panic and grief. To the inner children, this change of plan was tantamount to abandonment, and suddenly I couldn't remember what she looked like.

The Havening session only a few days before had been a moving, almost spiritual experience and I had imagined it would happen many times over the coming months until I was healed but it never did. It was the first and only time Ronnie would ever Haven me.

That night, I fell into grief when I thought about Ronnie and her son, a grown man now. My own boy, had he been born, would have been a 34-year-old man.

My desire to have children had always clashed with an intuitive knowledge that I would only ever repeat, rather than overcome, the devastating patterns I had learned as a child, and the spectre of certain failure clashed with my deep, deep longing, with the mysterious, primal urge to make a child, the ultimate act of Divine creation.

I remember thinking as a teenager it would be irresponsible have a child to suffer as I had suffered, but when I fell in love with Mac a few years later, the thought shut itself away. Inevitably, I succumbed to my biological programming and fell pregnant but then reversed it, as a subconscious message warned me that to give birth to a child in my unstable state and without partner and familial support, might break apart the fractured pieces of my psyche.

Mac was of my mother's generation. He and his wife Hetty were in her circle of friends and we met when I was 19 and he nearly 39. We began our affair a couple of years later and although Mac did eventually leave his wife and we lived together for a time, I never again fell pregnant.

I first met Mac at his holiday house in Mt Beauty, a little town 45 minutes from the ski resort of Falls Creek in the Victorian Alps. The year was 1983, and I was completing my first year at the Conservatorium of Music. He and his wife co-owned the house with Dave, who was Mum's boyfriend at the time. Dave was Mac's best mate and owned a Porsche and his own mechanics business, servicing big trucks. Dave was tall and skinny and looked like an ageing rock star. Mum told all her friends he was hopeless in bed, "I bought him a book on sex for teenagers. I gave it to him, and he said, 'Oh no,' and tried to push it away," she would say, laughing.

One cold winter's night, Luke and I and Dave's two kids piled into the back seat of Dave's Porshe, Mum in the front and we zoomed up the Hume Highway to Mt Beauty. At midnight, we arrived at the 1950s fibro holiday house, which had been built for workers of the great Snowy Hydro-Electric scheme. We clattered directly into the dim lounge room with its old gas heater, lumpy sofas and lounge chairs covered in faded, corduroy material and posters of European ski scenes. Mac and his family were already in bed.

The next morning, looking like the Michelin Man in my hired ski outfit, I wandered into the deserted lounge room and sat perusing an old *Women's Weekly* magazine. A man entered in tight, navy-blue racing pants and light-grey skivvy and sat casually in a squashy chair, throwing a leg over one arm.

I glanced surreptitiously over the top of my magazine and he caught my eye. His eyes were green and friendly and held a lively curiosity. He was very good looking and I intuited he was intelligent and worldly. I felt very childish and self-conscious and looked away but reflexively back again. He smiled and introduced himself. There was something familiar about him.

In her bedroom, Mum was fussing with her hair, staring intently into the mirror. Dave's ten-year-old daughter wandered into the room looking for her Dad but stopped in her tracks and stared at Mum's back. I could tell it was because Mum was wearing the girl's mother's old orange one-piece ski suit. She stood staring, rooted to the spot, then suddenly unfroze and dashed away like a little rabbit. Mum hadn't taken her eyes off of her reflection and hadn't noticed the girl's distress.

A couple of nights later, we squeezed together into two cars and headed out to a local restaurant for dinner. I happened to sit next to Mac and our thighs couldn't help but touch. It came into my head that I already knew him. It must have been in a past life I mused, before reminding myself that I didn't believe in past lives.

The next time I saw Mac was a couple of years later at one of

Mum's famous birthday parties, in the late August of 1985. Mum was born in the sign of Leo, on the cusp of Virgo and I thought she embodied the most irritating traits of both: exhibitionism, attention-seeking, and the withering criticism of an unhealthy Virgo.

The theme of the party was classically Leo — 'Glamour, Glitter, Gloss', and Mum was all feather boas and sequins, tits spilling out of her tight black bodice, laughing and flirting. My tits weren't on show but without realising, I had dressed as 'my mother's daughter', exclusively in Christmas tinsel and baubles.

As the evening shimmied its way to midnight, we all gathered around Stuart, an old man in his 60s, to receive his verdict on the most glitzily dressed woman. He studiously avoided looking in my direction, as did everybody else. Suddenly, I felt uncomfortable, like in a dream when you realise you are naked. I had thought I looked really good and couldn't understand why Mac's wife won. She'd been wearing a high-necked skivvy under a bright green feather boa. Hardly glamourous, I had thought, puzzled.

A voice spoke quietly in my ear. It was Mac whispering, "Of course, he couldn't give you the prize, no woman here can compete with your youth, your physique, your looks, you know". Suddenly his eyes lit up and he grabbed my arm and led me through the kitchen to the back room where a few people had started dancing.

"Ah, do you know who this is?" he crooned. I paused to listen. It sounded like 50s rock and roll, which I hated and shook my head, but not wanting to appear rude, feigned interest. "It's Buddy Holly, he's my idol, since I was a kid. My parents told me I'd grow out of it, but I never did," he said triumphantly, grabbing my hand and starting to dance. I could relate to this, as

Mum had told me I would grow out of the 60s sci-fi TV series *Lost In Space* but still loved it.

Mac leaned in grinning boyishly and breathed into my ear, "You're gorgeous". He backed away to look at me, his long, black-lashed, green eyes smiling rakishly. He leaned forward again and kissed my mouth. I could feel his tongue against my lips. I felt flattered and his boyish exuberance lent me a feeling of recklessness, but I also felt uncomfortable and wondered where his wife was. "You're gorgeous," he said again, and I thought he must be quite drunk.

I glanced around surreptitiously and although everyone seemed not to be looking at us, still I could feel their 'watching' and a frisson of disapproval. But Mac seemed not to notice or to care and continued to dance and flirt and then said, "I want to see you".

Suddenly he looked over my shoulder, stood back and said, "Hetty wants to go." As he passed me, he whispered, "I'll ring you," and was gone, taking with him his big green eyes, his boyish grin and all the colour from the room.

Two weeks later, after my final uni lecture of the day, I caught the tram down Elizabeth Steet and headed up Bourke Street to the culinary institution that was Mietta's Restaurant. I walked in nervously, looking around, taking in the grandeur, the decorative high-ceiling, gilded mirror and towering candle holders, huge flower displays, and the air of hushed elegance.

I was painfully conscious of my shabby garb of old jeans, coarse bomber jacket and dirty runners. An immaculate waiter glided to my side as I looked around desperately. With relief I suddenly spied Mac, lounging comfortably in a far corner. Ignoring the waiter, I made my way self-consciously across the room. Mac looked divine in his fine, light-grey woollen suit, crisp white shirt, midnight blue silk tie and black loafers. He smelled gorgeous too and his grin, all white teeth and black-fringed green eyes put me at once at ease and heightened my self-consciousness.

"What would you like to drink?" he asked, as another waiter suddenly appeared, like those creepy angels in *Dr Who* that sneak up when you blink. My mind was a blank and I couldn't think of a single thing, so I asked for a lemon squash. Mac ordered a glass of champagne and I immediately wished I had too.

After our drinks, we walked around the corner to a Japanese restaurant. I groaned inwardly as I considered the daunting prospect of raw fish, which I'd never tried. Mac was consulting on an LNG project involving the Japanese government and he spent much of his time in both Japan and Western Australia.

We sat on tatami mats and Mac ordered sashimi, sukiyaki and sake to share from a beautiful doll-like woman in an exquisite silk kimono. It was a most entrancing experience and as we ate the delicate artwork of sashimi and drank the warm sake and chatted, I began to relax. I watched him strolling off to the loo, wondering again why such a gorgeous, worldly man found me the slightest bit interesting.

On a sunny spring morning a little over one year later Mac and I were lying in my king single bed in the same white bedroom that had been mine as a child, when we had first come to Melbourne. We had lived with Uncle Arthur for five years, and then wanderlust had hit and Mum wanted to strike out on her own, and so the three of us had moved to a little unrenovated semi-detached house in East Hawthorn, where we'd lived for just over three years before moving to the outer east of Melbourne, for one year. Finally, we had come full circle, returning to Uncle Arthur's as I had entered my first year at uni.

By this time, Uncle Arthur had built himself a 'granny flat' and lived out the back, while Mum, Luke and I lived in the house. He had no cooking facilities though, and so needed to use our kitchen and if I was unlucky, would come unexpectedly upon him, lurking. He would let himself in without permission whenever he wished, usually when I was home studying and Mum was at work. When no one was home, he would snoop.

"I saw Arthur with his secateurs when I came down the drive. I think he listens at the window."

"Oh yuck!" I clamoured over Mac to quietly shut the window in case he was still about. "I brought lunch," Mac announced with the enthusiasm of a little boy, as he thrust a large paper bag under my nose. "Well, early lunch," he corrected, as it was only 11am. Mac had gone into his office in the city and had left soon after for his weekly Wednesday visit. I had no lectures that day, Mum was at work and Luke at school.

"What is this?" I laughed as he pulled the carboard tray from the paper bag. Chocolate eclairs and an almond croissant, "For lunch!" I rolled my eyes. He laughed too and bit an eclair in half, cream squeezing between the gap in his big, white, front teeth.

"Yum," he grinned. I licked the cream off his top lip and then tore off a piece of the croissant.

"These are so fattening," I told him.

"Got any wine?" Mac asked hopefully. Knowing Uncle Arthur may well be in the vicinity, I put on the beautiful silk kimono Mac had brought back for me from Japan and returned carrying a small cask of rosé and two tumblers. We ate the pastries and sipped the cordial-like wine while I told him all about my final singing exam, which was to take place in mid-November in the form of a concert.

Soon after, Mac headed back to work and I lolled about for a while in bed, finally making myself get up, planning to study and sing, which would give my position away to Uncle Arthur. Instead though, I mooched disconsolately about the house, careful to stay away from the windows, feeling like a fugitive in my own home. It was the same each Wednesday; when I was with Mac I felt alive and the world full of colour and possibility but when he had gone, I felt like a small, unprotected child, accidentally left behind at the fair as the lights were dowsed for the night.

# 7

MARIA CALLAS

I first fell in love with opera after reading a biography of the great Greek soprano Maria Callas when I was 18. Subconsciously, I identified with the suffering Callas had experienced throughout her life, especially during her childhood, precipitated by the cruelty of her mother, and was captivated by her passionate and volatile, yet kind and sensitive personality. Callas was an accomplished actress, and her rendition of the tragic heroine Tosca in Puccini's famous opera was legendary.

I resonated with drama and tragedy, and drama and tragedy resonated with me. When the curtain lifted, it revealed a parallel universe of chaos and loss, of pointless banality but elevated, the pain of betrayal and grief, shimmering on a sea of exquisite music. In that stylised world, it was acceptable to cry for Violetta and Mimi and Butterfly. Like Christ on the cross, the tragic heroines of opera in their suffering gave legitimacy to my own invisible pain.

The story of Maria Callas ignited a small flame that flared into an all-consuming fire a couple of years later when I was unhappily ensconced with my tuba in second year at the Conservatorium of Music. Suddenly the urge to open my mouth and sing was irresistible, a spiritual calling.

The tuba, the instrument that had until then given me such joy to play, and a surrogate home in the music department at Chadstone High School, had lost its appeal. It had saved me from succumbing to depression and worse in my teenage years but now I couldn't wait to throw it over for the mystique and emotionality of opera.

I auditioned for a very well-respected singing teacher, Bettine McCaughan, who was one of two singing teachers at the Conservatorium (the other was Loris Synan, who Bettine referred to as 'Boris'). "I've taught people with a lot less talent than you," she told me backhandedly, after she'd tested my range. I had climbed steadily up the scales, until she had stopped and beaming beatifically, had told me I'd hit top C and I had a lyric soprano voice. With training, I could one day be singing the roles of Mimi in 'La Boheme' and Susanna in 'The Marriage of Figaro', among many others.

The next day I rushed off to Allans Music in the city to purchase my very own copies of *The Melba Method*, written by Dame Nelli herself and *Twenty Italian Songs and Arias*. At home I reverently poured over Melba's scales and vocal exercises in the *Method* and the Neapolitan love songs for high voice, some of which had been made famous by Pavarotti.

Lessons began the following week, and I was given scales and vocal exercises to learn and an enchanting German lied by Schumann, about a lotus flower and her lover, the moon. Bursting with excitement, I hurried home and immediately began to practice. That night Uncle Arthur, who was in the kitchen preparing his dinner, which he would take back up to his lair to consume, looked at me quizzically and asked, "Michele, have you been standing on the cat's tail?"

"Wha…" I exclaimed, looking at him puzzled. He was smirking and suddenly I realised he was referring to my singing practice. "I don't go in for all that caterwauling," he told me witheringly and I blushed with shame.

Neither Mum nor Uncle Arthur could bear to see me happy or successful in any undertaking. Uncle Arthur satisfied himself with snide remarks but Mum's approach was more subtle and more cruel. From the very first day I started singing, she made a point of making no comment or reference to my practice. After a couple of weeks, curiosity overcame my wariness and I asked, "Mum, why don't you ever comment on my singing?"

"Because I was taught to only comment when something is good," she said briskly. She walked off again, leaving me feeling devastated.

I had stepped onto an enchanted path, a golden road of creative potential. My unfailing intuition had shown me the way and I had begun joyously, full of hope and sparkling intent but as the weeks went by, I walked, then stumbled and fell to my knees to crawl like a beaten dog. I must sound truly terrible I thought, feeling mortified, my insides wreathing like a pot of eels set to boil.

What had begun as a magical journey had turned into an excruciating ordeal and I began to avoid practicing at home, resolving to practice at the Conservatorium. Once the door closed on the practice room, I felt even more self-conscious, if that were possible, and resolved to practice at home instead. The practice rooms were not soundproofed, and I imagined genuinely talented students and teachers with international performing careers walking past and wincing to hear such shit.

The voice is so personal, an instrument that is literally a part of you, it *is* you, unlike a piano or clarinet, so the hedging left me feeling naked and exposed and my dream, my yearning to fulfil my creative destiny, spoiled. I was forced to limp on using a combination of dissociation and willpower, all the while searching, searching for an opening through which I could escape my self-consciousness to be free.

8

GREEN-EYED MONSTER

I was bitterly disappointed that Mac could not attend my examination concert but by way of meagre consolation he promised to drop in to wish me luck. It was almost time to leave when he finally arrived in a state of high anxiety and dashed into the lounge room, glanced at me, then dashed out again. Almost immediately, he came back and hurried over to kiss me saying, "I didn't recognise you". He seemed more up tight than I, as he distractedly handed me a bunch of beautiful flowers and said, "Good luck."

"Don't say that," I said faintly, "Say, 'break a leg' or 'Chookers'," but he had already gone, off to a 'do' with his wife.

The day of my final singing exam marked the end of 19 years of educational institutionalisation. I and five fellow honours students were to perform in our public concert. I was to sing the Willow Song from the opera *'Otello'* by Verdi, and as the pieces were to be performed in chronological order, I was placed second from last on the program, leaving plenty of time to sit backstage and sweat.

The Melba Hall at the Conservatorium of Music, University of Melbourne, was packed, every seat taken. The overflowing crowd stood in the isles and sat on the steps. I sat backstage in an acute state of nervous tension, staring straight ahead, not speaking. One by one my companions walked, wooden and dazed for their turn until finally I rose from my seat, pushed through the door to the back of the stage and zigzagged my way through the orchestra to stand in front of the audience.

I stared unseeing at the restless, amorphous mass. Suddenly, applause erupted again and I turned to smile automatically as the conductor came to stand next to me, beside his podium, smiling warmly. He stepped up and turned to the orchestra. The players shuffled deeper into their seats and after a moment, the maestro lifted his baton and the audience subsided into stillness. The auditorium was now deathly quiet, the air electrified.

The Willow Song starts with the lonely wail of a reedy cor anglais, perfuming the hushed auditorium with its melancholy tune. Although the long orchestral introduction helped my nerves to settle a little, I was still blinded by the sea of staring eyes and the flood of heat from the lights as I waited. Finally my cue arrived, my mouth opened automatically and I sang to my maid:

"Emilia, please
Lay out my pure white wedding garments
Upon my bed.
Listen! If I happen to die before you
Bury me in one of those veils..."

Then Desdemona sings of a poor woman, abandoned by her lover, who wept under a willow tree and died of grief. Verdi's music is lyrical and sad and I managed it well until the climax, a top B. Rather than supporting the note with my diaphragm, I launched my throat upward to sing a thin, sustained note. I was in no doubt that 'Boris' my examiner, was sitting somewhere in the auditorium scribbling madly. The aria then came to a swift end. Otello would strangle Desdemona in a fit of blinding jealousy while I guzzled alcohol in the green room, in glorious relief.

The audience let loose a deafening soundwave of applause that broke like a wall of water onto the stage. Feeling tremendously light, as if a huge weight had been removed from my shoulders, I smiled and glanced into the audience for the first time. People were smiling broadly, whistling, clapping their hands. The orchestra was applauding too and the conductor beaming.

Suddenly, I became aware that my friend George was standing below and I bent to scoop up the bouquet of flowers he handed me with a wide smile. Someone else was inching along in front of the stage... my mother. I had asked for her guidance in choosing an evening gown to wear on my big night but she had refused with a smirk and had remained true to her word and made no comment on my vocal preparations, yet here she was, the proud, supportive mother, smiling warmly and handing me a bunch of flowers. I held them to my heart, daring to hope she finally approved.

The next morning, Mac tapped gently on my bedroom window. Despite the very late night, and the drinking, I felt uncharacteristically relaxed and almost carefree as I stole quietly from my room to let him in through the front door. I was wearing a skimpy white tee shirt with a big green tree frog on the front. The frog smiled benignly up at Mac as he whispered keenly, "Well, how did you go?"

My smile widened. "Really well," I said, and then added, as

I slipped back into bed, "Do you want to get in?" It was very snuggly under the doona.

"I've just gone to get the paper, so..." he grimaced. "I'd better go and get one." He kissed me again and was gone.

That night in celebration we, the triumphant soloists were off to a restaurant to celebrate our successes, warm and easy in each other's company after our trial the previous night and four years together at 'The Con'. We had booked a table at a cool Italian restaurant in Toorak Rd, South Yarra. It was vibrant and fun with big mirrors, garish modern paintings, Italian waiters, and delicious food.

Half an hour before I was due to leave, Mum intercepted me as I walked through the lounge room. Her best friend Jane and Jane's daughter Sam, who was 17, were staying with us for a few days. Mum blocked my path to the bathroom. "Michele, you're taking Sam and your brother with you tonight."

"Wha... but Mum," I protested awkwardly under my breath as Jane and Sam were watching, "It's our special dinner together, you know, after last night. Please, please can't they stay with you?" I pleaded.

"No, they can't," snapped Mum, "Jane and I are going to a party."

9

LITTLE DANCE

Little Dance, little dew drop, little mist,
Caressing sleepy feathers of the crimson, grey gang gangs.
Little stream over woody roots,
Lithe torpedoes silver fins undulating, drunk in your purity.
Jewel-bright, dazzling, sun captures kiss and dance,
And you are gone.

One night a few months after the end of uni, I took my red lipstick from the dressing table and Mum's car keys from the small stand by the front door and let myself out quietly. He only lived a couple of suburbs away, Mac, his wife and their two teenage daughters. Sunday night was turning to Monday morning, and in a few hours the mad rush, the commuter clash, would start up again and chaos would resume.

I drove through the deserted night and turned the car into his street, killing the engine to sit for a moment, light-headed, heart pounding. I often drove past his street, eyes darting from the busy road to peer with longing toward his house and the life I so coveted.

Whisps of grey mist partially obscured the streetlights and stars glittered against the patchwork sky. All was quiet, still, asleep. I stole up the circular driveway. Elegant bay windows shone dimly to the right of the big front door. I climbed the three wide stone steps to the tiled veranda and stood in the pale light like a wraith at his bedroom window. I bent down and pressed my red lips to the glass pane. I pressed again and again, leaving a pattern like falling leaves in autumn.

My formal education was finished and the structure that had held my life together for almost 20 years had completely dissolved. The safe bubble of university life had popped and rather than leaping into the future, I clutched at tenuous threads linking me to my unhappy but known past. The future loomed menacingly through a hazy fog.

One morning, Mum burst into my bedroom and sounding put out told me I needed to leave. "Honestly Michele, I've supported you for long enough," she chided and my guts slid into my bowels. I felt I was being rejected, thrown out onto the street because, as bad as living with Mum and Uncle Arthur had been, I assumed living in the big wide world must be so much worse. I felt ill-equipped, childish, afraid. Meanwhile, Mum told a procession of her friends, who dropped in to chat over glasses of cask white, "Well, I had to kick her out of the nest, I mean, she's an adult now. Why should I keep supporting her?"

I moved into a big, old terrace house in North Melbourne in January, on the eve of my 23rd birthday, to share with some friends from the Conservatorium. My dream of becoming an opera singer had been subsumed by existential fear and uncertainty. My future survival and happiness now depended solely on Mac rescuing me by leaving his wife.

I returned to work at the same jewellery store I'd worked at each holiday from uni for the last four years. Time passed in a dissociative daze until seven months later, almost to the day when the previous year, Mac and I had lolled about in bed, eating pastries and drinking cask wine, when I caught up with an old high school friend and we made plans to go on a week's skiing holiday. He had wealthy friends with a ski lodge at Mt Hotham and accommodation was free, so the next week I said goodbye to Mac, hoping he might miss me and decide to leave his wife. I only managed to ski for two days though, before subsiding into anxiety; anxiety that he had forgotten me. Feeling miserable, I made an excuse to my friend and headed back home again. As soon as I arrived back in Melbourne, I invited Mac over to visit, since I was house minding and had it to myself.

For some strange reason, I had unconsciously stopped taking the pill at the ski lodge, complying with some faint, dream-like instruction. Five weeks later, as my old family doctor withdrew his fingers and met my anxious gaze, he nodded grimly. "What do you want to do?" he asked, giving me a stony look, as I put my undies back on.

"Well, I can't have it," I blurted out. The doctor had known me since we'd first come to Melbourne when I was nine and he was devoutly Catholic. I felt chastised and when I described his disapproval as Mac drove me home and I started to cry, Mac snapped, "Stop feeling so bloody sorry for yourself."

I hadn't realised I would need to make a case for an abortion, that it wasn't a given, and so when the kindly nurse asked why I didn't want to keep it, I said, "I'll be too depressed, waking up to feed it at 2am, all by myself… The father is married." I knew

I couldn't rely on Mum either. Approval was given and a time arranged for the termination.

A few days later, Mac drove me to the abortion clinic in East Melbourne and I sat dazed, staring straight ahead, with other silent, white-faced women. After changing into a hospital gown, I was called into a white room and told to lie on a sloping stainless-steel platform. The doctor then indicated I bring my heels up to my bum, keeping my knees together. I had a sudden vision of what would happen when the anaesthetic took effect and thought it ridiculously funny. I felt hysteria rising, and then it went black.

I woke from the procedure and after a moment's disorientation, remembered where I was and realised it must be over. I began to cry for my baby, for what I had done but then it was time to get up and get dressed, to walk out into the same street, returned but lesser, to meet Mac. Soon after, I forgot about the termination and got back to fretting over Mac's lack of action where his marriage was concerned. I shut what I'd done in a box marked 'do not open . . . ever'.

As the days and weeks slid by, my desire for a happy, safe life with Mac became more intense. I daydreamed about starting a family with him, fantasised about slipping into his current wife's place as if she had never existed. We'd be an instant family, me, Mac and his two girls and we'd go on skiing holidays and watch movies together, sit around drinking tea and chatting, and I'd cook for them. I would be cosseted in bliss. They would love me and finally, I would have a safe place in this world.

Nothing changed though and as the months trickled by, I decided I must finally give up on his empty promises and leave.

10

THE STAIRCASE SPUR

Mac wore a medallion with a sad-faced blue sun on a silver chain, and I wore a little gold heart. We were going to climb to the top of Mt Bogong, Victoria's highest peak and bury them, so these metallic avatars resonating with our energy would be together when we went our separate ways. Mac told Hetty he was going away with me for the one and only time, to say goodbye. I didn't tell anyone.

Mac picked me up from the flat I was now sharing with one other uni friend in Hawthorn. It was seven months after the abortion and the days were shortening again, another winter on the horizon. We travelled up the Hume Highway and turned onto the 'Snow Road' as dusk fell. I wound down the window to smell the air, which was sweet and mellow, the warmth of the day lingering in the scent of ripe grass. Hulking mountains, ancient and impassive crouched against the violet sky as we sped past.

The next day was a perfect autumn picture of fiery reds and amber and promised to be hot. We toured all the family's favourite haunts: the secret swimming hole on the Kiewa River, where Mac told me they had spent many idyllic hours floating peacefully under the clear blue sky on lilos, before heading home to sit under the huge, green leaves of the old bean tree to sip cold wine. We walked around Bogong Village and its dark, creepy lake, impenetrable and gloomy, and hiked on the Bogong High Plains, visiting old cattlemen's huts. I felt at once privileged and grief-stricken, envious of the sweet life I was denied.

On the eve of the ascent, we had an argument. I told Mac in a fit of petulant rage that it was a stupid idea to bury our trinkets together, what was the point? He became defensive and surly and lay down on the sofa with his back to me, feigning sleep. Immediately, I begged him to forgive me and to take me into his arms as our time was running out. Why did we have to part, I had asked him. "Well, that's entirely your decision, isn't it?" he said, rising from the sofa, looking smug.

We started afresh the next day, our altercation forgotten, as we had made the tough, five-hour trudge up the Staircase Spur. The physical activity was intense and the scenery spectacular and for a time I forgot this was to be our last complete day together, forever. We arrived at the summit and left our jewellery, which Mac had sealed in an old earthenware jar, hidden under loose rocks at the foot of the summit cairn. Then we started the decent, hardly talking, just concentrating on keeping our feet on the steep, stony path.

In the early evening of the following day, Mac dropped me outside my flat. I let myself in and stood at the threshold dazed and uncomprehending. The silence buzzed. I found wine, which I drank in one of the Dartington crystal glasses Mac had given me with a bottle of Verve Cliquot when we had first started going out. It had been my first taste of real champagne and we had sipped the delicate nectar while reclining together on a blanket in the long summer grass. We had chatted away for hours. The sun's shadows had lengthened, but I would see him again tomorrow. I dropped the flute onto the parquet floor and padded barefooted to find the other one so I could smash it too. Now the memories of our time together were imprisoned in the shattered crystal shards.

Somehow, I managed to get up and dressed for work the next day. Mac's office was on the corner of Bourke and Elizabeth Streets and the jewellery store, 50 metres up the hill in Bourke Street. I craned my neck up to the 39th floor. He'd be up there right now I thought, in the elegant hush of the office, sitting at his desk in his beautiful suit, smelling of Paco Rabanne.

Time crawled by in an empty, dissociated haze until one evening a few weeks after the split when, as I set off down Bourke Street to the train station with a colleague, Mac suddenly stepped from the open foyer of his building and handed me a small gift, catching my eye and smiling his gorgeous smile.

Silently I took it and he stepped aside to let me pass. I hurried after my colleague clutching the small box, a ray of pure joy almost lifting my feet off the pavement.

The next evening he was there again, waiting to ask if I would like to go for a quick drink on my way home. With profound relief I gave up all resistance and agreed. It was as easy as offering heroin to an addict and our relationship started up again, the agonising farewell and ensuing weeks instantly forgotten.

The passage of time, which had stuttered to a leaden stop began to move again and pick up speed. Suddenly Christmas was on the near horizon and Mac informed me he and Hetty were going home to England for six weeks, to spend Christmas with their families. The news was galvanising. Mac would go away to the other side of the world and when he got back, I would be gone, I told myself with resolve.

The father of a university friend, a senior executive in a big mining company, agreed to write me a reference for the position of geological assistant in an open-cut mine in the Western Australian outback. I was successful, securing the job at a small town called Laverton. I didn't tell Mac I was planning to leave, and a week before Christmas, on the eve of his trip, we said goodbye.

I never wanted to see him again and although my heart ached, having a plan provided a little insulation from the loss and uncertainty and I felt a small measure of control, which afforded me a fledgling sense of empowerment. I was determined to make a clean start, with the physical distance a barrier against being drawn back to him yet again.

It was around the time Mac was due back from the UK that I put my belongings into storage, packed my suitcase and caught a cab to Mum's place. She was still living in Uncle Arthur's home, with him in his 'granny flat' above, but Mum was leaving Melbourne too, as was Luke. My brother had turned 18 a few months earlier and was finally moving to Sydney to live with Dad. It had been his dearest wish since he'd been plucked away as a small child.

Mum was off to Spain to do a Spanish speaking course. The 'bohemian traveller' had sold all her belongings and thrown numerous farewell parties. The trip was the latest in a catalogue of new starts, the first of which was leaving Dad. In the future she'd try her hand at writing romance novels, and then photography, and then teaching.

That late January night, Mum, Luke and I ate dinner together for the last time ever. I was to sleep in my old room, the bright white one where Mac and I had drunk wine and eaten

French pastries in bed one fine spring morning, when my future as a classical singer still shone with promise.

I was just about to change into my nightdress when a familiar tapping sounded on the bedroom window. I stole into the hall, to the front door and slipped outside, motioning Mac to walk up the drive to the street, out of Mum's ear shot. As soon as we had passed the gate, Mac turned his anxious face to mine and said urgently, "I've just heard you're leaving".

"Yes," I told him, "I'm going to WA to work in an open-cut mine, as a geologist's assistant. I'm not coming back."

"Come away with me," Mac pleaded. "Look, I'll leave her right now . . . *right now*," he reiterated, turning to walk away, as if to make good his promise. "Right this minute," he finished, peering intensely into my eyes.

A part of me wished he had never come back to utter the words I had so desperately wished to hear those past five years. "Look, I have to go," I said. "They've paid my fare, the flight is tomorrow morning."

"I own a flat," he said, ignoring my protest and taking my hand. "We can live there." He kissed me and I took in the familiar smell of him and the feel of his lips.

"Well, if you move out, then I will come back," I told him. "But I must stay for three months or I will have to pay back the cost of the airfare."

11

MEETINGS AND SCISSORS

When I was nine years old, a young woman attempted suicide by cutting her wrists beside the Gardiners Creek, which was over our back fence.

All the kids had gone to see the spot, to stare transfixed at the spray of dried blood on the leaves of the bush under which she had hidden.

Where were those wretched nail scissors? I'd emptied the entire bathroom cabinet of old toothbrushes, face-cream sachets, tweezers, little soaps, dental floss and the plethora of old sample bottles from overseas hotels that would one day end up in landfill. The mess spilled over the basin and onto the floor and I'd just split a small shampoo bottle with my slippered foot.

I was looking for the black-handled pair, with the fine pointed blades. I spotted another, lying among the debris and half-heartedly picked them up and put the point of one blade to my left wrist and pressed. A small purple bruise marked the spot, between purple veins. I tried again and again. The little valleys became deeper and deeper but still no blood. I kept on pressing until little purple points patterned my skin, like shotgun pellets.

I had a thought—perhaps I'd left the good scissors in the kitchen—and dropped the dud pair back in the drawer, hurrying out of the bathroom and into the lounge room, nearly tripping over Pepper who was sprawled like a shagpile rug on the floor in the doorway, fast asleep. My computer was sitting on the dresser, lid open with a reminder box standing out against the screen's black background. For a few seconds I stood irresolute, then stepped closer to read what the little box had to say.

Suddenly, I remembered. I was working from home due to COVID 19 and had been editing a work document but had taken a break to go to the loo. That had been 30 minutes ago, according to the display on the laptop. I read the words in the box. Oh shit! The meeting I was chairing with work colleagues and external consultants had started five minutes before. I dived for the mouse and ping, the screen came alive with the faces of the participants.

"Hello everyone," I said brightly. "Sorry I'm late."

Where had this sudden urge come from? Why had I become enamoured of scissors and the big carving knife in the kitchen? The previous week, as I had sat distraught and sleepless in bed at 1am, a feeling of such powerful contempt and loathing had erupted that I whacked my fist against the side of my head. It had happened without warning and I had sat dazed, my head throbbing, my neck strained from the impact.

I had finally gone to sleep and fallen into a nightmare, wandering through a quiet forest in the early morning gloom. The path led to a river. Tendrils of fog laced the black marble surface and I could see a formless lump had washed up at its boggy edge. Cautiously I stepped out onto the open ground and approached. It was a corpse, its face bloated and unrecognisable, the skin pulled tight to bursting. I thought it must be me.

The alarm had exploded and I groped blindly for the off button on my phone. It said 8.55am and I had hurriedly stumbled out of bed, thrown on some clothes, splashed cold water on my face, applied mascara, then flicked the switch of the kettle and hurriedly opened my laptop at 9.07am, late for the daily team catch up. Thank God for COVID, I'd thought, because working from home allowed me to get up later and I didn't have to endure public transport or crowds and could wear my tracky dacks all day.

The early days of trauma therapy with Ronnie were painful, confusing and even dangerous. I had subconsciously supressed the unbearable feelings associated with overwhelming childhood experiences and this had enabled me to function in the world (to a point) but, with the advent of the therapy, the damaged parts of me that had been locked behind a wall of dissociation were leaking into consciousness causing nightmares, emotional dysregulation, and intense psychic pain.

Ronnie used the psychosensory modalities of EFT and Havening to facilitate the discharge of blocked energy caused by trauma and neglect. When a traumatic memory is activated, tapping on a sequence of meridian points sends calming signals to the nervous system and the enormous energetic charge that was generated when the trauma was created is released from the body, bringing lasting relief.

At 4pm each Saturday afternoon, Ronnie and I would work to resolve painful emotions, memories, and unhealthy beliefs. Ronnie would tap or Haven with me and because our energy bodies were connected even over distance, the healing effect was amplified. During initial rounds of tapping, I would receive snippets of information from my subconscious in the form of bodily sensations and/or images or emotions. Focusing on these cues would lead us to a frightened, sad or lonely child, isolated in the past, reliving a particular trauma over and over, not realising time had moved on while she had been left behind.

If we were using EFT, I would tap on my body and when the discomfort had reduced, would imagine tapping on my child 'part'. Miraculously the child, who I felt as a palpable presence, would begin to calm down. I could feel it happening in my body and feel the sense of relief. Once the young me was feeling better, I'd ask her what she needed. The child parts would usually want to climb onto my lap for a cuddle. Sometimes it happened spontaneously, before I could ask, the little one snuggling in and as I put my arms around her, Ronnie would tell her how brave she was and how much we loved her.

The release of negative emotions indicated the 'part' had been recouped or 'integrated' into my personality and the specific 'burden' she had carried, that triggered emotional dysregulation, was resolved.

For every child who could be reached and rescued, there were others who were too afraid to trust, or too angry or frightened to show up and would hide in dark places where we couldn't reach them. There were also 'parts' who resisted healing because they feared that if they felt better, Ronnie would abandon them. These were the parts who cried the loudest and were at odds with others who desperately wanted to be free of their pain, to be normal, happy kids. As the year progressed, the tug of war became more intense, causing more and more pain and emotional dysregulation. I felt I was being torn apart.

12

THE BEE

From the moment Ronnie had 'seen' my 'inner children' or 'parts', I had developed a great fear that she would suddenly leave. All children are biologically programmed to seek attachment with their caregiver, usually a parent, most commonly a mother. Ronnie's kindness had activated the 'parts' of me who had never experienced loving regard, who had never felt safe or cherished, had never been held, who had sought connection with Mum in vain.

For a child growing up in an emotionally nourishing environment, the inevitable upsets causing distress and pain don't interfere with the development of an integrated, cohesive personality, but for children experiencing abuse and/or neglect, traumatic experiences cause the developing personality to fragment. As the child grows, these split-off 'parts' remain stuck in time, and the learning of relational skills is arrested; the brain is literally damaged.

The fragmentation of the personality is an adaptive response to chronic childhood trauma and/or neglect. It is described by the 'structural dissociation' model of trauma, among others. In Janina Fisher's workbook, *Transforming the Living Legacy of Trauma*, she explains the term:

> "The model theorizes that, in a traumatic environment, the more instinctive right brain is stimulated to anticipate danger by maintaining hypervigilance or readiness for action, while the left-brain side of the personality 'keeps on keeping on', getting through the day, keeping life going no matter what. This allows an abused child to be on guard and ready to hide but still able to walk to school, play with other children and do homework. While the right-brain side might be afraid and ashamed, the left-brain side could be confidently developing skills as a student, athlete, artist, or scientist ... with repeated and chronic experiences of trauma, more complex splitting and fragmentation is often adaptive and necessary ... The model is clear that fragmentation or structural dissociation is a normal instinctive reaction to repeated trauma ... " (p77)

One Saturday, as Ronnie and I sat and tapped together, I had a flashing vision of Mum reading a story to my little three-year-old self. Mum thought it was novel, funny even, that I was crying for the ugly duckling. Sitting in front of Ronnie in 2020, I could tell the little 'part' felt shame and embarrassment, although I was unable feel the emotions in my body. The inability to feel or recognise emotions is called alexithymia and is a common adaptive response in trauma survivors.

Luckily, I didn't need to feel the emotions to process them with EFT. "Freeze the scene," Ronnie told me. In my mind's eye, I clicked my fingers and imagined stepping into my childhood bedroom. I turned Mum into a frozen block while smiling reassuringly at the small, ashamed girl on the bed. Approaching the girl slowly, I told her I was her, all grown up and had come to help her to feel better. "Would you mind if I tap on you? Look, like this," I said, demonstrating on myself. She nodded and as I tapped on the little me and Ronnie also tapped along, my three-year-old part stopped crying, then looked up and smiled, my face smiling with her. She wanted to be held and cuddled so, in my mind's eye, I took her little body into my arms and held her to my heart.

The comfort of this experience lingered for a day or two but by the next Tuesday, I couldn't imagine how I could possibly last another minute without seeing Ronnie again. I tried to remember what she looked like but her face had disappeared from my memory and I felt acutely abandoned.

Finally, the next Saturday arrived and as usual, I was completely flooded by the little 'parts' and rendered mute. For the first few minutes, I sat in exquisite agony, besotted, self-conscious and unable to speak.

After a time, and with great effort, I managed to regain access to my voice and because my feelings of dependency were so strong, I asked Ronnie, "If the unthinkable was to happen and you couldn't be my therapist anymore, who would you recommend we see?" She gave me the name of a social worker who practiced the Internal Family Systems (IFS) model ('parts' work) and Havening and told me reassuringly, "I'm here for the long haul. I had a client for a good eight years, on and off and I love this work, so I'm not going anywhere."

"Thanks, good to know," I replied, while inside the three-year-olds shuffled about like anxious little chicks, wholly unconvinced. They knew that one day she would leave them.

Between sessions, I spent many hours going over the highlights of previous sessions, trying to re-capture the visceral feelings of being seen and safe, of feeling accepted and even admired, trying to remember exactly what she had said, her smile, what we'd discussed and her kind eyes that held the kids in thrall.

Ronnie would tell me I was amazing to have survived my childhood, but I felt like a fraud as I hadn't consciously done anything remarkable to make it through, it had just happened. I would then imagine the pain Ronnie had endured in her life and feelings of guilt and shame would take my breath away. She'd had it so much worse, suffering from bipolar and borderline, yet the fact I hadn't developed borderline seemed to fascinate and inspire her. She told me that suffering neglect and trauma as a child interfered with the process of personality development, referring to it as having 'no architecture of self', implying I had a 'me'.

Whenever we talked about borderline and that I didn't have it, I would feel secretly disappointed, because having BPD would validate my suffering and give me something in common with Ronnie. One the other hand, I would agonise that Ronnie would not think me so remarkable.

"And you had no one," she continued one session. "Most people who have significant childhood trauma, have one place where they feel safe or one person who lets them know they are OK, but you had no one. Most people have a grandmother or an aunt," she raised her eyebrows and shook her head in kindly amazement.

"Did you have someone?" I asked, hoping she would tell me more about her life.

"I had my grandmother," she replied.

As Ronnie said this, my eyes unfocused. I was remembering my own grandmother, Mum's mum. She had not 'been there for me' either, like Ronnie's had. A vivid scene unfolded and I was seven years old again, wandering in bare feet over lush green grass. We were in our backyard in Sydney, which was next door to Nanna and Grandad's house. Mum and Nanna were walking slowly around the yard, deep in conversation, while I trailed along behind.

Suddenly a hot, sharp pain in my foot caused me to cry out and Mum whipped around to hiss, "I told you to be quiet, you'll wake your brother." Luke, who was only a baby, was having his morning sleep. She turned back to continue her conversation. I limped along behind, biting my lip anxiously to stop from crying.

Nanna must have realised I had been stung by a bee, and although she didn't say anything, abruptly changed direction and we found ourselves in her kitchen. She silently patted the table, indicating I climb up. I sat with my legs dangling over the edge while she went to find a needle and prepare of bowl of some liquid. She began her ministrations saying to Mum, who was staring silently out of the kitchen window, "She's trodden on a bee." Mum appeared not to hear, as she made no reply and didn't turn around. When Nanna had removed the sting, they drifted off again to resume their conversation.

That was it, another session over, and Ronnie disappeared from the computer screen. I was alone with another week to endure.

13

MARBLES

I dreamed I was walking along an unfamiliar street with little Luke in tow. We were ten and five years old, tired out and hungry because we'd been wandering for hours and it was getting dark. Suddenly, a crossroads loomed out of the gloom and I peered anxiously up at the road sign but it was blank. I looked around for someone to ask for directions but there was no one to be seen.

I was born in Sydney, in January 1964. Mum and Dad had taken me home from the Royal North Shore Hospital to a flat, one of eight in a bungalow complex on the beach-side, north shore suburb of Manly. When I was two and a half, we moved to a house in Willoughby, next door to Mum's parents, Tom and Ruth, my Nanna and Grandad.

Mum and Dad had desperately wanted a boy and when I was nearly six years old, in September 1969, Luke had been born. Three years later, in the winter of 1972, Mum and Dad underwent a trial separation for five months. Dad rented a pokey flat in Mossman with his younger brother, who had also separated from his wife. When he returned home again in late November, I was ecstatic and everything seemed as it had been before, except Luke was always crying, even at the beach.

A beautiful summer unfolded, full of seemingly endless, hot sunny days under the azure sky, the humid air fragrant with the scent of Chinese jasmine and gardenia. Thunderstorms blew in from the south, leaving behind cool, refreshing air and a glittering cascade of diamonds that twinkled against the black velvet cloth of the night. Weekends were spent at the surf, with noses covered in zinc cream and sometimes, as a treat, fish and chips for lunch. Long afternoons followed in a kind of glorious trance, amid the roar and ozone of crashing waves, the rippling dips and banks of sand filled with cool, lime-tinted glass made liquid, sprays of silver fry embedded in the brine.

It was during that glorious summer, when Mum and Dad were giving their marriage another go, that he had turned up—Uncle Arthur. After he'd gone again, the school holidays continued uneventfully until school resumed in late January 1973. I had just turned nine years old and was in Mr Wendell's grade four class at Willoughby Public School.

It was a few months later, on a cool autumn morning before school, that I asked Mum, yet again, if she had found my Lego set, as I wanted to take it to school. "No," she snapped, "I told you, I'll find it when I have a minute. Now, has Kandy got water?" Kandy was our large, gentle, blond Labrador cross. The black Labrador Satan, from next door had arrived home with her years before. She had been starving and pregnant and had given birth to ten gorgeous puppies in the disused shower recess in our laundry. I was absentmindedly scratching the top of her velvety head when, a short time later, Mum came up behind me, making me jump, "I told you to give her water."

"I have," I replied.

An hour later, I was absorbed in a game of marbles with a kid I'd stumbled upon some three weeks before, playing by himself in the school playground. I had asked if I could play too and he had kindly gifted me a small handful of his marbles to get started. Since then, we would meet up each morning for a game before the bell went for the first class of the day. I had never asked him his name, nor he mine, but it didn't matter, we just played.

The marbles clinked and rolled, glinting in the sun as they found little indents in the pitted, black asphalt surface. On this particular morning we were as usual, deeply engrossed in our game, when my head turned, the boy's turning too, to follow my gaze. We watched silently as a distant figure marched toward us. I could tell it was Mum wearing her cream woollen pant suit, carrying Luke on one hip.

As she approached I rose uncertainly to my feet. Without a word, she held out my little brown school case that smelled of Perkins Paste and Twisties and my hand reached automatically to grasp the handle. I hardly noticed as it fell and knocked against my knee. She was already turning away when she said, "Come on Michele, we're going to live in Melbourne." Leaving my marbles scattered over the ground and without a thought for the boy, I trailed after her to the waiting taxi.

We were checking in at the Ansett Airlines flight desk when a voice called Mum's name and she tensed. "How good to see you," said a man who was smiling at us all. Mum laughed and stuttered slightly as she replied, "Oh h-h-hello Ken... just off to Melbourne for a holiday." She turned back to grab the tickets from the counter, before turning again to leave.

"Well, come back here," said the affable Ken, one of Dad's work colleagues. "We'll have to get you an upgrade." He then spoke swiftly to the woman behind the desk and she handed over updated passes for business class.

"Lovely to see you," he said with a swift smile, before striding away. Mum's smile vanished and she sped off with her characteristic short-stepped march toward the boarding gate as I ran to keep up.

On board, the smiling air hostess asked what I'd like to drink and I told her Coke, glancing at Mum to see if she would object. Uncharacteristically she didn't and the smiling air hostess returned with a small glass filled with ice and a frosty can of Coke. I sipped my drink happily, unaware we were flying toward the 'death zone'. An hour later, we landed in Melbourne to start our new life with Uncle Arthur, a man 27 years' Mum's senior.

At 6 o'clock the following evening, as Uncle Arthur was arriving home to a house full of light and company, Dad would have been stepping through the front door of our home. He would have wondered why the house was uncharacteristically dark and would have walked into the bedroom, to hang up his suit jacket as he always did but would find the wardrobe empty of Mum's clothes. Confused, he would rush to his children's room to find our clothes and toys gone too.

He would find a note on the kitchen table. My beloved Kandy would be waiting outside the back door, hungry but tail wagging excitedly. Next door, Nanna and Grandad would be worried and perplexed, wondering where we had gone—Mum had not told them she was planning to run away either.

A week later, a big trunk arrived for us from Sydney. It was full of toys and clothes and my Lego set.

14

THE JACARANDA TREE

Our first cold winter in Melbourne was on the wane; the days lengthened into a summer of sorts, not consistently warm but an improvement. My two girlfriends—the twins—and I had just ridden our bikes into the backyard. We'd been riding around the streets chasing and being chased by 'the boys' for hours. The twins had dropped theirs on the grass, while I had propped mine against the wide trunk of the jacaranda tree. We were racing off for a glass of Cottee's orange cordial when Uncle Arthur, who was gardening, left his roses with secateurs in hand, and strode over to block my path.

"Look here, I told you to put your bike up in there," he snarled, pointing with his twisted index finger at the narrow, dank passageway up the side of the house.

He drew back the hand that was pointing and with full swing, cracked it across my face. My head jerked sideways, eyes watering with the stinging pain and shock. Blood rushed to my cheek, but I managed to swallow down the tears as mortified, I avoided my friends' gaze. Uncle Arthur stood glowering and

I quickly took my bike from the thick trunk and wheeled it up the side of the house. I stood for a moment, unsure of whether to lean it against the house and risk scratching the paint or to lay it on the ground, which he had emphatically told me not to do. I don't remember the decision I made but it must have been the right one because he strode back to his precious roses without another word and the twins and I continued inside for a drink.

That evening Mum, Uncle Arthur, Luke and I were invited to 'The Aunties' for dinner. The Aunties were Uncle Arthur's deceased wife's sisters and cousins, and I adored them. Although they were 'colonialists', The Aunties were not completely Caucasian and it showed in their raven hair, dark eyes and light, chai-coloured skin, and they spoke in a beautiful sing song accent. Uncle Arthur had trained himself to sound 'English' although he couldn't help but pronounce his 'Vs' as 'Ws', and he only laughed when Mum teased his pronunciation of Vicki as 'Wicki'.

There had been a hierarchy in Uncle Arthur's Ceylon (modern Sri Lanka). The British held the top spot, considering themselves the pinnacle of breeding and refinement. Only English men and women patronised the English clubs and they held the most senior positions in government. The Dutch were below the English but above the Portuguese, while the native Singhalese were at the bottom, servants and menial workers in their own land.

Uncle Arthur had tried to make himself sound English—mind you, not Cockney or Liverpudlian but like Prince Philip. He hated to be 'lesser' and had a large photo of the Queen on the lounge room mantlepiece. She had presented him with a medal on her visit to Ceylon in 1954 for his work as a high-ranking policeman.

Unlike Uncle Arthur, The Aunties, The Lovely Ladies, were unfailingly warm and playful, kind and generous. Bowls of delicious Bhuja mix were scattered around the big, warm lounge room (coming from a tropical country, they hated the cold) and I loved to pick out the peanuts. There were also bowls of roasted cashews and trays of 'short eats', which were delicious, crispy fried parcels containing fish or chicken or vegetable curry, served with sweet, spicy mango chutney.

This night as usual, Luke and I were allowed to stay up until 9pm before being put to bed in Aunty Leslie and Uncle Johann's bed. Luke went straight to sleep, but I fought to stay awake, comforted by the sounds of laughter and fond reminiscing of the 'good old days' in their Ceylon.

"Michele, look here! Get that bird off your damned cat," Uncle Arthur ordered as we arrived home from tennis the following afternoon. Smocker was holding a starling in his mouth. Uncle Arthur said he loved birds but his fruit trees dripped with pesticides. He loved wild 'life' too but the heads of his prey lined the hallway to my bedroom. By day their sad, glass eyes were fixed in what I took to be melancholy contemplation of their former jungle lives, before he'd put a bullet through them, but by night, the leopardess and black bears became restive and watchful and the elephant feet umbrella holders still had hair.

Reluctantly, I dawdled down the drive toward the cat until he roared, "Hurry up!" It had happened before—Smocker had caught a bird and Uncle Arthur had told me, if the poor thing was still alive, I would have to put it out of its misery.

"Arthur, she's afraid of what she might find," Mum told him, in an uncharacteristic display of solidarity. Why don't you get it yourself, I thought resentfully. Reluctantly, the cat released his prize into my hand, limp and mercifully for us both, dead.

Uncle Arthur only ever gave an instruction (order) once. If I did it again, at best I received a severe dressing down, at worse, a violent crack across the face. When we'd first arrived in Melbourne, I had had trouble remembering to turn off my bedroom light and was constantly berated as selfish and stupid. I wasn't to run in the house or put my feet on the furniture, or squeal and yell when playing in the street, or accidentally bang the lid of the toilet seat as I jumped off because my feet couldn't touch the ground. If I did, he'd be waiting outside the bathroom door.

One time, I'd forgotten the rule about running in the house and had collided with his hand as he'd strode around a corner. He had grabbed me by the scruff of the neck and shaken me, my feet dangling off the floor until I didn't know where I was. When he released his grip, I crumpled like a deflated paper bag into a limp pile at his feet. "I told you not to run in the house," he said, stepping over my dazed body and striding away.

At some point, Mum intervened and asked him not to hit me, so the next time he felt the urge, he raised his hand and swung but stopped just short of my cheek. I was braced, eyes squeezed shut, back rigid, everything tight. When nothing happened, I opened one eye and winced up into his face. He was watching me and as our eyes met, he dropped his hand and laughed uproariously, striding ebulliently away.

Uncle Arthur had been beaten as a child by his strict, austere, Baptist priest father, my great grandfather. After the beatings, apparently Arthur would stand on the church steps as the Sunday parishioners arrived, showing them his bruised body, telling them, "Look, my father, your priest did this."

Although he was never assessed, I'm sure Uncle Arthur was suffering post-traumatic stress disorder (PTSD) as he was easily startled, irritable and aggressive, rageful, controlling, obsessive, inflexible, had constant stomach pain and arthritis and had had a breakdown in his 40s.

"Now look here Michele," Uncle Arthur looked down his craggy nose at me one Saturday after lunch, not long after we'd arrived in Melbourne. "Your poor Mummy has to wash and cook and clean for you. She walks you to school." He looked outraged. I stared at his mouth non-plussed, so he continued, "From now on, you are going to clean the house for Mummy."

Each Saturday afternoon from then on, he followed me around the house, watching with severe scrutiny as I cleaned the toilet, basin, shower recess and bath and then did the vacuuming, making sure to move every piece of furniture, minding I didn't knock the skirting boards. The ordeal took hours and hours.

In Ceylon, the Dutch colonialists had had servants, including children (a servant boy used to run to Dad's school each day with his hot lunch) to cook and clean their sprawling bungalows, while the 'masters' ran tea plantations or held white collar positions. Their wives drank tea and gossiped or worked as schoolteachers.

Conveniently, Uncle Arthur had acquired a servant girl in me, to 'Mummy's' fragile princess. He had proudly rescued her from an unfulfilling union and the drudgery of domestic duties and she loved the special treatment, although... "Look at this..." she told me on her 35th birthday, "Arthur brought me a child's watch." He had also given her a child's tennis racquet the previous Christmas. His adoration came at the cost of infantilisation.

15

THE IMP

Whereas I had largely been ignored by Mum and Dad, I was always under intense scrutiny from Uncle Arthur. He relished finding fault and demonstrating his superiority. He would randomly bark at me to spell some word or other, and wait for me to stutter and flounder. I was an easy target as I was a hopeless speller and ashamed of and unconfident in my academic abilities.

Another of his favourite pastimes was to spring random questions on me, which I invariably could not answer. If by some miracle I did get one right, he would patronisingly parrot the answer back, in the same tone as a correction but nine times out of ten, I got the answer wrong and he would utter the same inevitable refrain, "Don't they teach you anything at that school of yours!?"

On weekends I was constantly summoned to his side, "Michele, come here," he would command and I would hasten to him, doing my best to look alert and eager. He would have thought up the solution to a non-existent problem and we'd be off to the bathroom where instructions ensued with a demonstration,

"Look here, that toilet roll rubs against the wallpaper if you put it on that way. When you replace it, you must put it on the holder so the paper feeds out from the back."

"Yes, Uncle Arthur," I would answer diffidently, not brave or stupid enough to tell him what was obvious even to a ten-year-old child, that the roll rubbed the wall whichever way you put it.

Another memorable money-saving initiative involved unnecessary wear and tear to a patch of high-traffic carpet. "Come here Michele." I was in my bedroom but immediately left my doodling to walk swiftly to his side, careful not to break into a run. I stood respectfully, looking politely curious, an eager dog ready to do his bidding lest he belt me. The main route from the bedrooms to the kitchen received more through-traffic than the slightly longer, less direct route, that split off via the lounge room.

"Now, you need to walk from the hallway through the lounge room door to the dining room, not the quicker way from the hall directly into the dining room. Do you understand?"

"Yes, Uncle Arthur."

From then on if he was in the vicinity, he would make a point to stop what he was doing and watch to see which route I took. He never told Mum or Luke to do these things and he never did them himself.

I obeyed Uncle Arthur's every order because intuitively, I knew it was too dangerous to openly defy him, he could kill me with a single blow but to be relentlessly bullied, used and invalidated was galling. Uncle Arthur relished telling stories of catching his officers sleeping on the job at midnight. He'd laugh, remembering how they'd jump to attention, shaking in their boots. I was terrified too but there was a part of me that unconsciously fought Uncle Arthur's authority, in subtle, passive ways, which he hated. He was intensely irritated that a mere girl would not completely submit to his will and from time to time that 'part' engaged in small acts of defiance that made 'our' lives more difficult.

'She' would 'steal' a biscuit, would scowl every morning and refused to say 'It's a pleasure' after doing what he had ordered me to do. Other parts of me craved his love and approval, wanted to be free of his scrutiny and sadism, would happily submit but the defiant part would never accept being treated like scum, even if she was only ten years old. 'She' would occasionally get her own back, the mischievous Imp making our lives just that little bit more difficult.

There was the time Mum and Uncle Arthur went out for an hour after dinner, leaving a plate of Arnott's Mint Slices temptingly on the kitchen table, with strict instructions by Uncle Arthur to not eat any more. I'll have another one if I want, 'I' thought and took one from the plate. The rest of the packet was in the tin in the pantry, which I doubted he had counted, but my hand reached out and took another from the plate. I set about nibbling the chocolate and mint layer off like a mouse. When that was all gone, I crunched up the chocolate biscuit base and feeling satisfied went to my room.

"I told you not to take another biscuit Michele," came Uncle Arthur's inevitable rebuke. "Now clean your teeth and go to bed." Phew, I had got off lightly and relieved and a little self-satisfied, bounced into bed and reached for my book, *Five On Kirran Island Again*.

I had avoided books until the age of ten when one day Mum and Uncle Arthur had barged into my bedroom and told me to start reading. Books made me feel stupid and so I had cried, but my lovely grade 5 teacher Miss Godfrey, had gifted me an Enid Blyton book, *The Island of Adventure*, which I had put away in the bookcase. Reluctantly, I retrieved it and began and after a few tortuous chapters was hooked on Enid Blyton, at least.

My fear of reading began in my first years at primary school. I'd found it difficult to learn to read as I was an undiagnosed dyslexic but would only discover the source of my academic difficulties in the final semester of my master's degree some 30 years later.

Thanks to Enid Blyton, reading became a wonderful escape. No matter how upsetting the day had been, when it came to bedtime, I fell eagerly into the adventures of The Famous Five—four brave kids and Timmy the dog. These children weren't cowed by the Uncle Arthurs of the world, and they spent their holidays slurping delicious ice creams, eating entire fruit cakes for lunch (not that I liked fruit cake) after demolishing piles of sandwiches, and then swam off George's boat and searched for treasure, which they actually found on George's very own island. And they even lived with an explosive uncle and weren't fazed in the slightest.

16

SOFT-BOILED EGGS

I'd been seeing Ronnie for four months and was fighting to hold myself together until my work contract expired the following month. My sleep quality was poor and I was bone tired, exhausted by the emotional distress of the many fragmented parts sharing my body. The urge to cut properly, grew steadily stronger.

If 'I' was triggered, it meant a traumatised child 'part' was leaking her pain or shock or grief or fear into consciousness, which resulted in emotional dysregulation or painful bodily symptoms. The 'parts' were of all ages and stages of development, although the ones who were most often triggered were three years old, terrified their 'Lovely Lady' would suddenly reject them and leave. I was re-enacting my early years with my unpredictable and emotionally neglectful but occasionally attentive Mummy.

One Tuesday morning three weeks before I finished work I texted, *Hi Ronnie, I am struggling a bit today. Have two important meetings on Zoom at 2.00 and 3.30pm, which I need to attend. I want to use the scissors again. Sorry to be a pain. Michele.*

Ronnie replied, *OK then, let's talk. I'll be free around 12.00. Does that work for you?* Ronnie sent me a Zoom meeting invite and we had an 'emergency' session.

The effects of Uncle Arthur's abuse, suppressed for so long, could no longer be subdued and I began to experience a visceral sense that I was being physically attacked. My reflexes warned me to duck my head and my back and shoulder muscles were frozen in rigid knots.

Not long after we had moved to Melbourne, I had begun to suffer migraine headaches. I'd get one every six months or so, especially at the start of the school holidays when I first arrived back 'home' in Sydney. The sudden let down in tension seemed to trigger the appearance of the dreaded point of light, flashing when I blinked. It would grow into a large, sickening kaleidoscopic ball of swimming lights, obscuring half my sight. Then the horrible ball would recede and a blinding headache and sometimes nausea would follow.

Because they only seemed to happen when I let down my guard, for example coming 'home' to Sydney, or when I was having an energetically fun time—bouncing around on a trampoline, or trail riding—I began to associate relaxing and exciting outdoor adventures with developing migraines. I feared becoming incapacitated with pain in a public place, surrounded by people and forced to let my mask drop. The fear followed me into my adult life, reinforcing again and again that it was not ever safe to have fun or to relax. If 'fun' ever happened spontaneously, the next day I would dread developing a migraine in retribution for daring to enjoy myself.

One day when I was 11, a migraine started during the third quarter of a netball match and on the way home, I sank to my knees on someone's nature strip and threw up the orange segment I'd eaten at half time, with a lot of bile. I immediately felt better, climbed to my feet and with renewed vigour and my usual after school appetite, continued home. I told Mum I had had a migraine and been sick a mere ten minutes before but was now starving and asked if I could have some toast.

Mum had a phobia about vomiting (which she passed on to me) and once I hit ten years of age, she made herself scarce if she thought I was going to throw up. I assume the migraine incident made some impact on her because the following week she took me to Uncle Arthur's chiropractor. A tall, serious-looking man, he placed little pads on my neck and shoulders and they delivered a rhythmic pulse. He then attempted to massage my shoulders, but I squirmed away from his hands because it hurt. When I groaned, he stopped and asked me to go back into the waiting room without Mum. I felt chastened, assuming he thought me naughty or ill mannered. If he had smiled, perhaps I would have known he was on my side.

A few days after that session, Mum told me she had instructed Uncle Arthur to stop hitting me, hence the 'pretend' whack when he'd caught me running in the house, but the migraines continued.

Mum once told me she admired Uncle Arthur because he was a man of action unlike my pathetic Dad. He demonstrated his love for her by chastising me and by doing practical things to make her life easier, like making the breakfast on weekday mornings.

The servants had prepared all the meals in Ceylon and so, like many ex-pats, when Uncle Arthur's wife had been killed in a car crash, he had to teach himself. Menu items included: cold, lumpy porridge made with water not milk and served with his sugar-free stewed apples rather than brown sugar; stinking kippers; and overly soft-boiled eggs. He preferred his eggs almost raw and after making the mistake of trying to eat one, I ate toast on egg days.

One evening, as Mum was cooking dinner and Uncle Arthur was standing with one arm leaning on the high, deep window ledge above the cupboard surveying us imperiously, Mum and I were enthusing about the perfect boiled eggs Grandad always cooked. The whites of Grandad's boiled eggs were always perfectly set, while the yolks were runny, ideal for dipping buttery soldiers into.

Because he seemed in such a benign mood, I piped up cheerfully, "Uncle Arthur, could you cook my eggs a bit more please?"

"Yes, alright," he replied with surprising grace.

"I like the whites hard Uncle Arthur," I told him beaming, just to make sure he got it.

"What's wrong with you? Eat your ruddy egg," he roared the next morning. He'd looked over from his lunch preparations, the same fishfinger sandwiches he made each day to take to work. It stank out the kitchen.

He must have boiled my egg for ages because the yolk was desiccated, too dry to swallow. He left his fishfingers to glare gleefully, "Come on," he sneered. "I told you to eat that ruddy egg." I resumed my swallowing routine until he ordered, "Drink your orange juice," and the mouthful finally went down. "Oh, thank you Uncle Arthur, that's better," I told him gratefully, after which I finished my breakfast very quickly and headed to school to play 'elastics' before the start of lessons.

Thankfully, the next weekend we were off to visit The Aunties again. "Go faster, Uncle Arthur," Luke and I pleaded excitedly. Mum looked worried but Luke and I grinned as Uncle Arthur let his huge 'Yank Tank' gather speed down the vertiginous road. We roared up the opposite hill and glided down the next. Breathless, we arrived to broad smiles of delight and I felt that wonderful feeling of maternal love, safe in the embrace of my aunties.

"Oh, Arthur, let her have another one," said Auntie Leslie, winking at me as she poked the plate of biscuits under my eager nose.

Hours later, back home in my bed, I woke with a tummy ache and puked up a lot of brown stuff into the bathroom basin. The next morning, I told Mum at breakfast. "Mum, guess what? Last night I got sick. It was all brown."

"Too many Tim Tams," observed Mum wryly.

"I hope you did it in the toilet," said Uncle Arthur. He shaved in the sink.

"Oh yes," said the Imp in a most convincing parody of diffidence, imagining him filling the basin with water and applying his shaving cream, then splashing water from that very basin onto his face. Some might even go in his mouth. Ha! The Imp smirked in a self-satisfied way, while the timid ones all giggled.

17

BLACK AND WHITE

I dreamed Matilda and I were police detectives and we had been called to the scene of a grisly murder. The pulpy mess, a severed head, had been discovered in the entry foyer of a bright new office tower by an early morning worker. We'd followed a lead and were in the library on an upper floor. Despite the newness of the building, the stadium-sized room felt ancient. Motes of dust swirled in long sunlit columns and old tomes littered deserted desks. The place smelled of yellowing paper and neglect.

Each level was connected by a wide, central staircase of many dark steps, with a polished wooden handrail coiling like a bronze snake to connect the misplaced room with the rest of the ultra-modern building. I stood uncertainly on the dusty parquet, peering across the endless expanse of floor to the impenetrable darkness beyond.

All at once, Matilda was locked in a deadly battle, grappling with something black and fierce—a teenage girl, dressed like a punk all in black, silver studs decorating her face in a spray of dull metal. Her long hair that should have been blond, was jet black. It framed her white face, my face and the thing wore a sneer.

Matilda managed to tie her to one of the iron rails of the staircase balustrade, but almost immediately she escaped, disappearing swiftly into the gloom. I was very angry with Matilda for letting her get away and I looked around, fearing to see her at the edge of the darkness.

The savage, unpredictable creature was on the loose again.

After school one day, I raced inside and put my empty lunchbox in the sink, grabbed a couple of Nice biscuits from the tin, and ran out into the street to play. There was a group of kids in the opposite front yard bending excitedly over something. It was a baby mouse in a box, caught by the boy who lived there. Everyone was breathing excitedly over the tiny form, prodding it and I felt desperately sorry for the little creature.

I went home to have my bath and dinner, but distressed by the thought of the weight of its suffering, stole furtively from the house after dinner to search among dusty old shoes and broken toys and found it still lying in the box, on its dirty piece of cloth.

Perhaps it is already dead, I thought hopefully. Its tiny head lolled pathetically when I lifted it carefully from the box but I carefully put it back and went in search of a small rock. I wanted to make sure it was no longer suffering. I found a solitary stone on the desolate garden bed bordering the concrete porch and returned with it to the cardboard coffin. Holding my breath, I tapped its tiny head. The stone left an indent. I had expected it to be hard.

It must be dead now I thought, surely. Unable to bear the uncertainty, I decided its suffering, the agony of abandonment, a fate worse than death was over, and relieved, I ran home before I was discovered.

I was that kind-hearted 11-year-old child who had tried to save the baby mouse from suffering. I had an RSPCA sticker on my bedroom window. Uncle Arthur sneered when he caught sight of it. He would tell me I was too selfish to love animals. With the addition of teenage hormones, submitting to Uncle Arthur's intractable will became more difficult and I began to drown under his relentless torment, which I internalised and then acted out, siphoning off the accumulation of unconscious rage onto the only safe option, my cat.

The first time it happened, I got hold of Luke and went in search of Smocker. We found him snoozing peacefully on the sunny veranda overlooking the long garden, beyond which was a paddock, the Gardiners Creek, and distant playing fields. I picked him up and carried him down our street, turning into the road leading to the creek. He began to struggle as we crossed the footbridge, but I held him tightly by the scruff of his neck and continued, not stopping until we were standing alone in the middle of one of the big, grassy ovals.

I put him down at my feet and could sense his fear and competing urges to both freeze and run. His distress filled me with a such savage pleasure that I laughed as I started to walk back toward the distant footbridge. The terrified statue came slowly to life. It crept and crawled, its belly touching the short grass, until it broke into a trot, then a controlled run, and finally a desperate dash to the footbridge. I watched enthralled but also anxious. What if he can't find his way home again or a dog gets him, I thought with a pang of fear? Trying to look indifferent and unconcerned to Luke, I followed his track back across the oval and bridge, up through the streets, to thankfully find him safely back in the garden. He was washing himself furiously but slunk away when he saw us coming.

The next week the same feeling of pressured fury bubbled

up like hot lava and I grabbed the cat again and took him back down the street and over the footbridge, but this time we turned right to follow the tall bank of the creek until we were opposite our back fence.

I threw him and he sailed in a spectacular arc to hit the cold, silty water. There was a splash and he disappeared below the murky surface. I sensed his shock as my own but smirked as the little arsehole reappeared and swam to the opposite bank. I felt a blessed moment of release, of power, loathing and euphoria but almost immediately worry obliterated the relief. He had arrived at the opposite bank but it had been shored up with huge boulders to stop erosion and I suffered a deep stab of fear, worried he might not be able to get out. It took a moment's scrabbling but with the look of a sleek water rat he pulled himself over the obstruction. Feeling relieved and guilty I watched him bob his way through the long grass to our back fence, over which he leapt with one huge bound, to safety.

18

THE FOX CUBS

"Joan of Arc? Yeah, she's still standing over there in her shiny silver armour, contemplating a daisy."

She seems a bit dazed and doesn't appear to have noticed, she's standing in an antipodean sea of blond wavy grass, heads bowed with seed, surrounded by muddled toddlers and a middle-aged woman with kind, grey eyes.

The woman is hosting a charm of little red fox cubs on her lap. One is even licking and chewing a nipple. The little she-cub is lapping the sweet milk as it spreads like warm honey, in a flood over the fabric of her breast, staining it darkly red.

I'd been seeing Ronnie for five months when the end of the financial year arrived and my work contract finally expired. Due to the pandemic, my leaving lunch was put on an indefinite hold, for which I was thankful because I was exhausted and just wanted to be alone at home to sleep in, to think about Ronnie in peace and to let the internal firestorm rage unchecked by work commitments. It was such a strain to pretend

I felt OK, that everything was fine and I wasn't going mad. Managing the constant emotional overwhelm was like trying to hold back a bout of vomiting. Being sick is the pits but holding it in is unsustainable.

The idea I would suddenly find the motivation and confidence to train Tuala turned out to be a pipe dream. If anything, I felt even more triggered by her size, her reactivity and her majesty and catching and leading her to the stables became too difficult. When she needed her regular hoof trims, I asked the agistment owner to catch and lead her for me. All I could manage was to take a bucket of feed to her paddock and sit on the other side of the fence, next to her head, as she tucked in, and I watched.

Without work to pull me into the straitjacket of a routine, the days and weeks lost their wonky rhythm. It was now mid-winter—cold, grey and bleak and each day I would grab my headphones and walk the same route, which led to the All Nations Park as it provided a high vantage point from where I could stand and gaze with unrequited longing to the distant northeastern horizon, to the flat tabletop of Kinglake, beyond which was the town of Beechworth many kilometres away, where Ronnie lived.

What was she doing? I would wonder, my heart as heavy as a rock, icy fingers of wind insinuated their way through my clothing. Perhaps she was talking on the phone, the rich tones of her voice lulling the listener as an electric jug came to the boil. She could be hanging out her washing, or seeing another client on Zoom, or eating a piece of toast, or having coffee at a local café with one of her many friends, laughing and engaging. She might be crying, designing a new art installation, taking a shower or getting dressed, talking to her cat or her inner children, to whom she told me she fed ice cream when they were feeling bad. I hoped she wasn't kissing her wife—I couldn't stand the thought of that and so kept imagining she was.

Ronnie had worked from a number of different consulting suites before moving to Beechworth, one of which was in Northcote and on my frequent walks to the All Nations Park, I'd take a detour to pass them. The rooms were now a Pilates studio and I'd stand on the opposite side of the street and imagine it was one year ago and that I might see her rushing in or out of the double doors, on her way home or to grab something to cook for dinner at the nearby shopping centre. How many times had I wandered through Northcote Plaza Shopping Centre. We might have passed each other, I thought desperately and would never have known that one day I would love her.

One Saturday afternoon in early July, when I logged into Zoom for our weekly session, I found I couldn't speak. I opened my mouth a couple of times but nothing came out, so I had sat staring mutely at Ronnie.

After a bit, I scabbled around on the desk for a piece of paper and pen and wrote a note, which I held in front of the screen. *I have been hijacked, can't talk.*

"Do you know how old they are?" Ronnie asked, referring to the inner kids.

Nine plus . . . ? I wrote, but I wasn't sure.

"How are they feeling?" she asked.

I wrote back, *They are feeling loathsome.*

It was true, I felt like a disgusting, slimy slug but Ronnie just smiled reassuringly.

I wrote again, *One of them got cut.*

"Oh shit!" said Ronnie. "You could have sent me a text, you know?" She sounded put out, which we liked. It showed she cared.

But they thought there was no point. They wanted to do it, had made up their minds. I grimaced apologetically and tried again to speak but the block was still in place.

Can't feel anything, just numb, I continued to scribe.

"Do you know what triggered the cutting?" she asked.

God, what a fraud. The one who had done it had only managed deep scratches. They hadn't even bled and I felt my insides squeeze with embarrassment. How pathetic, someone else thought.

Felt too big, might go crazy, I wrote, referring to the feeling of overwhelm that led to the episode. Then an intuitive thought told me these 'new' children were younger, around two years of age and there were many of them, little split-off, traumatised parts, hijacking my body and pre-frontal cortex. They were all alone in the dark, afraid and distraught. They had been hiding for 54 years and I hadn't realised it.

As I sat quietly, more information came into my head in the form of thoughts and images. Someone told me it hadn't been the two-year-old parts who had cut but older protector parts, whose role it was to suppress negative, overwhelming feelings that might derail our outward appearance of normality.

Slowly the vision of an inner world began to materialise, and I could perceive in the deep gloom, the naked backs of many pale little bodies, hunching protectively, their spines visible through fine, translucent skin. They looked naked, unformed and exposed, like tortoises without their shells. All were lying in a vast underground, earthen cave. In the cave there was no light and down at the far end, there was a big hole in the floor, the abyss which threatened to suck them down, to annihilate them, if they dared move or make a sound.

After some tapping, I regained my ability to speak and Ronnie and I worked together to place a fine, translucent shell over each little body for containment and protection, until our next session.

After another long, long week, overwhelmed by what had been thrown up from my subconscious, I went back inside to find them all still there. Ronnie suggested I take Tuala down to them in their cave, so they could smell her beautiful, hay-smelling body and feel its exquisite heat and vitality. Tuala stood like red marble in the gloom of the cave but was suddenly engulfed by a mass of black insects that crawled all over her, like black beetles. I felt disgusted and overwhelmed. There were so very many, and they were hungry.

I was afraid of these damaged, deprived parts. Mum must have been too, as it was her revulsion I had internalised, at the age of two. As the natural drive to independence exerted itself, perhaps Mum had felt overwhelmed by my demands, which were greater than she was capable of meeting. The fact there were many fragments, many beetles, meant I had felt overwhelmed on many occasions and as a result, had developed a disorganised/fearful attachment style.

Meanwhile Ronnie had had another idea and asked, "Could we take some light down to them, do you think?" Immediately I was blinded by an impossibly brilliant explosion that illuminated the cave, subsuming the darkness. The little ones cringed away from the source, looking like white petals around a glowing anther. The fine, tall flame resolved itself into the shining figure of Saint Joan of Arc.

There she stood, bright and fierce, loving and protective of these fragile, emotionally malnourished fragments of humanity. Suddenly they were safe under their fine, mother of pearl 'tortoise' shells. "Make the shells translucent," suggested Ronnie, "So they can feel the warmth of the Divine light."

Time was up again and I looked back one last time to see them safe and curled under their shells of organic armour with St Joan, the 'Maid', sword in hand, silently standing guard.

For some reason I pictured this underground cave, which was both their refuge and prison, to be located at the farm where Tuala was agisted. It lay under the grassy slope leading down to a small dam, the land rising again on the opposite bank, where live a beautiful cinnamon-coloured Arab colt and filly, who are brother and sister, called Henry and Lolly. Opposite them, diagonally across from the two-year-old's paddock, lived Tuala (she has since been moved to another agistment).

Over the course of many weeks with Ronnie's support, I managed to make a hole in the roof of the cave but hadn't the emotional strength to erase the abyss. Over time, the hole in the roof became bigger and the deprived children were given a carpet of exquisitely soft, green moss to lie on. Fireflies provided a soft light and when night fell, stars could be seen blinking sleepily down through the hole in the roof.

EFT (Matrix Reimprinting) had enabled the slow transformation of their inner landscape and although the little ones didn't seem to hear or feel Ronnie's nurturing words, the toddlers did eventually venture out above ground, blinking like owls in the morning light. Many were children but some did not feel safe in human form and appeared instead as little red fox cubs, their senses more finely attuned, able to respond more nimbly to threat. They didn't trust humans and I wondered how it was possible they were so damaged. Surely my infancy hadn't been that bad?

One Sunday afternoon in the middle of the work with the two-year-olds, Matilda and I went out for lunch (between COVID lockdowns) to Warrandyte, a bushy suburb in Melbourne's outer east. After lunch we amused ourselves browsing in the art and craft shops. One little shop sold children's toys and there I bought the two-year-olds a cute, pale-green, velvet dinosaur, whom they called Dolly. She was utterly gorgeous but when I picked her up that night to cuddle her, I felt the same sickening urge I had felt when I had tormented my cat all those years before. I put her down, before they could rip her to pieces.

19

LOLITA

I dreamed of a bright, sunny morning. I was standing on the corner of Victoria and Lygon Streets, the city centre to my left and the Exhibition Gardens behind. Usually noisy and congested, the intersection was now deserted.

Making its way slowly up Victoria Street from the west was a rickety cart, drawn by a motheaten old nag. A throng of pubescent children jostled around the cart, like street urchins from a Dickensian novel. I worked my way through the throng to peer over the edge of the cart, which was laden with what looked like mounds of dirty tissue paper.

One of the children had a long pole and was prodding clumps of the paper. I wished he wouldn't. A piece of the stained pulp tore to reveal the pale, immobile face of a corpse, a man with smooth black hair and porcelain white skin. The child continued to prod and probe and uncovered the white face of a dead woman.

Suddenly their eyes sprang open and they leapt with lightning speed and unnatural agility off the cart. The urchins screamed and ran helter-skelter in all directions. The man lunged and I took *off at a dead run up Victoria Street. Even as I sprinted away, I knew he would never give up until he caught me.*

It was on those hottest of summer nights that I would shrug off my long nightie and lay naked, searching out cool patches under the cotton sheet. One school morning, Uncle Arthur, rather than 'Mummy' came to wake me. He ripped the sheet off and held it up. I lay still, staring up at the ceiling, feeling his eyes raking my hairless, 11-year-old body.

After that morning, on hot nights I would try with all my might to keep my nightie on until I couldn't stand its cloying twist around my legs for another second. *I'll make myself wake up before he comes*, I would tell myself.

One morning I managed to wake just as the door slid open and had the presence of mind to grab a handful of sheet. I lay with eyes closed, playing possum. I could feel him standing quietly watching me until the air moved against my cheek. He had bent down to the sheet, then pulled but feeling resistance, snarled and ripped it from my grasp. I could feel him glaring and feasting as he held it up for what felt like ages, before letting it fall like a shroud over my face.

Ronnie and I tapped on the dream of the cart in our next session, while images floated into consciousness like rubbish on an incoming tide. As we tapped on the fear and shame of my helplessness and guilt at being naked 'on purpose', another more distressing memory flashed up. I tried to push it back down but my ten-year-old self felt compelled to confess.

Before we moved to Melbourne, I would sleep in Mum and Dad's bed when he went away on intrastate business. One day, when I was around the age of ten, Mum announced she was going away for a night to a work conference and without thinking I piped up triumphantly in front of Uncle Arthur, "Mum, I can sleep in your bed!"

Immediately, I felt the horror of the implication. It would mean sleeping with Uncle Arthur, not Mum and although I was a child, I knew there was no backing out. No one rejected Arthur, especially not me. As I reddened, Mum laughed non-committally and nothing more was said.

I stewed with dread on the day Mum would leave and all too soon she was gone. Now Uncle Arthur had me all to himself. It never occurred to me to go to bed in my own room and hope there was no retribution. That night, I slowly got myself ready for bed and finally dawdled to his bedroom wearing my short cotton nightie with orange rabbits nibbling bright green carrots. I stood uncertainly next to his bed on Mum's side until he said, "Alright," in a tone that implied he was doing me a favour, "You can get in for 15 minutes." I climbed in feeling a mixture of self-consciousness and relief. Fifteen minutes was strange but was better than all night.

Uncle Arthur turned off the light as I lay on my back like a plank, eyes wide in the dark. After a moment, the bed creaked and I felt his huge, calloused hand stroke my arm. After a time, his hand roamed from arm, to chest, down the length of my torso to my legs, which he stroked and stroked. I became aware of the sound of his breathing and with each stroke it became louder. There was heat and intensity as he fixated on my legs and his breath became laboured until suddenly he pushed me roughly away and growled, "Now get out." In a strange way, I felt rejected and had no idea what had just happened.

The next morning as I was getting dressed, he burst into my bedroom, "What the hell are you doing?" he roared and I jumped violently. Laughing, he strode away down the hall.

20

TEACHERS

Ever since Ronnie had told had me she had recovered from borderline personality disorder, I felt periodically drawn to review the diagnostic criteria because I had an intuitive feeling I might also have it. Each time though, I would dismiss myself as pathetic. Who would want to suffer such a crippling mental illness just for someone's approval?

"I would," said a hopeful little voice.

BPD is a mental illness characterised by intense psychic pain. To be diagnosed with the disorder a person must display five of the following nine symptoms: explosive anger; intense fear of abandonment; suicidal behaviour or ideation; black and white thinking (splitting); self-injurious behaviour; impulsive, self-destructive behaviours; extreme emotional swings; chronic feelings of emptiness; and an unstable sense of self.

Late one Saturday night following one of our weekly sessions, I had re-read the diagnostic criteria yet again and decided yet again, that I didn't fit the stereotypical picture of the angry, suicidal, highly dysregulated, crazy person. That sounded more like Mum but then, what about Ronnie? Was she like my mother? I couldn't imagine my lovely, enthusiastic, supportive, creative, warm-hearted, empathetic Ronnie to be like Mum. I could imagine Ronnie had perhaps been needy and highly dysregulated, self-destructive, even difficult to please and critical at times, but not like Mum.

I reasoned that having suffered both BPD and bipolar, Ronnie would have attempted suicide at least once and I imagined her as a young woman lying in a hospital bed, desolate and disappointed because she hadn't succeeded. I started to cry. That I had never attempted suicide felt like a betrayal of Ronnie and that I had let myself down.

By contrast, when I thought back to Mum's suicide attempt, I felt no empathy, no pangs of guilt or shame. I remember being sick and tired of her mood swings, of walking on eggshells, of being used and neglected, and the unrelenting chaos and drama she generated. When she had swallowed the bottle of pills, I had wished the attempt had succeeded because, already world weary, I considered life would be much easier with only my brother to look after and my father to worry about.

Interestingly, Mum's borderline behaviour only became evident after we'd moved out of Uncle Arthur's and she was back 'on the market'. We had taken our unexpected flight from Sydney to Uncle Arthur's in 1973 when I was nine years old. Mum, Luke and I had lived with him for five long years, until we moved again in 1978 and I was a 14-year-old adolescent and Luke was nine. Mum purchased a small, unrenovated, semi-detached weatherboard house in East Hawthorn. It was the worst house in one of the best suburbs and she bought it without telling Luke or me. A week before we were due to move, Uncle Arthur and

Mum 'surprised' us with the announcement as we drove around the new neighbourhood.

I nearly cried out in desperation as Uncle Arthur pointed to an ugly, dark brown, brick building and told me airily it was to be my new school. "Does it have a music department?" I asked miserably. The idea I would leave my haven, Chadstone High School, the only real 'home' I had, was unthinkable. It was there I hid my battered heart for safe keeping with her, my wonderful music teacher. I must have said something to Mum, made a case to stay, I don't remember, but thankfully she made the effort to discover a bus route accessible from the new house to my school.

Going to school was a place of escape from Uncle Arthur, a sanctuary and I felt safe and nurtured there, and even liked. I loved my school uniform and locker, the sour tinge of acid scenting the science room on hot February afternoons, the unhealthy canteen speciality of a hot sausage roll with sauce inside a buttered white roll, and most of all, Room 115, which was the music room—the domain of Miss Hann our classroom music teacher.

Each morning as I walked through the school gate, I would glance over to the teacher's carpark to make sure Miss Hann's car was there, the Toyota with the fluffy steering wheel. Once I'd confirmed she wasn't away, I would look up to the first floor, to the window of the staff room, and a buoyant feeling would fill my chest. She is in there right now, I would think.

One day after school, I looked up her address in the White Pages and with the twins who I'd convinced to come with me for moral support, we rode our bikes the five-odd kilometres to her home. When we finally arrived, forgetting all about my companions, I stood transfixed, taking in the large, dark, overgrown front garden, dusty old porch, diamond-paned lead-light windows and her trusty white Toyota sleeping quietly on the concrete driveway, like a loyal dog. When she wasn't reigning over Room 115 with its smelly, hormonal teens shaking maracas and belting xylophones, she was here, in her house, where she slept.

I remember my beloved music teacher, my 'Lovely Lady' as kind, independent, opinionated and a bit dowdy. Her musical domain, the classroom, was filled with a fine collection of classical records, an upright Yamaha piano, recorders of various sizes and pitches, a blackboard covered in musical squiggles and her classically trained, contralto voice.

21

THE BUS

My fondest memories from childhood are of the beach, especially the surf. According to Mum, I took my first steps on the Corso at South Steyne beach, Manly, one summer's afternoon when I was 11 months old.

When I was big enough, Dad used to take me past the breakers to float on the gentle sea beyond. He'd tuck me under his left arm and we'd set out, through the tumble of smaller waves. As the sand sloped away from the shore and the water became deeper, Dad would press me snuggly to his side and we'd dive through the churning maelstrom, eyes shut tight against the swirling grit, breath held for what felt like an age.

We'd surface nose-first like seals, streaming and gasping in the sharp ozone-tinged air. Daddy would say, "And another one, ready," as the next towering wall charged us like a bull elephant and we dove. "Almost there," he'd say, dashing forward to meet the next wall just before it broke. With an exhilarating whoosh, the wave carried us up toward the sky, its clear crystal tip tapping my head playfully in passing.

Now all was tranquil and serene and we floated blissfully on the glassy green sea, the gentle swell cradling us in a secure embrace. Above, pinned to the sapphire sky, seagulls shone white like stars.

On a grey autumn morning in March, a few months after we'd moved to Hawthorn, Mum pulled open the bedroom curtains and bustled to my bedside to give me a quick kiss. "Good morning," she said brightly, "Time to get up." I rose reluctantly, the weight of a depressive funk pressing me to the bed. I'd been carrying it since returning from school holidays in Sydney a month before. I idolised Dad and missed him dreadfully, although his level of self-absorption and irritability had escalated since Mum had left him, but perhaps he'd always been that way and I had been too small to notice.

Although it wasn't mandatory, I loved to wear the full school uniform of charcoal-grey, woollen, pleated skirt and matching jumper, white shirt, maroon blazer and charcoal tie with fine diagonal white and maroon stripes. The school felt more homelike than the house I shared with my 'family', and wearing the full uniform reinforced my sense of belonging.

Mum was making toast for Luke and a cup of tea for herself and when I arrived in the kitchen she announced proudly, "Michele, I've broken the cycle."

"What do you mean?" I asked.

"No one ever said 'good morning' when I was growing up ... Nanna and Grandad were always fighting and once Grandad gave me a black eye when I stepped between them to protect Mum, but she told me, 'Get away from me, you're just like him.'" I ate my toast, cleaned my teeth and rushed out of the front door to catch the 7.45am bus from Camberwell Junction, which was 14 minutes from home. I walked swiftly to the bus stop in a kind of miserable trance.

Leaving Dad was always a wrench, and I would pine for him and my former life for weeks upon my return, marking the days off on the calendar until I could see him again but after this latest holiday, I was feeling particularly anxious and fretful. The day before Luke and I left, Dad told my Aunty Anne he had almost killed himself. She had interrupted, saying awkwardly, "Do you think you should say this in front of..." trailing off, nodding her head in my direction, looking concerned, but he replied, "It's good for her to know these things."

There was something implied in his statement, which in hindsight I intuited to mean he wanted me to tell Mum he was suicidal, hoping to make her feel guilty for leaving. I didn't though, because I couldn't bear to hear Mum put Dad down. I never shared Mum's 'crazy' behaviour with Dad either, it never occurred to me, nor did it occur to me, in fact, that their behaviour was 'crazy', until I was much older.

Dad completed his story, telling us he had been drunk one rainy night just before Christmas and had 'almost' turned his car into the oncoming stream of traffic on a six-lane expressway. After hearing his horrifying story, I became overwhelmed with worry, fearing I would never see him again. I felt his life was my responsibility and being in Melbourne I could do nothing to save him.

I had felt a crushing sense of responsibility for Dad's welfare ever since I had returned to Sydney that first time following our departure to Melbourne. He had appeared so broken.

That first summer school holiday, Luke had remained in Melbourne because Mum thought he was too young to travel without her. He was only three, while I was nine. A couple of nights after arriving, I woke suddenly in the middle of the night and feeling something wasn't right, stumbled from my bedroom in search of Dad. The lounge room was ablaze but deserted. A bottle was standing next to a fallen wine glass on the mosaic coffee table, a small red puddle of claret was all that was left of the wine. I remembered watching enthralled as Mum had glued the iridescent blue and mustard yellow tiles onto the blond wooden surface and applied the grout, so long ago. Shirley Bassey was singing Never Never Never to the empty room on an endless loop.

I searched the entire house before wandering through the brightly lit kitchen and laundry to stand uncertainly at the top of the back steps. It was a black, moonless night and I couldn't see beyond the bright imprint left by the kitchen light. I strained to see and gradually the night revealed a black shape on the dark expanse of lawn. It was Dad. He was unconscious, snoring heavily, spooning our dog Kandy. As I approached, Kandy's soft eyes met mine but she continued to lay unmoving except for her tail, which beat a gentle greeting.

Although I was afraid Dad would be angry with me for waking him, I stretched out a tentative hand and touched his arm gently, but he continued to snore. I pressed a little harder, but he kept on sleeping. I began to cry and shook his shoulder saying, "Daddy, wake up," but he didn't. I stood indecisively staring from Dad's unresponsive form to the dark house and back again. The house looked forbidding, its black windows sinister. I looked into the sky but there was no help there, no friendly god of small, frightened children, only the indifferent stars, so I willed myself back inside and to bed.

When they were together, Mum had lamented the fact that despite working for an airline company, Dad never organised family holidays, for which he would pay almost nothing. One Christmas holiday, in a bid to show her what she was now missing, Dad took me to Fiji and the following year, Disney Land via Hawaii. His newfound enthusiasm for overseas travel was obviously for show, because he was aloof, critical and neglectful and I felt like an annoying gate crasher on his holiday. Like the 'snow trip', my stomach was clenched in a perpetual knot.

In Hawaii, he'd left me alone in our hotel room one night while he slept with an air hostess he'd met on the plane. I'd woken alone and feeling anxious and distraught, had repeatedly called reception until the woman stopped taking my calls. She had offered to send me some ginger ale for my nausea but fearing I would be in trouble for not asking permission, I had declined. The next morning, he'd sent me alone to Waikiki beach, where I had sat as close to a family of four as I could without drawing attention to myself, feeling self-conscious and exposed.

I was now 14 and worried Dad might kill himself at any time, might even be dead already. I sat at the bus stop on my way to school, eyes unfocused in a numb daze. The bus arrived and I trudged up the steps, paid the driver, slouched up the aisle and sank down into a seat near the back. I sat still, petrified, the world outside the window rushing past in a grey blur. I wished I could sit on the bus all day, as I hardly had the energy to move.

At lunch time, ignoring the cold, I made my way to the deserted lawn at the front of the school and sank down heavily onto the grass, mouth sagging, eyes drooping. I never dreamed of confiding in anyone, student or teacher, as I had never learned the concept of trust.

22

THE TENNIS MATCH

When Mum was with her friends, she was extroverted, vibrant, energetic and outgoing. She collected male admirers easily and while she wasn't classically beautiful, she had been described as 'striking' and 'sexy'.

Despite the positive attention, Mum constantly obsessed about her 'looks', complaining her hair was a 'horrible, mousy brown', pouting and fingering it with blunt, insensitive fingers. She hated her eyes too and I secretly agreed, as they resembled a reedy pond after heavy rain. One of her front teeth was slightly angled and she'd complain about it catching the light in photos. "No, you stand here," she'd cry, grabbing my arm and pushing me to her 'bad side'. She'd stand naked in front of the mirror scrutinising her breasts and tell me miserably they were saggy because she had breast-fed me. Paradoxically, she had also told me breast-feeding Luke and me for eight months each had been her greatest achievement in life.

I dropped my school bag on the floor. "Don't drop your bag like that, it will split," said Mum. I took two slices of white bread and margarine from the fridge and went to the pantry for the jar of vegemite. Luke was playing in his room and Mum had started making dinner, a lamb chop casserole made with a packet of dried French onion soup mix.

"Poor Luke," Mum started to say, before ducking her head around the corner to make sure he was out of earshot. "His teacher told me he's been sitting by himself at lunchtime."

I thought about telling her I was doing the same thing but didn't bother.

"Get a plate for that toast, Michele... How many times do I have to tell you... Oh, he's missing Dad and getting used to his new primary school, poor Lukie. Are you listening to me?"

"Yes."

"The casserole will be ready in an hour. Steam some potatoes and broccoli to go with it".

"Wha... where are you going?" I asked, coming out of my trance.

"I'm meeting Sandy. Don't forget the washing up and make sure you help Luke with his homework."

I had been Uncle Arthur-free for a couple of months, free from his sadistic bullying and I should have felt a sense of lightness, but didn't. I had survived for five years in perpetual hypervigilance and 'freeze' mode but now the pressure was off, hyperarousal had been replaced with depression. Life had gone from a puppet dance in the paralysing glare of his scrutiny to wading through a river of treacle, all alone, just a different version of misery.

Years later, Mum had hinted that we'd moved for my benefit and I knew intuitively she was referring to the time I beat up Smocker in a third and final 'acting out' session. I hit him on the top of his head once, then did it again and suddenly couldn't stop, even though I felt sick to my stomach. I had felt possessed. I had only stopped when I felt someone watching. It had been Mum behind the glass wall of the back room, the vacuum cleaner sucking the air as she stood frozen, watching.

Had she finally realised how damaged I was becoming, or was she bored with Uncle Arthur's lack of interest in her social set? Perhaps it was a bit of both. Once we'd moved to Hawthorn, Mum's social life had exploded. She was single again and went out most nights to dinner parties, drinks with friends, on dates and to the over-40s disco, 'Chasers'. She even gave up work to become a full-time student.

I steamed the veggies and called Luke for dinner, which we ate at the dining room table. I did the washing up and offhandedly offered to help Luke with his homework, which according to him, he'd already completed. I supposed I should do my homework too, but instead I lay on the sofa contemplating my nails.

I didn't have many friends and the ones I did have lived too far away to visit, so on weekends, when I'd finished my homework, I would lie on my bed, bored out of my skull but too lethargic to 'do' anything. I'd stare at the ceiling in a trance until inexplicably, I would jump off the bed as if stung, to pound the pavements around the streets of Hawthorn. I usually ended up at a particular park with a sweeping view and there I would sit, back against a large tree, heavy and torpid. Restlessness would eventually prod me back to my feet and I'd wander aimlessly home to mooch about the small house before sinking despondently onto the bed again.

I must have told Mum I was bored, although I can't remember doing so because one day she announced she had organised for me to play tennis at a club in Camberwell. Reluctantly, I walked the two kilometres to the courts and was matched with a girl around my age. We played a couple of sets and while we hit the ball back and forth and no conversation was required, I quite enjoyed the friendly rivalry but as soon as we'd skipped to the net to shake hands, I became self-conscious and shy. She seemed too nice for me, warm and easy going and inside my stomach crawled with self-consciousness and shame. We both agreed it would be nice to meet up again the following Sunday and left each other with a smile.

"Well, how did that go?" Mum asked when I had wandered back into the kitchen a few hours later.

"OK," I replied defensively.

"Well, are you going back then?" she snapped.

"No," I snapped back, even though I wanted to. I couldn't risk being 'seen'.

"Honestly, I don't know what's wrong with you Michele."

The following day, I sloped off to the bus stop, wishing I could sit there all day.

23

MUSIC THERAPY

Allegro non troppo

When I was five years old, I constantly pestered Nanna to play for me on her lovely old piano. One day as I plonked away on the keyboard, making a dreadful racket, she suggested I ask Mum if I could take piano lessons. Full of excitement and anticipation, I raced next door. Mum, who was placing a casserole in the old Kooka oven, took her time to consider my proposition while I stared beseechingly at her on tenterhooks. She straightened up, stood silently for a moment contemplating the ivy on the fence outside the kitchen window before answering, "No Michele, you'll never practice".

From the time I can remember, music has been my passion. When I was three years old, I would shut myself in the lounge room and play records on the huge old record player. I'd burble along to Hollywood film themes and Hungarian dances, making up words and dancing with carefree abandon. Music was a gateway to another world; a better, magical one, where time was suspended and I was free. It wasn't until age 15 that I could fulfil my great desire to learn a musical instrument when, at Chadstone High School, instrument loan and tuition were free and didn't require Mum's permission.

Like a kid in a lolly shop, I tried out the flute, clarinet and trombone before deciding to learn the tuba. 'Freddy' was awkward and heavy to lug around but fun to play, his tone rich and deep like treacle toffee. He had served in the army and had acquired various dints and even a burn but these superficial flaws added character to his silver-plated brass curves.

After a handful of lessons, I joined the junior band, then the Chadstone High School Concert Band and by year 12 was playing in the Melbourne Youth Symphonic Band. Playing the tuba was exciting yet calming and my depression lifted. The music department and Miss Hann became my surrogate home and family, and favourite classical pieces, lifelong friends. Music was my world and I set my sights on completing a Bachelor of Music at the Conservatorium of Music.

Two years later, while I was completing my final school year, Mum turned up with a new man in tow and the relative stability of our lives began to falter. I'm saying 'relative' because, although Mum's serial dating and neglect had continued, it had been easier to cope with because I had my own surrogate family in Miss Hann and Freddy and the school band.

Still, Mum's relationships with men had been turbulent (especially if she fell in love) and always short-lived. When I had turned 16, Mum had decided I was old enough to become her 'friend', which was code for inappropriate sharing of her sexual exploits... "John, has the biggest penis of any man I've ever known and last night he asked if he could put it up my arse," she drawled, taking off his American accent, and, "I had to stop seeing Peter because he drools so much, it runs down my throat, it's disgusting." She only laughed when I protested.

A few years later, she and Dave would masturbate each other off in a spa at my 21st birthday party, not stopping (until they'd 'finished') as my friends and I tumbled in around them. She had told me what they'd been up to a couple of weeks later. It explained the spaced-out looks on their faces.

Worse even than the oversharing were her histrionic outbursts. One evening, when I thought she was out, Mum stumbled dramatically into the lounge room interrupting my tinkering on the piano and sobbing, threw her arms around me, clinging like wet seaweed to my neck. Feeling overwhelmed, embarrassed and wretched, I gently disengaged her arms and escaped back to the refuge of the piano, wishing I could disappear. Instantly her grief turned to rage and she spat, "You are so cold Michele, you are so hard on me."

The new man James was introduced as I tidied the kitchen after dinner. He was a tall, ruddy-faced bear, with a boyish grin. They'd met the previous weekend at a dinner party and I could tell Mum was smitten.

The next morning she chatted excitedly while I was eating breakfast, telling me James was 'the one' and she'd always known she would marry an engineer. That night, as she prepared herself for a date at a fancy restaurant with James, the usual instructions eschewed from the bathroom, "Get the dinner Michele! There's some left-over spaghetti bolognaise in the fridge. You can have ice cream and tinned peaches for dessert."

Mum hurried from the bathroom leaving behind a floral waft of YSL 'Paris', a gift from another male lover. She almost always slept with the men she went out with, even if only once. Some became 'friends' and ever-hopeful, hung around like stray dogs in heat. New arrivals sometimes gave me gifts, usually a record and once AFL grand final tickets. Perhaps they assumed Mum cared about my opinion of them? Then predictably, they'd tell us we looked like sisters, glancing rakishly at Mum, who would giggle and flirt as if I wasn't there.

The phone rang and I answered it. "Mum, it's Lindsay," I yelled. She came bustling back into the lounge room, grabbed the receiver and started to tell her best friend all about her 'new man'. Here she goes again I thought, my eyes rolling. She was constantly on the phone, which was in the lounge room, so I heard the same story over and over again.

As the pace of life quickened and exams rolled ever closer, James spent more and more time at our house, drinking wine and kissing Mum as they sat ensconced on the sofa, while I studied in my room for my Victorian Certificate of Education (VCE). James' favourite classical piece was the Manfred Symphony by Tchaikovsky and whenever he was staying, he would play it and I'd be woken by the pounding of the first movement finale because the stereo speakers were on the other side of my flimsy bedroom wall, on either side of my bedhead.

The pressure of the final school year continued to mount and one morning in desperation I begged Mum, "Can't you stay at his place for a change?" I was finding it more and more difficult to sleep and had noticed with horror that, rather than absorbing the contents of class lessons, they had begun to wash over me like rain on parched earth and I began to panic. My entire future depended on getting into the Conservatorium.

She didn't reply. "Mum?" I raised my voice, "I can't sleep because of his music."

"No, I can't," she replied, coming to herself, her voice rising to match mine.

"Why not?" I retorted, scowling.

"Because his children wouldn't like it."

Mum and James had been going out for six months, but Luke and I had never met his three kids; didn't even know their names.

The following week Mum suddenly announced we were going to live with my aunty and cousins. Then, a couple of weeks later, she told me she and James were to marry and we were all going to live together in a big house. It was September, only two months from the first exam and I stared open-mouthed. "You should be pleased for me Michele," came her indignant response.

That night I woke to the thudding boom but rather than stuffing the pillow over my head, I leapt out of bed as if stung and scrabbled under the bed for my slippers. I searched blindly for the arm holes of my dressing gown and while the hapless Manfred blundered about in the wilderness, I stole silently (not that they could hear me over the racket) up the hallway and out through the front door, into the midnight, moonlit street.

I jumped as a cat broke cover at my feet and ran ninja-like up a high wall, casting a huge shadow in the bright moon shine. I stole furtively up the centre line of the asphalt, away from invisible monsters I imagined might drag me into their dank gardens. I rounded the corner into Riversdale Road to the Sanderson's gate. Hardly breathing, I pushed it open, hoping it wouldn't creak and like a wispy shadow, slipped through the tranquil garden to a path leading around the side of the house, to the back door. I let myself in; they never locked the door.

The house was warm and smelled of the previous night's dinner. The little spare room off to the left smelled dusty but familiar and I immediately felt a sense of safety and comfort. The little single bed was made up and as I slipped between the cool sheets, an irresistible wave of relief and sleep washed me into a deep, dreamless slumber. The next morning, I woke up before the household stirred and ran home before I was discovered or missed.

The Sanderson's, a family of four, lived in a beautiful, high-ceilinged house with an inground swimming pool. Henry, a short, wiry-haired man in his 50s was married to 30-year-old Ella, his second wife. Their two children were Oliver, who was a few years younger than Luke, and Mila who was 12, the same age as Luke.

Luke had met little Oliver and his Dad one day at a nearby park soon after we'd moved to East Hawthorn. Luke and Oliver had become friends and when Luke had mentioned he had an older sister, Ella had invited me to babysit. Ella was a wonderfully kind and generous person and I quickly became close to her. We spent many hours together chatting about school, life and music. Opera and ballet were her passions.

Henry owned a successful small business and was very easy going and generous with his time and money. By comparison, Mum struggled to make ends meet, especially as she had given up work to study to become a teacher. At that time, she relied solely on the Supporting Mothers Benefit and the pittance of child maintenance Dad paid, with resentment. So, when Henry invited Mum, Luke and I to the Palace Hotel in Hawthorn one Friday night for a counter meal, it was a real treat and became a Friday night ritual. Ella became the mentor I so desperately craved and Henry, a generous, good-natured substitute father.

Final exams were to commence in November, the first being the music practical/tuba exam and this was held at the Conservatorium of Music at Melbourne University. Three days before the exam, Mum gave me a shock, telling me she would be away. She refused to say where she was going but that her best friend Lindsay would take me to the university for my tuba exam. "Oh, and you had better stay with the Sanderson's," she said walking off and then threw over her shoulder. "You'd better ask them." She was off to the cinema with James.

"Michele," she called from the bathroom and I doubled back and stood at the open doorway waiting. "Oh, there you are, I've put our house on the market. We are going to live with James."

"But when?" I stammered, reeling.

"Get that look off your face," she snapped.

"When will that be Mum?" I tried to sound polite.

"In January, after your birthday."

I tottered off before coming to and turned back to ask, "Where are we going to live?"

She didn't answer that question but added, "Oh and Ray is coming to stay in a few weeks." Ray was Mum's younger brother, married to Janet and living in Canberra.

"But Mum, written exams start then."

"He can sleep in Luke's room. I think he's met someone else."

24

BLACK CHERRIES AND CHAMPAGNE

When I was small, Mum never had much time for me, she did what she wanted to do.

At the beach, she would rub zinc cream on my nose and shoulders, then ignoring me, lie down to sunbake for the entire day. She never played sandcastles at the water's edge and wouldn't swim, as she hated being cold and didn't believe me when I told her the water was really, really warm when you got used to it.

Mum took me to 'The Nutcracker' because she loved ballet. She'd had lessons when she was a girl, but two hours was too long for a five-year-old and after the first 20 minutes, I squirmed restlessly until it was over.

I watched fascinated but was never allowed to help as Mum mosaiced tables and lampshade stands and cut snowflakes from thin strips of polystyrene and decorated them with silver glitter at Christmas time. She fed me bowls of her lightly stewed black cherries as I sat on the grass in the backyard entranced, as Dad looked to the overcast sky and told me Santa would need to fly low tonight.

The tumult of exams crashed over me like a disordered wave and when Luke's school year had finished, we flew straight to

Sydney to spend Christmas with Dad, Nanna and Grandad. I flew back to Melbourne earlier than I would normally have done to get my VCE results.

Faint with anxiety and forgetting to breathe, I opened the envelope and withdrew the small, typed slip of paper. I saw As and Bs and one C and feverishly tallied my marks. With a rush of profound relief and excitement, I realised I had achieved the requisite score and would be studying at the Conservatorium of Music, and WOW, I'd received As for both my music subjects! I raced inside to phone Miss Hann to tell her of our wonderful achievement. I was the first person in my family to go to university and Mum proudly told anyone who would listen, her daughter was off to the Conservatorium of Music, not that she ever actually congratulated me.

I had arrived back home from Sydney to find a strange guy sprawled on our lounge room sofa in the place of James. Raven was a tall, good looking, 27-year-old Canadian, with curly black hair and goatee. He had the air of an eager-to-please retriever and I assumed, was just another of Mum's many male admirers, although too young to be anything other than a friend.

Mum had told me in few words on the way home from the airport that there had been a change of plan and we would not be moving in with James and his three children after all. He had suddenly changed his mind after she had sold our house in December and consequently had been forced to buy another one, in a far outer suburb of Melbourne and we'd be moving in a couple of weeks.

The next afternoon Henry Sanderson turned up, obviously hoping to be invited to stay for a glass of wine with Mum. He had tried to kiss her one night in the front doorway when he'd walked me home from babysitting. Unable to get inside, I had stood awkwardly as Mum laughed and batted him away, saying "Don't try that with me Henry Sanderson." Seeing Raven ensconced on the sofa, Henry caught my eye, winked and mouthed, 'Your boyfriend'. Grinning, he gave me a surreptitious thumbs up and I blushed furiously.

January 14 1982 was my 18th birthday. Dad didn't want to cut Luke's holiday short and anyway he hated Melbourne, so they both stayed in Sydney but Mum surprised me with a special dinner at an expensive restaurant. She was quieter than usual but I was too busy sipping a delectable champagne cocktail, my first, to pay this unusual state of affairs much attention. We ordered succulent, crispy-skinned duck in a delicious sweet and savoury, cherry and port sauce and for dessert, a warm, chocolate pudding with a molten centre, accompanied by creamy vanilla bean ice cream. To end the dinner, Mum toasted my future success with a glass of bubbly.

The next day was to be our last in the little house and as we made our final preparations to depart, I wished Raven would leave us alone for once, as I felt discombobulated. Without advice or support from Mum, I had had to make what felt like a momentous decision to defer the start of my uni degree for one year, to save up to buy my own tuba. They were expensive and all Mum had said on the topic was that she was not going to extend the mortgage.

I was officially an adult but had never felt so small. Boxes containing my clothes and nick-nacks hunched around my bed like black boulders, ready for the removalist the next morning. I lay awake staring at the dark green corrugated cardboard ceiling (mine was the only room Mum hadn't redecorated) through the gloom when I heard a soft moan. It came from

Mum's room and was followed by another and another, each one louder. Disgusted and embarrassed, I wrapped the pillow around my head in a vain attempt to block out the sound of her voice, so intimate and desperate. "Shut up, shut up, shut up," I muttered. Finally, she cried out and the brooding silence returned.

They had kept their physical relationship a secret all the while Raven had smiled and talked to me with his cute, deep brown eyes and thrown Mum's sedate Mazda around corners, executing impressive racing changes. I had been flattered by his attention and had secretly hoped he might ask me out. It never occurred to me he and Mum were 'an item' because the absence of James was so palpable. Anyway, Raven was closer to my age and like a moron I had fallen for the usual ploy, completely sucked in by his attention. "What a fucking idiot you are," I told a peeling corner of corrugated cardboard ceiling.

25

MUSIC CAMP

After the move to Ringwood, Mum disappeared for a break with Raven. Luke was still in Sydney with Dad, and so I went to stay with the Sanderson's at their holiday home in Anglesea for a week. On the Sunday night, I returned to Melbourne with Henry who was heading back to work while I was to attend the annual music camp at Melbourne High School run by the Melbourne Youth Music Council.

I was so looking forward to the week-long camp and also to staying with Henry, as he was self-assured and easy going compared with Dad and I couldn't wait to have him all to myself. As a treat, we stopped for fish and chips on the way home and didn't arrive in Melbourne until late. I laid my things out for the following morning's adventure and flopped into bed, falling instantly to sleep.

Minutes later it seemed, the door of the spare room slid open and early morning light filtered into the dim room. I heard muffled footsteps and felt myself tilt slightly as Henry sat on the edge of the little single bed. Yawning, I smiled in greeting and stretched sleepily.

I watched his hand float down through the gloom and come to rest on my right breast. It stayed crouching for a moment like a large, fat spider, then levitated a little into the air. I felt his finger make a circle around the periphery of my breast. Gradually the circles became smaller and smaller until his short sausage of a middle finger was skipping lightly over the tiny, soft lumps on the areola. He brushed the nipple as lightly as a feather and it puckered up, erect. With a jolt, I felt wetness between my legs. The bed springs creaked again. "Come on love, time to get up," he said, his tone matter of fact. I heard the scrape of the sliding door and dim twilight returned.

That afternoon Henry picked me up from music camp and we drove straight to the pub. I chatted away through dinner pretending I had forgotten all about the morning and as the evening progressed, I began to think it must not have happened because Henry acted as he always did and the memory was taking on a dream-like quality. We drove home and I went straight to bed, waving Henry goodnight before sliding the door closed. I put on my nightie, turned off the light and got into bed.

I had inadvertently left the door open a few centimetres and after a time became aware of soft murmuring voices on the TV. The quiet conversation turned to soft groaning and mystified, I rose on one elbow to peer through the crack in the door. Shocked and fascinated in equal measure, I saw a woman dressed in a French maid's outfit kneeling in front of a naked man, who reared above her, his penis hugely erect. "Can I suck your cock sir?" she asked him politely, before leaning in to take its swollen head between her glossy red lips. My body responded reflexively, a tattoo of blood in my head, a sweet ache in my loins.

A shadow passed across the screen and I quickly lay back down, feigning sleep. Henry stole into my room again, and this time squatted by my head. I felt cool air on my arm as the sheet lifted and his hand found the bottom of my long, satin tee shirt. He slid his hand up to my breast and my nipples contracted at his touch. I really didn't want them to, he was short and old and washed his hair with soap, unlike like tall, lean, silky Raven with his jet-black goatee and smooth smile.

I saw the dim shape of Henry's curly head leaning over me, his thin lips latching onto mine, pointy tongue probing, wet and slimy. His breath was hot and smelled of beer and I felt sick. I stared past him to the distant ceiling, beyond which was the dark night sky, wholesome and twinkling with stars. "I'm not giving in to you," I thought fiercely, thinking of lovely Ella.

Suddenly, Henry lifted his head and I thought it was over. I let my shoulders relax. I felt aroused, it made me feel dirty and I didn't want him to know. There was wetness and the ache I needed to soothe. I was turning into my mother . . . How disgusting, I thought, please God, no!

His voice broke through the storm in my head like a whip crack, "You know love, I thought you were a giver . . ." Forgetting to avert my gaze, I found his small, shrewd eyes, ". . . but you're a taker, just like your mother." Was it true? The thought careened inside my skull, like a chook with no head, running round and round, shitting everywhere, spraying blood. The choice was simple, I would do anything not to be like my mother, so I opened my mouth.

After that night, I gradually forgot he was ancient and repulsive and married to my lovely mentor. My blind, traitorous body loved his touch and so I began to await our assignations with eager enthusiasm. As soon as we were alone, he would lift my top and suck my nipples, breaking into an enormous sweat. We kissed, he sucked my nipples and I caressed his penis, first with my hand but it soon became my mouth. He told me what we were doing didn't count as sex and I suppose if asked, he would say, "I did not have sexual relations with that woman."

He only ever returned the favour once, bringing me to the point of orgasm before stopping at the brink, feigning concern, "Oh, sorry love, I didn't realise I was getting you so worked up."

Henry was always quick to warn me about other 'men'—"Love," he'd say, and I knew what was coming, "men will use and abuse you." He'd remind me regularly, even as he felt me up and stuck his tongue in my mouth. I took his 'fatherly' advice seriously, oblivious to the irony, but it did resonate. I had come to the unconscious conclusion all men except for fathers were demanding, critical, violent and cruel and I would repulse them. They all looked like Uncle Arthur and I could not discern if they were good people or abusers.

Although 'Daddy', my idol, was a 'good guy', he often teased me when I visited him during the school holidays, telling me it was only a matter of time before I forgot him for 'long-haired gits'. "No Daddy," I would plead tearfully, "I won't." I knew I must keep myself for my Daddy and give surfy dudes a wide berth.

Mum's contradictory attitude toward men added to my confusion and wariness. Mum was never without a lover for long and was either completely and madly in love or, when those relationships ended, both histrionic and depressed until the replacement came along, which never took longer than three weeks, or she would complain relentlessly about 'men'. "Oh, men are hopeless," was her constant refrain. She split up with one guy because she didn't like the way he pronounced Sunday. He said 'Sundee', and she thought he sounded uneducated, although he wasn't.

And as a teenager and young adult, there had been boyfriends of Mum's who took an inappropriate interest in me, throwing me covert, lecherous looks when they thought Mum wasn't looking, using me as a confident when things weren't going well and trying to seduce me, like 'German George' who kissed me one night when Mum had left us alone. Bright and early the next morning he had waited for me outside our house and offered to drive me to uni. That evening he had just happened to find me at Melbourne Central Station and ride the train all the way to my stop. I told Mum, risking her wrath but the next time he visited, she had just slapped him playfully on the chest and told him he was a naughty boy.

Occasionally, I would force myself to go out with men of my own generation, mainly to ease the pressure of Mum's expectations, as she thought I was weird because I didn't have a boyfriend. She had begun dating at age 16 but I found male attention excruciating, not flattering and going on the occasional date was an ordeal to be endured—I felt so horribly exposed. They never asked for a second, my mask of aloofness was impenetrable. Ironically, it was only with older men like Henry and Mac that I felt safe and relaxed.

The fondling and kissing and sucking of Henry's penis continued for three years, until the day I met up with Mac and we sipped warm sake in that beautiful Japanese restaurant. Suddenly I'd had enough of Henry sticking his tongue down my throat and I told him it was over.

26

THE ROCKS

It was the beginning of February, a few weeks after my 18th birthday and it was time to commence the search for my first job. I was overwhelmed at the thought though and began to procrastinate, telling myself I would start in a couple of weeks. One day I decided to catch the train to the city to see a film. It finished in the late afternoon and I used the public phone at the cinema to call Mum to organise a lift home.

The receptionist at Mum's work informed me she had not been in that day, which I thought odd because I had assumed she'd gone to work. I had been asleep when she left to drop Luke off to school, presumably on her way. "No, she was taken ill with food poisoning and is in hospital," said the receptionist.

At a loss, I hung up. After a moment's indecision, I decided to go to the Sanderson's. To my surprise, Luke was already there, Uncle Arthur had unexpectedly collected him from school and dropped him off. Henry took me aside, out of Luke's earshot and told me Mum had been admitted to the Alfred Hospital as she'd tried to kill herself. She'd taken an overdose of sleeping pills at

Black Rock Beach, walked out onto the rocks and collapsed, unconscious. A man had thought her behaviour odd and had followed her. By the time he reached her to pull her above the high-water line, the rising tide had reached her hair, which I could see in my mind's eye, floating like brown seaweed in a rock pool and she was frothing at the mouth. Henry warned me not to tell Luke, who was only 12 and the official story was that Mum had contracted food poisoning.

She had apparently written a suicide note but Henry told me Uncle Arthur had destroyed it and this brought to mind her uncharacteristically thoughtful gesture on my 18th birthday; the dinner at the expensive restaurant, the champagne, and the good wishes for my future... a future she was planning to miss.

We stayed the night at the Sanderson's and the next day Uncle Arthur took Luke and me to visit Mum in hospital. We were ushered into a stark, white-tiled room by a sniffy, unsmiling nurse who made me feel guilty. Mum lay like a corpse on a narrow trolley-like bed. Her body looked impossibly heavy under the white hospital gown. Her grey-streaked brown hair looked greasy and the way it was arranged stiffly around her white face for some reason filled me with disgust. She had had her stomach pumped and I shuddered in the antiseptic chill. I imagined I could see a smudge of black at the corner of her mouth. Uncle Arthur immediately went to her side and began to stroke her forehead and hair. Luke and I stood at a safe distance from the body on the trolley until he eyed me coldly. "Come here and kiss your mother," he ordered, stepping back and motioning me forward.

I moved reluctantly to Mum's side, opposite Uncle Arthur. Her chest was rising and falling ponderously, as if she was drowning in sleep, and the purple line of her lips was turned down. I lowered my face to her forehead and the pounding of my heart migrated to my skull. With the briefest brush of lips, I kissed the rubbery, cold of her forehead and involuntarily snapped my head back upright.

The day after the visit, the Sanderson's took Luke and me out for a day in the country. It worked as a distraction until we were driving home, sitting on the back seat with Luke and the Sanderson children and I had the urge to broach the subject of what had happened. The time wasn't right though, somehow it never was.

The next day, Uncle Arthur turned up unannounced, to take Luke and me to clean the house in Ringwood before Mum's discharge from hospital. Luke and I sat in tense silence as Uncle Arthur drove, hunched over the steering wheel, brooding.

I sat in shock, staring blankly out the window thinking about Mum. What had happened to her, how could she lose control like that? How could she kill herself and leave her children, especially Lukie, who was the apple of her eye?

Ella had said the day Mum had chosen to end her life was the day James had left Australia for a three-month civil engineering posting to Indonesia. This piece of information must have been in the note Mum had left, I thought, and Uncle Arthur must have told Ella. I wondered what else the note had said. She must have started to plan it from the time James dumped her. She must have gone to a doctor to request a script for sleeping pills. My thoughts then drifted to the time just after James had left and I wondered how Mum could have slept with Raven when she was so in love with James, the man she literally couldn't live without. And I couldn't seem to remember how the Sanderson's had become involved in all of this, the series of events that had brought us back together. They had explained it a couple of times, but I kept forgetting and to this day, still can't remember.

    As I vacuumed the house, Luke was supposed to be tidying his room. I looked in and he was sitting on his bed reading a comic book. Uncle Arthur came up silently behind me. "Good-oh son," he said encouragingly over my shoulder, indicating Luke's still untidy room. I turned back to the vacuum cleaner. "Well come on, hurry up," he snarled and returned to the kitchen bench, to lean on one elbow, eyeing me like I was dog shit on his shoe.

    Finally, we returned to the familiar homeliness, the normality of the Sanderson's and Ella asked, "Arthur, would you like to stay for dinner?"

    Please say no, please say no, I intoned under my breath. "No, thank you," Uncle Arthur replied graciously and thankfully left soon after.

    When he'd disappeared though the front door, I couldn't help but say to Henry and Ella, "He can be really mean, you know?" but they smiled benignly. I felt like Cassandra, never to be believed, unable to make myself understood. I couldn't seem to find the words to impress upon them the side he kept hidden, his sadism and cruelty, the patronising chauvinism and rage, the aura of physical danger he exuded, of how he seemed truly to hate me. As Henry continued to smile non-committally, Ella said, smiling kindly, "Oh well, this must be a shock for him, don't judge him too harshly."

27

RIVALS

Mum was due for release from hospital a few days after the cleaning day but the next morning she called the Sanderson's and asked to speak with me. "Hello... Mum?" I asked tentatively.

"I need to get out of here, they put me in the psychiatric ward, it's barbaric," she blurted without preamble. "I want you to come and pick me up tomorrow at 11am."

"Oh... OK," I replied.

"Is Luke there?"

The next morning just before 11, I parked opposite the hospital, got out of the car and stood leaning against the door, waiting to cross the busy road. The broad, once luscious, emerald-green leaves of the shady plane trees hung limp and unmoving in the oppressive heat, and dust billowed in an enveloping cloud as a tram clattered past.

I spied Mum in the distance, on my side of the road and stepped onto the pavement to wait as she hurried toward me with her characteristic short-stepped march. As she approached, she lifted her arms and pointed the index finger of each hand at her chest. I stared uncomprehendingly until she stopped a little too close and said shortly, "You forgot to pack my bra."

I can't remember what we did when we arrived home, what was said, what we had for dinner but the next day a small group of Mum's friends turn up to 'support' her. I opened the front door and without a word they entered in single file, avoiding my gaze. I went back to my bedroom and through the door could discern their subdued, compassionate murmurings.

The next weekend, Mum told Luke and I that we were going to the local shopping centre to get groceries for lunch. Obligingly we got into the car, fastened our seatbelts and headed off.

"Hey, Mum, what are you doing, the shops are that way?" I said pointing behind me. She didn't answer. "Mum, where are we going?" I asked again. "I thought we were going to the shopping centre ... MUM!" I yelled. Now what, I thought rolling my eyes?

"We're going somewhere first."

"Well, take me back and pick me up when you've done it," I said, feeling deeply resentful. When she didn't respond, I continued in an accusing tone, "You said we were going shopping. Why did you LIE?" I finished with a yell. She continued to ignore me, so I subsided into a well-practiced, surly silence.

As we drove on, the house blocks became larger and were increasingly interspersed with paddocks containing peacefully grazing horses. Finally, the car slowed and Mum pulled off onto the driveway of a large house with a wide veranda surrounded by sweeping lawns. Mt Dandenong's green, wooded slopes sat impassively behind, framing the house.

Mum turned off the engine and alighted onto the gravel drive, slamming the door behind her. She started to walk up the drive but hearing nothing from the car, turned and motioned me to get out too. I sat resolutely but wound down the window as she doubled back. "So, where are we?" I demanded but in a quiet voice. "Get out," she hissed and took a menacing step toward the car.

Luke, who had also been waiting, opened his door and got out. Reluctantly, I followed suit. We trailed behind Mum, our steps crunching loudly on the gravel. To our left, little blue wrens flitted in an out of a low hedge, chasing tiny insects and chirping excitedly to each other. Industrious bees hummed a soporific chorus to the deep blue of the late-summer sky as they buzzed here and there, collecting their precious bounty of pollen.

A harsh banging shattered the afternoon's peace and I jumped. Mum was pounding on the front door. She stopped and an ominous silence fell.

Perhaps the person Mum has come to see won't be home, I thought hopefully, then we can just go away again and get lunch. I was on the verge of turning back when the door opened and a short, dark-haired woman around Mum's age stood framed in the doorway. She looked forbidding and suddenly the air felt as thick as custard. I could tell she knew who we were.

The two women stood frozen like statues facing off, until the dark-haired woman said, as if to an unspoken question, "Yes, this is our home."

She stepped back drawing us inside and retreated to a closed door off the large, open-plan living room into which we had stepped. She opened the door and said, "This is where we sleep." Mum strode brazenly to the door and glared balefully into the room, eyes narrowed, resentful and suspicious.

Without realising it, Luke and I had crept forward and were watched silently as Mum took in the neatly made double bed and the large, framed photo of James, the woman and their three children standing on a tall oak dresser. "We are married, and he'll come home to me."

Without a word, Mum turned and marched from the house. Luke and I scurried after her embarrassed, avoiding the woman's scorching glare.

28

THE STORM

I continued the obsessive search for myself in a greater understanding of BPD and one day came across an article titled *Quiet Borderline Personality Disorder—Signs, Symptoms, Healing and Reaching Out*, by Imi Lo of Eggshell Therapy and Coaching. Finally, I had found what I was looking for.

Relieved and excited, I re-read the article several times. It described a version of borderline in which sufferers react to emotional dysregulation by 'acting in', rather than acting out in stereotypical ways, hiding it from the world and even from themselves.

The article could have been written by me, as it was an account of my own emotional torment and interpersonal struggles but written by a stranger. All at once a veil lifted and I was able to recognise my maladaptive patterns of behaviour as indications of traumatic abuse and neglect, not weakness of character. They were coping mechanisms, ingenious survival strategies, and my suffering was validated.

Excitedly, I sent a precis of the article along with the link to

Ronnie, then sat staring impatiently at the computer, expecting an instant, validatory response. As the minutes crept by, doubt took the place of heady excitement and I began to panic. Perhaps the article didn't reflect my experiences the way I thought they did? What if having quiet borderline was not enough for her? What if Ronnie was disappointed in me for developing a personality disorder when she'd been so impressed I hadn't. She had told me a number of times my survival had been 'heroic' and I was incredible to have survived and to have not developed BPD. Would she now be disappointed? What if she was angry? What if she stopped seeing us?

I slept fitfully and woke with a start wondering what was wrong. I remembered, I was waiting. Finally, mid-morning her response hit my inbox with a clarion ping and I began to read with heart in mouth. My stomach fell. The tone of her email lacked its usual inclusiveness. My lungs contracted as the little parts became afraid and collapsed in distress. They wondered where their 'Lovely Lady' had gone.

Ronnie's email sounded like a high-handed lecture on the role of ego in mental illness and it seemed unrelated to the email and article I had sent her. She had never taken such an impersonal tone before and someone inside felt ashamed, another unaccountably angry, another afraid. I wandered the house, yelling and crying. Some parts hated her, and others believed she was angry with them and would not come back the next Saturday.

I had been 'flooded' by traumatised, fragmented pieces of my personality, the child parts who still thought they lived with their dysregulated, BPD/narcissistic mother, their moody, neglectful father and terrifying uncle. With a supreme effort, I managed to regain some agency and texted Ronnie, trying to explain how everyone was feeling. She emailed back, sounding more like her usual self as she asked, *How old are these kids who are in a rage?* I thought they might be around 14 years of age.

Ronnie suggested she send the children a Havening video, to help them through to the next session but explained she needed my help to understand their feelings before recording it. The request caused more fury, as some parts expected Ronnie to automatically know what they needed. The feelings of anger triggered the three-year-olds, who were fearful the angry parts would in turn, anger Ronnie and she would abandon them.

Energised by the flood of indignant anger that masked feelings of intolerable vulnerability, hurt and fear, I closed my laptop with a snap. It was mid-afternoon and a big storm was brewing. I made hasty preparations to travel to Arthurs Creek, to secure Tuala's hay stash. It was stacked on pallets in her paddock and the tarp protecting it from rain had come loose in the gale of the previous night. I didn't fancy fiddling about with metal tent pegs in an electrical storm, so sped off toward the black smudge on the distant horizon.

As the car took the winding curves of the road like a skier on fine powder, a text popped onto my smart phone. It said, *Hi Michele* (we noted the friendly tone), *do you have a few minutes now for a quick Zoom?* and then another followed almost immediately, *I have until 5.45 for us to talk if you have the time. I'd like to do that if it's possible.*

I kept driving as there was nowhere to pull over on the narrow, tree-lined road but I had no desire to. After the agony of the previous 24 hours, the fact that Ronnie was reaching out felt supremely relieving and comforting, like a 'hit' to an addict. I drove on through a fog of dreamy dissociation, lulled by the feel of the swaying car, mesmerised by the beauty of the bush and the heavy, water-laden air, as it throbbed with a glorious electrical intensity that was as soothing as a weighted blanket.

A few minutes later, the phone rang and it was Ronnie. I took lazy delight in ignoring that too. It felt dreamy, heady to see her name pop onto the screen and then ghost her. The little three-year-olds felt soothed and replete and the 14-year-olds powerful—the shoe was on the other foot now. The feeling of control provided an enormous sense of relief but most importantly it proved that Ronnie cared. No one had ever even noticed or empathised when we were upset, and for a brief time everyone felt sated and content.

Sheet lightening was flickering over the rolling hills and a few heavy drops of rain 'thunked' on the tarp as I secured the last tent peg. I left Tuala with a final scratch. She was happily occupied, her nose buried in a biscuit of sweet-smelling hay, munching contentedly, oblivious to the weather. A gust of wind spread her long, blond-red tail over muscular haunches like a fan, and it really started to rain. I ran down the hill laughing and splashed through a wide, cold rivulet at the bottom and back up the slippery slope to the car. I was soaked, panting and alive in a wild, stormy spring evening and Ronnie still loved us.

As the electrical storm receded and the city approached, the final vestiges of the 'drug' drained away to replace euphoria with feelings of guilt and fear. I had ignored Ronnie's earnest attempts to connect and support and repair. The three-year old parts were now quietly fretful, their terror of being abandoned never leaving them for long, no matter how attentive Ronnie was.

When Ronnie's face finally popped up on Zoom the following Saturday it was as if aeons had passed since the previous Saturday's session. I felt a huge sense of relief, safe in her capable and loving hands. We discussed the 'splitting', which is a characteristic of borderline. I told her we'd felt utterly betrayed when she'd ignored all the kids and written instead to my so-called 'adult self'. I told Ronnie she could do 99 things right but any misstep, no matter how small and seemingly inconsequential, was a sign of absolute betrayal. It caused 'us' to become suspicious, confused, disappointed, grief-stricken, fearful and angry. All the kindness, effort and care she had shown over the previous months were wiped out in a moment and she had gone from 'all good' to 'all bad'.

"I read the quiet borderline article," Ronnie told me and my eyes snapped to hers. Was she about to tell me I was making it all up?

"Yes," she said, "although the presentation is different, along with the splitting, there's the self-harm, suicidal ideation, intense fear of abandonment, the idea you don't exist and the feelings of emptiness. It is not uncommon for borderlines to have a disorganised attachment style, which you do display and this, along with your childhood history of abuse and neglect, does point to borderline... so interesting you know, I've not come across this internalised presentation before," she concluded.

I felt enormously relieved, a mystery finally solved. Now I had a framework upon which to hang my feelings of unworthiness and unrelenting emotional pain, chronic depression and anxiety, difficulty navigating work relationships, especially with other damaged people and my avoidance of personal relationships. It also explained my inability to trust people, the ever-present feeling of emptiness, that I didn't exist and my embarrassingly needy behaviour toward Ronnie.

Ronnie told me the clincher for her was that any love I received drained away, like water through a sieve. She told me simply, "Your bucket has no bottom and that's borderline." I told her yes, "There's a hole where my heart should be," and we then did a Havening session together, focusing on building the strength of my heart, letting it know it was safe, so that love could be retained.

I'd kept the dysfunction hidden from every doctor, psychiatrist, psychotherapist and psychologist I'd ever seen, not that I'd done it consciously. Even Ronnie herself had not recognised my version of borderline in its introverted form.

Imi Lo says, "You may not have stereotypical BPD symptoms such as frequent anger outbursts—instead you suffer in silence. You may appear calm and 'high functioning', instead of exploding you implode and collapse from within." Because quiet borderlines attempt to hide their pain and dysfunction, it is even harder to diagnose and Lo says this is a dangerous problem because we are less likely to end up in therapy.

Many health professionals are likely to associate borderlines with explosive anger and extreme mood swings, suicide attempts and self-harming behaviours. Some mental health professionals will not treat a person with BPD because they believe the sufferer is 'untreatable' or too 'difficult', and some are reluctant to formally diagnose borderline because it is such a stigmatised disorder.

When a person is formally diagnosed with BPD, they will most commonly be prescribed antipsychotics and/or antidepressants. Pharmaceutical drugs may be warranted for short-term stabilisation of severe symptoms but ultimately should be included as part of a wider treatment plan that includes trauma-informed psychotherapy, the use of trauma resolving modalities (EMDR, EFT, Havening, Somatic Experiencing, 'parts' work) and creative hobbies.

Most sufferers of borderline experienced childhood trauma and/or neglect but trauma therapy is never recommended by psychiatrists and through no fault of their own, trauma survivors are labelled wilfully 'crazy', 'manipulative' and attention-seeking. In short, they are pathologised and so rendered impotent.

Borderline personality disorder is an extremely painful condition and people who suffer it deserve to be treated as heroines/heroes for enduring the unendurable. Rather than vilification, sufferers of BPD require and deserve dedicated, professional support to heal.

The mental health system is massively under-funded and many, many sufferers of borderline are forced to wait weeks and even months to receive appropriate treatment, if at all. Lives are on hold, the sufferer surviving from day to day, hour to hour and even minute to minute. The emotional dysfunction affects not just the sufferer but spills into the lives of family and friends. Worst of all, if we have children and our illness remains untreated, we are likely to pass borderline on to a new generation, especially from mother to daughter.

29

TUG OF WAR

It was the winter of 1972, a year before we were to leave Sydney to live with Uncle Arthur. Luke was two and I was eight years old. Mum and Dad had separated a couple of weeks before and this was the first weekend we had spent with Dad since the trial began.

I'd woken in the middle of Saturday night and feeling claustrophobic and sick, had tiptoed through the lounge room to the balcony and vomited over the railing. Unfortunately, I'd splattered a car with sick from a great height and the man whose car it was happened to be looking up when next morning I peered over the balcony. He caught a glimpse of my face, shook his head at me in disgust and two minutes later was knocking on our door.

That Sunday evening, Dad drove us back home to Willoughby. He opened the front door and Luke and I filed past him and stood huddled together in the cold hallway. The house looked unfamiliar and had an unfriendly air, like it wanted to be left alone.

"Where's your mother?" Dad asked, sounding put out. I didn't know and just stared around the hallway, hoping she would appear out of thin air. "Where's your mother?" he repeated, sounding querulous. "I need to go." He jiggled his foot impatiently and looked around too.

Luke started to cry and tottered over to Dad, grabbing a handful of trouser just above the knee. Ignoring him, Dad said again, "Look, I have to go." He sounded angry and Luke cried harder, his chubby, screwed-up face, red and snotty. "Don't go, Daddy, don't go Daddy," he sobbed, peering beseechingly up through his tears to the distant face.

"I have to go, get him off me," Dad cried desperately.

With feigned cheerfulness I bent down, my face close to his and said, "It's OK Lukie." I peeled first one, then the other pudgy fist off Dad's leg but as soon as I'd managed to prize one hand off, the other would grab hold again. "Come on Lukie, it's OK," I lied again.

Dad stood staring impatiently into the distance, his foot still jiggling until I had finally freed him. He turned and strode to the front door and without waiting for Mum or looking back, stepped into the night and was gone.

The reference to 'high functioning' in Imi Lo's article brought with it another huge insight: the 'high functioning' 'part' of me, who went about daily life, was actually the parentified eight-year-old child who had been forced to take responsibility for Luke.

As Ronnie and I came to terms with the knowledge that an eight-year-old 'part' had been diligently showing up to therapy each week for the past eight months and had run my life until the breakdown four years earlier, I suddenly wondered who 'I' was. It was a disorienting thought.

'I' was actually an amorphous mass of child 'parts' with no coherent framework or hierarchy. The adult person I thought I was didn't seem to exist. In 'my' place was a child, occupying a role she had taken on by default because her parents had abnegated their adult responsibilities. The eight-year-old was stuck in time, unable to grow up, carrying an adult's load for almost 50 years. The ongoing trauma and neglect I had experienced from a very young age had interrupted normal childhood development, resulting in the comprehensive fragmentation of my personality.

This explained why, over the course of the year, the therapy sessions had become increasingly bogged down but finding the eight-year-old provided the answer—Ronnie had been inadvertently collaborating with the child 'part' rather than the 'adult'. Expecting an eight-year-old to 'rescue' other child 'parts' was way too much for her, only 'I' could do that, but 'I' was missing in action.

Overwhelmed by the realisation, I swept the contents of my desk onto the floor. I was 56 and didn't know who I was, how was that possible? "But I thought I was real," I cried to Ronnie. That wasn't entirely true though I thought, remembering the achingly 'empty' feeling I had endured on and off all my life. But still, it felt I had been waiting and waiting to become real so my life could truly start.

Feeling 'empty' is one of the nine borderline traits. God I thought, no wonder life had been such a struggle. I was an eight-year-old imposter, like in those comedies where mother and daughter swap bodies, but this wasn't funny, it was deeply disturbing.

In the world of psychotherapy, my lack of progress was referred to as 'resistance'. Ronnie preferred to explain the mechanism of 'resistance' using the Internal Family Systems (IFS) model because she believed it provided a more compassionate and helpful description.

In IFS, 'resistance' is described as the tug of war between the 'parts'. The 'parts' are categorised into three groups: the 'exiles' are parts who experienced and hold the traumas; 'manager parts' who attempt to suppress or mask the pain of the exiles, and 'firefighter parts', who attempt to manage the overwhelm caused by the pain of the exiles using unhealthy behaviours, including but not limited to: suicidal ideation (conjuring a sense of control and relief), suicide attempts (escape from pain), emotional and physical self-harming behaviours (attempts at nervous system regulation), alcohol and substance abuse (numbing), binge eating, engaging in unsafe sex, spending, gambling, dangerous driving (displacement and re-enactment) and dissociation (escape).

Early in his career as a family therapist, the developer of Internal Family Systems Therapy, Dr Richard Schwartz noted that even in highly dissociated individuals, there was always a 'part' who was free from dysfunction. This part displayed life-affirming characteristics such as calmness, creativity, courage and compassion. This 'part' he called the 'Self', the indestructible, eternal core of our being. We all have a 'Self' and in traumatised individuals it is waiting to be uncovered, to be re-discovered.

When Ronnie finally realised she had been collaborating with an eight-year-old rather than with my 'Self', she began to encourage 'me' to speak and act directly for the damaged 'parts'. In this way, she devised to lessen my dependence on her, which she hoped might reduce the 'resistance' and better enable the therapeutic process to flow.

As the weeks progressed, my fledgling 'Self' began to wake up and assert her Divine nature. Through the pain of trauma therapy, I found my core. She is the observer, the 'watcher'. 'She' is writing this book.

30

THE SERGEANT MAJOR

It was early December. Christmas was approaching and I started to worry about how I would cope if Ronnie took extended leave over the summer holidays. Matilda and I were to fly to Alice Springs to stay with Luke and his family on 23rd December and I hoped Ronnie would only take three weeks' holiday so we wouldn't be marooned without her for too long.

The next Saturday Ronnie popped up on Zoom with a new hairstyle. Startled, the kids stared and I was rendered mute. Where's Ronnie? they wondered, all at sea. From one week to the next, a change of hair, more or less eye liner, a more or less ebullient Ronnie, these were all different Ronnies to the inner kids and it eroded their trust in her.

Our fears were confirmed when Ronnie informed us that she would be taking a six-week holiday, three weeks' longer than we were to be away. It was a daunting prospect, as separation from week to week was difficult enough.

The new, brisk Ronnie continued, explaining she would be introducing a more Internal Family Systems approach to the therapy, with the objective of working with the 'parts' who 'sabotaged' the therapy. Our sessions had also blown out to two hours but next year we would stick to the hour. "Kids need structure," she said but they heard, "Kids need discipline," and 'discipline' meant Uncle Arthur. The eight-year-old wasn't impressed; she reckoned she was more 'disciplined' than Ronnie any day.

Ronnie continued, seeming not to notice our shock by announcing it would be a good idea to see a psychiatrist before the start of therapy the following year. "All my other clients with BPD have a psychiatrist and we work together," she told me. I, well we, were all united in gross mistrust of medical doctors including psychiatrists, who we believe are pimps for the trillion-dollar pharmaceuticals industry. A-typical antipsychotics like olanzapine and selective serotonin reuptake inhibitors, like Prozac and Celexa, were prescribed by the tonne, while 'trauma-informed therapy' is largely eschewed.

"It's hard enough doing this work when you are sleeping but without it, it is almost impossible. I was given huge doses at various times," she said and I snapped out of my reverie. "I was psychotic with my borderline… but it is helpful in small doses, for sleep. I took it like that when I was doing my own healing work."

There it was again, the feelings of guilt and failure and inadequacy, of unaccountable compassion and yearning, all mixed together. So, she had been psychotic too I thought, my eyes sliding out of focus as an image of her younger self appeared in my mind. I had found it one sleepless night, a picture of Ronnie on an advertising poster for a work she had curated 30 years before about madness—her madness. She had looked so beautiful, her hair wavy and dark, her lips curvaceous and red, glazed eyes staring.

I imagined stepping into the photo. Who was holding the camera, directing her pose? Who was the faceless man, one broad shoulder visible in the tailored sports blazer, standing like a mannequin beside her? Click, click, the shutter would turn her warm living flesh to timeless wax. The tired arm holding the twisted white sheet taut around her neck would drop with relief to her side. She'd reach for the printed dress she had thrown carelessly over a chair and distractedly button it over her silk camisole.

I made an effort to snap back to the present and nodded, pretending to listen but as Ronnie continued on enthusiastically about the new regime, my mind wandered away again, lulled by the sound of her voice. It played on my mind like the gentle murmur of a distant sea at midnight.

"Where did you just go?" She had stopped talking and was observing me intently.

I had been watching her mouth as she was speaking. "I dunno," I said and quickly looked away, afraid she would read my mind. The curving swell of her lips was mesmerising. I wondered how it would feel to lean in, to feel the warmth of her breath, to kiss her mouth.

She cocked her head and smiled and then we continued with the session. We finished up after some Havening, stroking our arms and faces while she told us reassuringly, "Even though Ronnie is going away, she will be back on February 6th, 2021, and she will see all the children again . . ."

I stumbled out to the kitchen, shellshocked and already thinking about how far away next Saturday's session was. It would be the penultimate one for the year. I greeted Matilda with an automatic, casual smile designed to hide my distress. She was making paella for our Saturday night dinner. I wondered what Ronnie was having for dinner and who was cooking it. I reached for the bottle of gin.

I was well-practiced at hiding my distress from Matilda but

not because she lacked empathy. As soon as my little parts had been triggered by fears of abandonment, to appear vulnerable was dangerous and this caused my protective parts to engage in subterfuge. They would hide feelings of anxiety and acute distress with officious, critical behaviour aimed at Matilda, leaving her feeling hurt, confused and unsure of how to reach me. She would quietly withdraw and the little parts would then interpret her avoidance as emotional neglect and this in turn reinforced feelings of abandonment. 'I' would feel hurt, wondering why she made no effort to soothe or understand my feelings, believing she was the cold, unresponsive one.

Late that night, when all was quiet the parts had the space to make their thoughts and feelings known—"How dare she lecture me about structure?" the parentified eight-year-old yelled in my head. Hadn't we completed multiple university degrees and held down important jobs? "We survived because of me," she said, outraged. "Ronnie isn't even an organised person, she's a 'P' preference for sure (Myers Briggs Personality Type Indicator) and they are hopeless, they never finish anything and she's always losing things and takes on too many clients and doesn't have enough energy for 'us'."

Other parts were less vocal but I could feel their terror at the thought they must have botched the therapy. Anything less than perfection was extremely dangerous. There was also the dread and grief of the little ones, who were sure this was the end of their 'Lovely Lady'.

There were so many polarised parts, I felt I was being torn apart. The war raged on inside, waged by a tribe of strange, traumatised children, all living in one, tired body.

I limped along sleeplessly until Wednesday in a state of hyperarousal, paralysed with anxiety. The little nail scissors happened to be sitting on the dining room table where Matilda had left them the night before. Suddenly, I couldn't stand it, couldn't bear for another minute the waiting, the uncertainty, the lack of control, the pain.

I'd worked with Ronnie to develop a grab bag of interventions to use when the 'Firefighters' showed up to 'take me out' but the pressure had built to an intolerable level, knocking my pre-frontal cortex 'off-line'. I didn't even consider texting her as I had done before for the emergency session months before because the parts didn't want to be a pain, an inconvenience. We could sense she was too busy, tired and distracted in the lead up to Christmas. She didn't have time for us.

I picked up the scissors and slowly inspected the little blades. I tested one against my thumb. It was blunt. Suddenly I had a thought... where is my Swiss army knife? I knew it was sharp as I used it to cut the twine on Tuala's hay bales. I found it stowed in my filthy old 'horsey' backpack, after rummaging in the front pocket, collecting dirt and tiny fragments of hay under my fingernails. The blade was small but elegant and much sharper than the scissors but still I took the blade to the carving knife sharpener and started to work it. The eight-year-old part wanted to make very sure everything was done perfectly this time.

With a job to do and the promise of release, the escalating panic and emotional overwhelm was replaced with a wonderful feeling of dissociative calm. The firefighter, who was working to short circuit the distress, watched patiently while the eight-year-old used alcohol swabs to thoroughly disinfect the blade and lower left arm.

Doing the job cleanly improved the likelihood of keeping this embarrassing lack of 'self' control a secret, even from Matilda. The only parts who might be a problem were the little three-year-old kids who would probably want to tell Ronnie about it on Saturday, so she could coo with concern and smile her beautiful smile at them.

I couldn't identify 'who' the firefighter was, as she took careful aim and raised the blade. Was she two, or 11 or 14 years old? Perhaps she was a twin to the organised eight-year-old? The blade was lowered again. The eight-year-old was telling her it would be more prudent to cut the inside upper arm because it would be less noticeable when the body needed a blood test or to have its blood pressure taken.

The stainless-steel blade sliced easily though the fine, white skin on the underside of the upper arm. It reminded me of peeling tomatoes after they have been soaked in boiling water. When the blade meets the skin of the fruit, it splits apart easily.

We all looked to see what kind of job the part had done. Shame and panic welled with the big red drops. It didn't look deep enough. How could we be counted as worthy when we couldn't even cut ourselves properly? Again, the blade was raised and brushed across the arm, this time with a little more speed and force, like the bow of a violin making contact with the string.

This time it really did sting and deep, deep ruby-red blood started to trickle from the slit, in a lazy rivulet which joined the ephemeral trickle of the lesser cut. The venal blood flowed down our arm to drip off the elbow into the bright silver kitchen sink. It was such a beautiful sight and the plunk, plunk, plunk of the drops falling onto the metal, sounded as sweet and reassuring as a magpie's warble.

There is stillness. We feel a profound sense of relief and peace and listen fondly as outside the kitchen window the wattle birds chide and chatter in the eucalyptus tree. The world slides into soft focus and the children admire the fat little house spider sunning herself on the window ledge, waiting good-naturedly for a fly to land obligingly on her web. On the kitchen bench beside us, golden rays of sunlight play on the soft, tawny fur of our big Maine coon Pepper, who is blissfully sprawled, twitching and chattering in his dreams.

The eight-year-old rouses us from our reverie. Matilda will be home soon. I am back now and take a shower, examining the cuts. They are both still bleeding freely. The second cut is deeper but I hope neither requires stitches. Inside me, the children feel a profound sense of achievement. Finally, they have cut properly and feel relieved, not like the other times when all they managed were deep scratches. These were proper cuts.

I find a couple of butterfly strips but can't hold the cuts together with only one hand, so I place another cotton wool swab, folded in half, over the cuts and stick a big band aide over them. I put on a long-sleeved top and place all the bloodied cotton wool pads in a plastic bag, tied up and placed under some rubbish in the bin outside. I am now ready for Matilda.

31

THE PSYCHIATRIST

After Christmas in Alice Springs with Luke and family, Matilda and I returned to Melbourne and dutifully, ten days before the first session with Ronnie for 2021, I went to see a psychiatrist. Ronnie had hunted down the name of a couple of psychiatrists who had a reputation for working successfully with borderline patients, but I was reluctant to book an appointment, such was my wariness of allopathic medicine. I was deeply distrustful of most psychiatrists, with their blinkered, outdated research, reliance on pharmaceutical drugs, scorn of complementary/alternative medicine, disinterest in trauma-informed modalities, wilful non-acceptance of the reality of dissociation as a response to trauma (especially in Australia) and gross lack of common sense.

When I'd cut myself in December, I'd visited a GP who practiced complementary medicine and she had given me the name of a psychiatrist who practiced complementary psychiatry. I'd Googled him and read on his site that he refused point blank to prescribe Ritalin and opioids, which I took as a promising sign and so went ahead and booked an appointment.

I put together a list of the supplements I take to manage anxiety, insomnia, Hashimoto Thyroiditis, irritable bowel syndrome and the other physical issues caused by childhood trauma. I handed it over and he sat quietly perusing it before saying, "I'd just suggest adding lithium orotate to your regime."

"What?" I blurted out, "But that's really hardcore… isn't it?"

He smiled knowingly, "Lithium carbonate is hard core yes, but I'm suggesting the organic version, lithium orotate." He handed me a photocopied article from a psychiatric journal and I read it is more easily absorbed and almost impossible to overdose on when compared with the inorganic version used to treat bipolar disorder. Apparently, lithium, a light, alkali metal, is as important to brain health as magnesium is to muscle health. He told me he, his wife and mother-in-law took it too and it's used in Holland to treat dementia. I ordered a bottle from I-Herb, which cost $4.00 and lasted almost two years.

When I'd finished scanning the article and he my notes, I told him I thought I had BPD, which he ignored, instead asking me for a brief history of my childhood. I gave him a very abridged synopsis and he followed up with a couple of questions: "Are you a perfectionist?"

"Yes," I replied.

"Did you receive counselling when your parents separated?" *Of course I hadn't.* "No," I told him, and he shook his head gravely.

Again, I broached the subject of my having quiet borderline. He raised his eyebrows and after appearing to think for a moment, told me in a categorical tone, no. In response, I outlined my symptoms and he admitted I might well have some individual borderline traits and some for obsessive compulsive personality disorder too. I thought he was probably right about the latter, I must have picked those up from Uncle Arthur, who had displayed all the hallmark symptoms. As to borderline, he had told me at the start of the session he did not make assessments. To satisfy my curiosity, I underwent a formal assessment process with a different psychiatrist in 2022 and he confirmed I do meet the criteria for BPD. He also diagnosed persistent depressive disorder (dysthymia), PTSD and generalised anxiety disorder.

To finish, the psychiatrist gave me a diagram with a line drawing of a child, adult and parent. It was supposed to represent the roles we play in our relationships, but it looked familiar and I realised with a jolt that I had first seen it when doing inner child work in my 30s. I'd really been hoping for more but hiding my disappointment, I thanked him and not wanting to sound crazy, kept to myself the fact that I didn't have an 'inner child', I had a tribe.

It really was not surprising the psychiatrist had dismissed my assertion I have BPD, as my trusty mask had been firmly in place. He would have seen a poised, slightly overweight middle-aged woman, sitting crossed legged on his couch, in a neatly ironed, pale blue linen shirt and white cotton chinos, blond, wavy hair expertly cut, charcoal eyeliner expertly applied, speckly, grey eyes holding his.

It was her again, the eight-year-old and the mask. I couldn't have been my 'self' if I had tried, so ingrained was the habit of projecting an air of calm competence, even when it might have been more helpful to show the empty, inner chaos. She had fooled Ronnie for many months, so it was not difficult to kid a middle-aged male psychiatrist, even a so-called 'progressive'.

32

THE SCREAM

I dreamed of a mellow evening in autumn. The traffic noise at the busy intersection was muted. I turned as I heard the door open behind me. Ronnie smiled and stepped aside to let me past into her old consulting room. She took my hand and led me to a chair and sat me down. She smiled into my eyes and began to stroke my arms.

It was Matilda's 60th birthday and we travelled down to the Mornington Peninsula to stay at a friend's place. After a long lunch at a local winery with a group of Matilda's closest friends, we spent the remainder of the afternoon and into the evening splashing around in the pool, soaking in the spa, drinking champagne and wondering how we had gotten so 'old'.

I had received a text from Ronnie as we were lolling about on banana lounges by the pool, reminding me of our first appointment for the year. *As if I need it*, I wrote back, joking. I closed my eyes against the late-afternoon sun and reviewed the long, six-week break without her. I allowed myself a small flutter of excitement. Only one more day, one more sleep and the long, long wait would be over.

I smiled inwardly, stretching out in the warm sun and sighed. The world suddenly felt safer. This time tomorrow, we would finally see our 'Lovely Lady' again. Perhaps COVID would be done in 2021 and we would be able to resume in-person sessions. She might Haven us, perhaps even hug us.

At 1pm the next day, Saturday, we left Mt Martha and headed back to Melbourne. What a year 2020 had been, with its astounding revelations and pain. The floor had fallen away and I had landed in a strange, almost mythical underworld, secret and hidden from the material reality of everyday life.

What would the next year bring? Ronnie had told me early in the treatment that I would start to feel better and although I hadn't, she had assured me we had made progress and intuitively I knew she was right. Still, there was a long, long way to go; the attachment wound still seemed raw.

I changed into my favourite pale blue linen shirt and went up to the loft 30 minutes before our scheduled start, allowing myself a moment of quiet congratulation. The effort Ronnie had put into the pre-holiday preparations and my adherence to them had got us all through in one piece. There had been no cutting or hitting the bottle and although I'd been flooded on several occasions, I had managed to soothe myself by playing the guitar or writing morning pages or watching a Havening video, reassuring the little ones that I knew she would come back to them.

The desk at which I sat was placed between two long windows and it gave a view over the top of next door's corrugated iron roof, to the tips of the city's skyscrapers, five kilometres away. It was a warm and sunny day, with a light, cool breeze. Perfect, I thought smiling.

On the dot of 4.30, an email invite to our Zoom meeting popped into my inbox. Here we go, I thought, feeling joyful and nervous. With a pounding heart, I clicked the link and with that dear, familiar 'ping', the screen came alive and finally, she was there.

Even though we were all ecstatic, a part of me noted she looked a little tired and not refreshed as she'd promised, with her 'tanks filled up'. She wasn't wearing any make up, although we reminded ourselves, she sometimes didn't. But again, why hadn't she made the effort on this, our first session and the beginning of a whole new year?

"See, there she is," I told the kids, smiling broadly. "See, she said she would come back and...", I trailed off, as Ronnie interrupted, smiling with, "So, how was your holiday?"

"Oh, it was pretty good; long but we did OK." I was flooded but did my best to describe Christmas and the delights of swimming in deep, clear freshwater holes, under the deep blue enamelled skies, surrounded by the ancient red earth of the central Australian desert. I stuttered to a halt.

"Tell me about your holiday," I smiled sheepishly saying, "I've been flooded."

"Oh well, it didn't turn out as I had expected..."

"What do you mean?" I asked sharply, my stomach clenching. This could not be happening. After that, I could only take in snippets of what she said. "...a relapse of my heart condition... was struggling in the heat and I took a medication that should only be taken... too much and it affected my kidneys... Dr was on holidays, of course... pacemaker really hadn't had to work hard until... don't know what I will do with all that time... said I have to give up work... I've been here before..."

We started to cry. Someone screamed, raw, like an animal.

We tapped together. "Even though Ronnie is leaving us and we'll never, ever see her again, I love and accept myself."

She made our last ever Havening video. She told the little fox cubs she hoped they would find their way out into the sunny meadow and we were all worthy and lovable. Then, as the time wore on and the hour was up, her façade started to crack and she cried, "I've gotta go." We watched her until the screen went blank and she was gone.

I just sat in stunned and confused silence. I looked down at my favourite shirt, wondering if perhaps it was jinxed and this was the reason she had left. The parts had been struck a mortal blow. Somewhere, someone was quietly moaning. And we'd survived that interminably long six weeks and now she had gone, just like that, forever.

We were never, ever going to see her again, we could not get our head around it. Ronnie had abandoned us, suddenly and without warning, way before we were ready to strike out on our own. I cried as I thought of the damaged little two-year-olds, so wary and untrusting of humans that they had to hide as animals. She had said she was "In it for the long haul," but she would never see them again, nor see them free of their pain, if they ever were.

The impossible had happened, as we had always known it would and her assurances, her smile, her magic was gone and we floated anchorless again, but now with full consciousness of our condition. She had just fucked off when she had promised she would be there for us for as long as we needed.

Ronnie and I had had a plan and I had been reading the Internal Family Systems Therapy book over the holiday and was looking forward to the next phase of our therapeutic journey together. With my emerging 'Self', a fledgling, Ronnie and

'I' would have worked in collaboration to reach and 'rescue' the many 'parts' who were so traumatised and lost. She would have mentored me through the process. Ronnie had also suggested she would be my creativity mentor, so even when we were all healed, she could still, if we wanted, play a role in our lives.

Almost exactly one year before, with a knowing look, she had opened Pandora's Box and I had fallen in. Now my therapist, my guide and mentor had gone, and somehow I had to navigate a way out of the orphanage, the labyrinth, while not losing my new found 'Self', simultaneously comforting, supporting and healing all the damaged children in the process.

Before I could lift my shocked body off the chair and descend the steps to join Matilda, I tapped "Even though we survived the six weeks, we are now on our own, and I love and accept myself." I hadn't been able to tap for myself all the previous year. Now in desperation I tapped, because she had gone and we had nothing more to lose.

PART II

33

THE 'WILD WEST'

I left Mac at Uncle Arthur's front gate with a kiss and promise to contact him once I'd settled into my job as geological assistant in Laverton, outback WA. The next morning, my head full of renewed uncertainty, I flew to Perth, then Kalgoorlie and finally, took a small plane to Laverton. Now I was actually leaving Mac and my life in Melbourne, I felt torn. A part of me was disappointed that it was not the clean start I had planned, but on the other hand, Mac was finally going to leave his wife and we were to start a life together in three months' time, if he stuck to his promise.

One scorching afternoon three weeks later, I walked into the delicious chill of the office and was called to the phone. "I've been trying to contact you for days," came Mac's harried voice.

"Hi," I managed, my heart squeezing in delight to hear his voice again.

"I'll be in Perth at the end of the month, can you get away and join me?"

"Dunno," I replied uncertainly. "I haven't accrued any holidays," but vowed to myself I would manage it somehow.

I could tell Mac was feeling insecure and it felt good. For the first time in our relationship, I held the power. The resources sector was heavily weighted with men, something he knew about, consulting to mining companies. Sounding eager to please, he told me he'd asked his tenants to vacate his flat and planned to move in five weeks' time.

Two weeks later I flew to Perth, accompanied by a plane full of men returning home for their allocated time off. I entered the terminal and there he was, grinning hugely, his appraising gaze engulfing me like a big, green sea. I smiled shyly as he took my arm and whisked me away to a luxurious new hotel on the beach at Scarborough. Because Mac held a senior position, he flew business class and always stayed in the best hotels.

We hadn't spent more than a few minutes together in over two months and now he felt almost a stranger again. He had gone home to England with Hetty in mid-December and upon returning had just happened to visit Deb, a mutual friend of his, Hetty and Mum's, the night before I was due to leave, at which point he raced around to beg me to stay.

It was now March, one year since our hike up Mt Bogong and in the holiday atmosphere, the dry heat of the Australian 'Wild West', we fell into bed together and the impossible anguish of the long months apart, the years of yearning, the rollercoaster of push and pull, fell away. For three nights and days we ate in the posh hotel restaurant or lolled about in fluffy, white robes on the enormous bed, working our way through the delicious room-service menu.

There was a huge spa bath to share, replete with savoury mineral soaks. We sipped fine wines and real champagne as we shared our respective news. At dusk we would wander along the shore, the Indian Ocean indigo and benign and watch the huge sun melt into her depths. It felt like a honeymoon.

I flew back to Laverton with renewed hope and spent the remainder of my tenure trudging around the dirt of an open-cut gold mine, loading shot that blew the crust off the ancient landscape, scraping samples into small bags to be sent for assay, going to parties that were monumental drink and drug-taking fests, and finally, almost three months later, with great relief, left the mine for good and began the journey back to Melbourne, to start my life.

3 4

INSTANT FAMILY

Eleven hours after setting out, the plane's wheels hit the slick, icy runway at Melbourne airport and I peered excitedly through the porthole window, reminding myself irresistibly of the ten-year-old me, returning to Sydney to see my precious Daddy. Finally I thought, the long, long wait is over. I felt a great rush of excitement and almost skipped up the ramp into the airport terminal, smiling gleefully, expecting to see him at any moment. The rest of my life was just about to start and at last I would be safe.

I stopped suddenly, causing someone to step on my heel and throw me a dirty look in passing. I couldn't see Mac, he wasn't in the crowd of friends, lovers and family. I stood indecisively for a moment, then reluctantly began to amble in the direction of the baggage retrieval, my anxious heart pounding in my chest. And then I spotted him, smirking as he sauntered casually against the tide of new arrivals toward me. I could tell he'd been drinking.

On the way to his flat, Mac took me to his local pizza restaurant for a late dinner. He smiled as he told the waiter, "See, here she is, I didn't make her up." He said it proudly but he had set the tone at the airport and I felt awkward and out of place, not sure if I had made a monumental mistake, as he seemed so different to the Mac in WA, cool and offhand. We drove around the corner and at the top of the road, parked outside Mac's ground-floor, two-bedroom pad. I dragged my suitcase inside and he showed me around. Finally, exhausted, I climbed into his bed, feeling like a child, uncertain of my place, a passenger on someone else's journey.

The next morning, Mac went to work and I set about unpacking and exploring all the nooks and crannies. He'd said I needed to contribute to the 'household' and not really sure what he meant, went off to Myers to spend some of the money I had saved in WA on a lavish new doona and sheet set. I bought a chicken to roast and as the afternoon wore away, began to prepare a special dinner. At 6.30 with the preparations complete, the small kitchen table set, the chicken spitting and sizzling in the oven, I sat down to wait for Mac to return from work. The time ticked by. Seven o'clock came and went. Then eight. When nine o'clock rolled around and he still hadn't appeared or called, I allowed the panic to overwhelm me. How could this be happening?

I seized the phone book to search out Dave's number. Dave was Mac's best mate and Mum's now-ex-boyfriend, the one who was allegedly hopeless in bed. Crying, I dialled his number. After three rings, he answered. "It's Michele," I blurted out. "Is Mac with you? Do you know where he is?"

Without waiting for Dave to reply, I continued hysterically, "It's our first day together and he hasn't come home from work and it's ten past nine and he finishes at five-thirty. He must have had an accident... Is he with you? Do you know where he is? Do you think he's had an accident? Should I call the hospitals?"

A bemused Dave stuttered, "Ah...nnnno, I, ah..."

I hung up abruptly, desperately racking my brains to think of somebody else who might know what had happened to him but couldn't. Chilled water doused my insides. Oh my God, I thought, I have no job, I have nowhere else to go. What if he's dead? They would call his wife if something had happened to him, not me. She'd kick me out. I'd be homeless. Becoming homeless was my greatest fear in the world.

A rattle sounded at the front door and then a key turned in the lock and with a huge surge of relief I ran into the hall. "Where have you been!?" I cried, anger rising unexpectedly to my throat. I pushed it down, not wanting to antagonise Mac, knowing intuitively he would lash out, would not tolerate it. He'd been drinking again and he smirked, as if daring me to protest and said, "Been out with John and the work crowd." He slurred slightly and grinned cruelly, his big, white teeth flashing a snarl.

"Oh, are you hungry?" I ventured.

"I've eaten," he said.

There was a strange settling-in period, tense and awkward and occasionally distressing but after a few weeks, Mac calmed down and I could relax a little. He intimated his cool reception was because I'd put on a few extra kilograms since we had met up in Perth. I had no job, only my savings and he, an executive salary, but I joined his exclusive gym in Armadale and began to lose the extra kilos. I remembered looking through one of his family photo albums and finding a snap of Hetty just out of the shower, with a towel around her head, only wearing underpants. "What's this about?" I had asked and he'd replied that he'd ambushed her so he could show her how much weight she had put on. He told me his woman's appearance reflected on him.

Our first trip away together was a skiing holiday. We stayed at Mac's holiday house in Mt Beauty, where I'd met him five years earlier and where we had said our goodbyes the previous year. As we headed up to Falls Creek on that first morning, I felt euphoric. Here we were, just the two of us, together as I'd always dreamed, going skiing. It was such a contrast to how I had felt when Mac had headed off with his family to ski without me. I had taken Valium to get through the days, the hours, the minutes until his return.

It was a beautiful morning, the surrounding slopes blindingly white and the sky the colour of bluebells. I stood contentedly next to Mac in the lift ticket queue, watching kids jostling excitedly, throwing snowballs, exuberant and free. "I'm not paying for you, you have to pay for yourself," Mac piped up suddenly.

Embarrassed and crestfallen, I shuffled to the end of the queue. I had this wonderful memory of Mac cheerfully handing out lift tickets to his wife and two laughing daughters and I felt a door slam in my face, shutting away the warmth and camaraderie of that scene, pushing it beyond my grasp. I had fantasised I'd step effortlessly into Hetty's shoes, into a ready-made family, his teenage daughters becoming instant friends, who looked up to and relied on me, more older sister than young step-mum.

We returned to Melbourne and I set about the task of looking for a job. I had no idea what I wanted to pursue now my dream of being an opera singer had faded away. Besides, I'd already achieved my life's ambition, I was living with him. After all the drama, the ups and downs, I'd finally 'secured' Mac but still felt insecure. The idea of becoming an opera singer, or of getting a job or hobby that didn't involve him filled me with a dreary dread.

My obsession with Mac extended to his two daughters,

Quincy who was 19 and Alexandra, her 16-year-old sibling. I desperately wanted to get to know them, to spend time with them, to become their indispensable support and confidant and I wanted them to love me unconditionally.

I'd first met Mac's daughters on the skiing trip with Mum and Dave when I was 19. On that trip, I had admired Quincy's confidence, had been snared by her charisma but also felt strangely drawn to Alexandra. I had learned snippets here and there over the years about both girls from Mac and even from Mum. I had intuited that Alexandra was the black sheep of the family. She was very pretty and shared with her father the same black hair and curling eyelashes, but eyes that were a deep and vivid blue, rather than green. Her nose was fine and straight and her smile enchanting but beneath the harmonious beauty of her face and perfect figure, raged an emotional maelstrom. She was sensitive, gentle and sweet but also impulsive and reckless, with a propensity to sudden anger that could flare dangerously, like a bushfire in late summer.

Mac seemed to dislike her immensely, was always putting her down and railing against her. She could do no right but the stories of her latest outburst or outrageous doings only fuelled my fascination. My desire to meet with her grew and grew but this was not possible because Alexandra hated me with white-hot intensity. She vowed to Mac that if ever she ran into me, she would kill me, and I believed her. She was at once savage panther and vulnerable kitten.

Mac's other daughter was the 'golden child' and could do no wrong. She looked more like her mother, with long brown hair and hazel eyes. Quincy wasn't so beautiful as Alexandra but her personality was vibrant and she had an innate confidence and ease with people and she was very popular. Quincy had recently enrolled to become a police officer, ahead of Alexandra, who was desperate to join the Victoria Police Force but who, in a cruel twist of fate, would be knocked back the next year due to a chronic health condition.

Quincy was a magnet for men and had many friends of both sexes. I became enamoured of her, of the way she looked, dressed and behaved, her lifestyle and personality and I desperately wanted Quincy to like me. I also wanted to be just like her, confident, engaging, extroverted and adventurous. She drank and partied with abandon and rather than fear it, delighted in male attention.

Quincy loved the clothing brand Country Road and Levi 501 jeans and I started to emulate her dress style. I bought pale blue 501s and white linen shirts with expensive, dark brown leather loafers, linen blazers and silk scarves.

Unlike Alexandra, Quincy would sometimes breeze in for a chat on her way to a party or an intimate dinner, cooked by some or other enamoured young, male police officer. She'd sit in our lounge room, chatting about her doings in the Force, busting crooks at midnight or entertaining interstate colleagues at trendy bars in South Yarra.

I'd sit in thrall, surreptitiously noting everything about her, from her choice of blouse, the jewellery she wore and the way she braided her long, dark brown hair. I would observe with surprise the gap between her front teeth, the same as Mac's, the freckles on her button nose and the scent of her perfume. I would invite her to Friday night drinks and with a knot of distracted impatience wait for her to arrive, feeling quietly devastated when she didn't show.

35

OLD IVORY

Mac and I had been living together for almost two years when he announced one day that he wanted me to move out of his flat. We were sitting side by side on tall stools in a wine bar, sipping a buttery chardonnay. "It's not fun anymore," he said and threw me a calculating look, green eyes hooded. It felt as if he had slid the blade of a knife between my ribs, to puncture my heart. I had not seen it coming and felt myself falling, falling, in slow motion but muttered, "Oh, OK... sure." He smirked and then with a look of mingled unconcern and satisfaction, turned his face away, to take a considered sip of his wine.

"You want children anyway," he continued in his lazy, rhetorical way. We had had brief discussions about children and the fact that he didn't want to start again, at age 45, complaining he didn't have enough money. I thought perhaps I did want children, believing he would change his mind if I became pregnant, sometime in the distant future. Suddenly though, I wasn't sure. Perhaps I didn't want children. All I knew with certainty was that I couldn't bear the thought of losing Mac again and that it had always been my dearest and most desperate desire since Mum and Dad had separated to have my own children and a family one day.

I had had the abortion three years earlier, when Mac was still with his wife because I had worried I would not cope as a single mother. I had aborted our child, a boy I was convinced. He would have been the most gorgeous three-year-old by now and we would have been a family… but perhaps Mac would not have left his wife if I'd had the child. He told me smugly he had avoided the 'crazy hour' when his girls were small, staying back at work until they were tucked up in bed.

Obediently, I found a little terrace house to rent in North Carlton and moved out a month later. Mac told me he had strategically chosen to send me packing before we had clocked up two years of living together, so I would have no claim on his assets. He had joked that Hetty would get half and I the other.

One evening a few days after I'd taken possession of the little house, Mac and I attended a dinner together. I had planned to stay the night at his place but when we arrived back there he was drunk. Although he was amicable, I knew his mood could change in an instant and although his aggression was usually limited to vile vitriol, I would never forget the one time he had kicked out at me but lost his balance. He had tumbled to the floor and convinced I had shoved him, rose like an enraged snake to slam me into the wall.

"I'm going to my place," I announced, feeling empowered and relieved as I grabbed my handbag and headed to the front door. A deluge of insults followed me to the car but I felt pleased because I no longer had to put up with his tantrums and congratulated myself for a lucky escape.

It was Sunday night and the roads were quiet as I drove for

20 minutes to my new home, as-yet unfurnished except for my new bed and a wardrobe containing a few clothes. I went to bed and fell instantly to sleep but woke suddenly, feeling disorientated, wondering where I was and what had woken me. I heard banging coming from somewhere and then remembered I had escaped to North Carlton and that it must be early morning.

I fumbled for my nightie, put it on and then padded down the carpeted hall to the lovely front door, with its two panels of red and blue lead light. I put my mouth to the door and said quietly, "Hello?"

"I have something for you, you bitch," came Mac's slurred voice. Jesus, I thought, he has driven all the way here and is absolutely drunk. I opened the door a crack, leaving the chain on but immediately closed it so as to remove the chain and open the door.

He had my little rabbit Sebastian and as he stepped inside I held out my hands to take him but rather than handing him to me, Mac threw him over my shoulder. "I've no idea where Happer is," he slurred. Happer was my guinea pig.

Mac stood swaying in the hallway, the dim light cast by the streetlight throwing his profile into ugly relief, his chin jutting out in a parody of Popeye's square jaw, his mouth an ugly slash. The tirade started up again but I hardly heard, so worried was I about my dear little rabbit, fearing he might hop out into the night and be lost. The fear was galvanising and a strength, a power rose in me that I did not know I possessed—a protective urge that subdued my fear. A sense of clarity and purpose took the place of the terror rageful men induce and I stopped backing up and began to walk purposefully toward Mac. I took the first step and he stepped back. He had been shouting but fell silent. I took another step toward him, my eyes fixed firmly on his and he stepped back again. I took another step forward and he, one back. I could feel my energy pushing him away from me until suddenly he stumbled over the threshold and off the small step. The door clicked shut in his face.

All at once he went berserk, screaming and smashing the door with his fist. I slid down the wall and started to cry. As soon as he'd given up and gone, I went in search of my little guy. He was sitting calmly on his hind legs on the carpet in the second bedroom, washing his furry face.

I took my doona and pillow and lay down next to him, waiting for the day. I drifted in and out of sleep until I woke with a start, my nerves taught, shell shocked and exhausted. I could hear the footsteps of people walking along the pavement to work in the cold, early morning mist. They would stop and after a pause, continue on their way. I heard one set of footsteps stop and a voice mutter, "How terrible!"

I got up and padded to the front door. The grey light penetrated numerous holes in the glass panes. I waited for another set of footsteps to fade and with trepidation, opened the door and peered out. The front doorstep was littered with red and blue glass, the black lead piping in the door was twisted and broken in places and the white door frame splattered with dark, reddy-brown blood. I felt shocked and then angry at the thought of explaining what had happened to the landlord, my record smeared after signing the lease only a few days before.

Later that day I drove to Mac's and found him wandering around his flat crying. He'd not gone to work and had clumsily bandaged his hand, which he took off to show me the damage. Puzzled, I noted his strange switch from raging demon to little boy. The cuts were only superficial and hardly warranted a bandage, let alone tears. "Did you find Happer?" I asked anxiously and he indicated the hutch. Happer was nibbling his cereal, looking OK as far as I could tell. When Mac had returned, he'd found him hiding under the stairs in the flat's ground-floor foyer.

Despite this latest drama, yet again I agreed to Mac's suggestion we continue to see each other on weekends and so we settled into a comfortable routine. Mac would come over each Friday night and we'd spend the weekend together. Weeknights we were left to our own devices.

The 'rabbit' incident had been put to bed somewhere in the many-roomed house of my mind but the door couldn't be completely closed and feelings of disquiet, of dissatisfaction and resentment began to erode my need for him. To hurt a small animal to get at me, was unforgivable and the shabby way he treated his younger daughter Alexandra was telling too. I began a dossier and his pedestal wobbled. I re-remembered Quincy telling me when she and Alex were children, Hetty had sometimes bundled them into the car to drive for hours to escape Mac's raging. I wondered whether I really wanted him to father my child, and if not Mac, then who? My resolve crystalised a few months later and I ended our relationship with relative ease. It had run its course.

I did still occasionally catch up with Mac for lunch and on one of those occasions he told me he had remarried, "You know her," he told me. "Joan, from the soccer club. She's divorced too and has her own house and superannuation." I couldn't remember meeting her but felt sure he had courted her while we were together.

It had been many years since I had seen Mac but one day he phoned out of the blue and invited me to lunch. I told Matilda I was catching up with him and suggested naively that perhaps we could all go out to lunch one day as Matilda, Mac and Joan were all English and would have lots in common. When I suggested this to Mac at the lunch, he mumbled something about Joan being the jealous type. "Well, do you give her reason to be jealous?" I asked and he shuffled about, looking awkward and mumbled that he didn't before reverting to type and flashing his winning, trademark smile, his teeth still strong but yellowing like old ivory.

That evening he followed up with an email telling me without preamble: "I'd like to spend more time with you next time we meet." Irritated by his air of entitlement, I replied saying I did not ever want to play the role of 'other woman' ever again. "It's hopeless then," he responded dramatically. Yep, I thought, you sure are.

36

BIG SISTER

Soon after moving to North Carlton, I found a lovely woman called Lee, also in her late-20s, to share the small house. We clicked instantly, both being introverted, sensitive animal lovers.

One weekday evening before Mac and I had split, Lee suggested we get dressed up and head down to Brunswick Street for a drink. This sounded fun, although I was not used to doing anything spontaneous and it felt a little daring. We set off down Canning Street and turned left into Johnston Street, Melbourne's 'Spanish quarter', only making it as far as The Tapas Bar, strains of the Gipsy Kings luring us inside. Liking what we saw, we climbed onto a bar stool and ordered sangria.

The Tapas Bar became our regular hang out and we'd sit chatting and drinking sangria, the bar's owner flirting with Lee. It was the early 1990s and tapas bars were a 'thing'. As the night progressed and the place became more crowded and rowdier, couples would climb onto the bar to dance. Stilettoed feet would stutter back and forth and we'd clutch our drinks to our chests. Once, a couple fell off the bar into the shelf opposite, causing a colourful cascade of glass and spirits to shower the good-natured owner. He didn't mind, it was good for business.

Sharing with Lee and seeing Mac on weekends was easy and life was uncharacteristically drama-free. Although Lee was my age, she seemed sophisticated and it lent her an air of worldliness and I felt safe in her big-sisterly presence. Mac was easier to get on with too and we enjoyed the best of each other. In this way life sailed pleasantly on until a year later, a few months after Mac and I had split, when Lee announced she was to be married to her on-again-off-again boyfriend and was moving out.

The eight-year-old part who had reeled when Mum and Dad separated, woke in the darkness of her perpetual now to feel it happening all over again, and her torment gushed into the present day. A cold, sick feeling of dread squeezed my insides. My safe world was falling apart, the ground was shifting under my feet again.

I would have preferred to live alone but couldn't afford the rent, so quickly found a replacement house mate—Jim, a young male professional who was very keen to move in. He seemed to instantaneously form a crush and followed me around like a love-sick puppy, which I found cloying and annoying and felt compelled to escape the house whenever he was there. I missed Lee dreadfully.

One day a few months after Jim had arrived, I inherited a modest sum of money and used it as a deposit for a small house. The boy planned on coming too. He was obsessed with Mustang cars and wanted to pull one apart in the big backyard. "No, sorry," I told him, "that grass is reserved for Sebastian the rabbit and Mr Happer the guinea pig."

The little weatherboard house was located ten kilometres from Melbourne's central business district in the suburb of West Footscray, which was to become a respectable refuge for 'yuppies' when they could no longer afford the inner city but for now, was strictly working class.

I had been in such a rush to escape 'the boy' that I had not done my homework. Not long after I'd moved in, the line of rundown houses opposite my front door were demolished to reveal the Tottenham Goods Yard, a barren industrial landscape, a sprawling iron and grey stone eyesore of train tracks, idle goods carriages and giant Tonka Toy engines.

This ugly wasteland generated a lot of noise, which again, I only became conscious of after I'd moved. Interstate diesel passenger and goods trains clattered and roared past, 40 metres from my home, wafting diesel fumes through open windows on what would otherwise be pleasant summer afternoons. Worst of all, for six nights a week, the entire night was given over to deafening booms and crashes as loose carriages were free shunted—that is, encouraged to roll down the slight incline to connect with a deafening bang, while the diesel engines revved and roared back and forth, like angry, testosterone-fuelled ants.

I found the incessant noise and smell deeply distressing, triggering a state of acute hypervigilance, not realising I suffered from PTSD. The intrusive noises reminding my body of Uncle Arthur's rage as he banged cupboards and doors and swore ferociously.

I managed to survive, living on my nerves for nine months until my house was broken into a second time while I was at work. The thieves stole my jewellery and large collection of CDs, and feeling profoundly violated and unsafe, I felt compelled to move again. I rented out my house and moved back to the inner city to share with a couple of university mates.

At first, I felt relieved to be back in North Calton, with its familiar beauty, the streets lined with quaint terrace houses and plane trees, rather than the bleak, dreary landscape, the noise and foul-smelling air of the western suburbs. Even so, as the months slipped by, despite my escape to this relative paradise, I felt more and more exiled from the world and my life. I didn't know I was depressed, that the gloom would always return after bouts of hypervigilance. I had been depressed on and off since I was a very small child. Depression was my 'ground state'.

One of my housemates would always come running when he heard me arriving home from work and would ask the same question each night, "How're you going?" Unaccountably, this question irritated me immensely, possibly because I couldn't begin to put into words just how dreadful, how lost and scared I felt, in an indefinable, dissociated sort of way. I began to creep up the stairs like a thief, to compose myself before descending again to face the gang, all bright and fresh and witty, and to drink wine.

Despite the alcohol, I often lay awake late into the night, feeling exhausted but unable to sleep. Each morning, I'd hang listlessly off the handrail in the packed tram on my way to work, listening over and over again to 'Wonderwall' on my Walkman. Of a lunchtime, I'd trudged to the Botanical Gardens and breathe a sigh as I passed through the wrought iron gates into the peace of nature: the fragrant grass, sweeping views down to the ornamental lake, glimpsed through the huge boughs of exotic trees. I'd slump onto the manicured lawn and eat my sandwich wishing I could sit there all afternoon.

Without the unstable stability of life with Mac, the loss of my operatic ambitions and the warmth and companionship of my 'big sister' Lee, life took on the aspect of a sickening, slow-motion carnival ride I couldn't get off. The world wobbled past my bedroom window, pale and indistinct, while my head was filled with a constant, intrusive stream of destructive self-talk. I cut myself to pieces with a relentless barrage of critical commentary, generated by the internalised voices of my childhood tormentors.

37

THE RED SEA

One morning I woke and felt too depressed to get up for work. I never usually cried but this day I'd hit rock bottom and hot tears suddenly spilled from my eyes, soaking into my hair and trickling into my ears. I associated crying with ridicule and hated succumbing, but the tears bestowed a quantum of relief and I began to feel a small measure of release.

Suddenly the bedroom door flew open and one of my housemates George, bustled over to sit on my bed. Embarrassed, I tried to wipe my eyes on the sheet without him seeing. He must have bionic hearing, I thought because I was well-practiced at crying silently.

He put an arm solicitously around my shoulder in a misguided attempt to cheer me up, to stop me crying. The welcome relief that had begun to soothe my heart with the flow of rusty tears was shut off, like a tap. I wanted to shrink away but instead hoisted the mask back on telling him I felt "Much better thank you." Business-like, he bustled off to get ready for work. I waited anxiously to hear the click of the front door and when it finally came, sank back down, the weight in my chest crushing.

The next morning, I felt the same heavy sense of hopelessness but there were no tears and no small measure of relief. On tenterhooks, expecting my space to be violated at any time, I lay in bed hardly breathing, waiting for George to go to work, praying he would leave me alone. When the front door finally shut and all was quiet, I slumped further into my pillow, still feeling depressed but also restless. It was at this point my intuition nudged me with a memory of a person from choir, who raved about an 'amazing' Kinesiologist. I didn't know what Kinesiologists did, but a tiny glimmer of hope flickered and I roused myself to go in search of the woman's card.

Her name was Binnie, a sought-after practitioner who was booked up for months in advance. She answered her phone on the first ring, something she would never do again and in a tentative voice I introduced myself and explained my connection with the woman from choir. Binnie asked some questions only one of which I remember, "Are you suicidal?" I didn't think I was, had no plans to kill myself but muttered that I might be, so desperate was I to find some relief. She told me to come over immediately.

Binnie got to work over my prone body, making strange movements while I surrendered to her process. After ten minutes or so, she stopped and looking grave asked if when I was a child, I had known a child who had died. I shook my head, puzzled. Without a word Binnie resumed her muscle testing and with sudden insight said, "It was you. A part of you died when you were five." I had started school when I was five and it had been a huge, traumatic shock, like being sent alone to a foreign, hostile planet. Binnie advised me to do 'inner child' work and gave me the name of a social worker who ran inner-child healing weekend workshops.

I left Binnie feeling a little better because I now had a plan, a plan on which I pinned all my hopes. I was 30, working for a publishing company in a role I hated, that played to my weaknesses, and was lonely but afraid of intimate relationships. I was depressed and anxious and at serious risk of going mad, literally mad with fear, fear of life, fear of the world, and that I was a total fuck up. My back was hard like a board, so hard I could hardly breathe. At any second life might suck my soul out through my arse. Luckily, I had learned to dissociate at a young age and this survival strategy got me through although it came at a cost—I moved through life like a rigid, straight-laced, spaced-out junkie.

Despite my desperation, I considered the weekend workshop quite a sacrifice. I mean, to give over an entire weekend? It is funny to think I was so naïve. I thought it marked the end of suffering, with the big party, a black forest cherry cake and party poppers, supportive family and friends dancing to an 80s soundtrack. No, it wasn't the wonderful start to the rest of my happy life, but it was the start of the beginning.

I'd been driving for approximately an hour and a half when the soft evening light suddenly gave way to the absolute blackness of a moonless night in the country. I slowed my little VW Golf to a crawl, picking my way carefully along the narrow, winding dirt road, minus one headlight. I could only see a few metres in front of the bonnet and sat hunched forward, shoulders strained as blackberry vines scraped along the passenger side of the car if I got too close to the weed-choked culvert. I've probably missed the turnoff, I thought fretfully. I have a dyslexic sense of direction, which often leads me astray. Sometimes, I even choose the opposite direction on purpose and it always proves to be right.

An animal loomed out of the gloom and quickly disappeared again. I thought it had antlers. The little car crawled along for what felt like ages until I decided I really must have missed the turnoff and should turn around, if that was even possible, when a small sign appeared on the left and the undergrowth relented its tangled grasp to reveal a driveway. Feeling greatly relieved, I turned in and proceeded up the long dirt drive to the first of two large, timber bungalows. A bright, golden light peeped from under the curtains, inviting me inside.

There were six participants including myself and the female facilitator, who I would instantly develop a crush on. The workshop location was in beautiful, hilly countryside, full of eucalyptus trees, bright, raucous birds and herbaceous scents and it was in this peaceful setting that we began our 'work' the next morning at 9am.

The workshop was wonderful and terrifying in equal measure. It was especially confronting to witness the torment of one participant, a beautiful, kind young woman who had been repeatedly raped by her 16-year-old brother when she was 12 and brutalised by her deranged policeman father who had locked her in his dark shed for hours and hours when she was a small child for being 'naughty'. She was now a psychiatric nurse.

When it was my turn to explore my own trauma, I found it beyond confronting to open up and express my feelings associated with the abuse in the presence of others and as with Ronnie, I became hyperaroused. We were engaged in 'psycho drama' and I felt excruciatingly self-conscious, unable to 'let go' of my anger at Uncle Arthur by belting the hell out of a pillow in front of everyone. Despite the unyielding barrier behind which I hid my emotions, the same 'wall' that shielded the myriad of child 'parts' I would stumble upon some 23 years later, it was also my first experience of sharing and of unconditional giving and receiving, camaraderie and connection and it was very nourishing and affirming. It felt like a 'home' of sorts.

On the Sunday evening, at the conclusion of the workshop, I found it difficult to leave, as I felt so warm and content on the inside, while outside the view was ethereal. I stood for ages, mesmerised by the sight of the changing sunset colours on the sky above Mt Dandenong, a procession through yellow, orange, pink and red, and then, as the sun dipped further below the horizon, lilac, purple and finally midnight blue. Crickets began to croak and glittering stars appeared shyly, to twinkle softly.

When everyone else had finally driven away to their homes and lives, I got into my car and headed back along the dark, tree-lined roads toward the city, feeling safe and replete, as if wrapped in a warm bubble of connection and belonging. I took a wrong turn and ended up on the main freeway into Melbourne and at that point, the feelings of connection and love began to falter. They progressively weakened like a spell wearing off, the wonderful memories already fading, becoming indistinct, like half-remembered dreams. I was not yet strong enough to hold the love, I did not yet know about 'object constancy' and it would be many years until I did. For now, I was a cracked glass, unable to hold onto love and joy. It drained away to emptiness.

The next weekend in a haze of depression and despair, I drove off without any idea of where I was going until I realised the car was meandering steadily toward the distant hills. A couple of hours later, I found myself at the workshop venue again. The place was now deserted. I parked at the gates and wandered up the verdant driveway, wattle birds swooping on the line of weeping shrubs laden with red bottle brush flowers. Furtively, I mounted the back steps and stood on the timber deck, seeing us drinking tea in the sun, swinging our legs off the edge, and marvelling at the spectacular, mountain views. It felt like aeons had passed.

I peered through the window into the deserted interior and could see us all as we had been the previous weekend. The sun rose higher in the sky and the air lost its rosy hew but still I stood, reliving the special moments. If only it was this time last week, was the constant refrain, the ear worm in my head. I smiled as I remembered the feelings of warmth and acceptance and closed my eyes in concentration, straining to grasp and hold them. With each repetition a little of their colour faded until they, like me, were empty. I turned away in despair. Despite the warm spring sunshine, the air had gone cold.

I wended my way back to civilisation, feeling as depressed as I had the morning I phoned Binnie but without any small seed of hope. It was dark when I arrived home and everyone was out, as it was Saturday night. I ran a bath. The big oak tree outside the first-floor bathroom window was bursting with new spring growth. I put on a CD of Prokofiev's ballet music to Cinderella and opened the window. The scent of jasmine wafted into the white-tiled room on a draught of balmy air. I looked down into the water. It was red and I could see myself motionless, floating, wrists cut, a river of blood emptying along with all my pain, into the salty ocean of my unshed tears. Into the black, starry night I watched my soul escape through the enveloping arms of the silent oak tree.

38

BORDERLAND

We inhabit Borderland.
Borderland is the surface below which we sink each night,
crying dry tears.
It's the bleak winter walk we take each day, past her old rooms.
It's watching paralysed, as someone else kisses her in our dreams.
It's reaching out to grasp her hand, that isn't there.
It's standing against the sucking tide that steals the sand
from beneath our feet, and the roar as panic grabs our guts.
It's forgetting again and again, we are not real. [1]

Ronnie had gone forever and the little three-year-olds were crying, their tears falling down my cheeks as they remembered the soothing feel of her hands on their chubby little arms and flushed cheeks. It had only happened once, but they thought about the session when Ronnie had Havened them,

---

[1] The title of 'Borderland' was inspired by Kevin Redmayne's *Wuthering Heights: Read the Story of Love, Borderline Personality Disorder, and Complex-PTSD* (2019).

over and over, into the wee small hours of Saturday night and into Sunday morning. They clung like limpets to that memory, eyes squeezed shut, sucking on the sweetness, feeling her skin on theirs.

It had been our last ever session together and the screen had died. I had sat reeling, as if a rock had crashed through the window to knock me senseless. This was the most monstrous of betrayals.

That night I managed to sleep for a couple of hours but woke to the sound of little children crying and calling for Ronnie. It was 3.30am and in desperation and because I am a 'doer', I grabbed the only lifeline she had thrown and drafted an email to the two therapists she had recommended, not that she had facilitated an introduction. I described what had happened and begged them, like a bedraggled stray cat, to take me in. I was desperate to maintain some form of connection with Ronnie through one of the women.

As the night wove its weary way to morning, I suddenly remembered my old therapist Iona, who I'd seen for a couple of years ten years earlier. I had had weekly sessions during a severe period of PTSD activation and I wrote another desperate email and begged for an emergency session as soon as possible. Iona responded almost immediately and agreed to see me the following day, for which I was desperately thankful. Still, I thought dismissively, as soon as Ronnie's therapists are available, I'll start with one of them.

In that last session, Ronnie had set out to make a final Havening video. There had been a false start and then she'd got the wording right. A couple of days after she had left, she had sent the aborted one by mistake. I had written her a desperate text just hours after she had left saying, "Please don't leave us, we can't stand the pain," which she had ignored but now addressed, writing that she would send the correct Havening video and reminding me I would get flooded and that I must 'honour the work'.

The days after Ronnie left were bathed in visceral, all-consuming grief. I felt I was drowning, that my worst nightmare was upon me. On the night it was over, I had stumbled into the lounge room crying, to tell Matilda that Ronnie had gone. I had sat down on the sofa and rested my head on her shoulder, and she had put her arms around me. It is a normal, natural urge for humans to seek physical comfort when distressed but I found it deeply shaming. On this occasion though, I was too overwhelmed to hide the grief and shock and so had endured the feelings of intense vulnerability while pretending to feel nourished.

39

MATILDA

It was Christmas time as I walked down the Bourke Street Mall in Melbourne. A large crowd of excited shoppers and small children jostled to glimpse the annual Myer department store's Christmas windows display. It was always beautifully put together and drew big crowds.

Drifts of soggy leaves huddled in brown heaps around the lamp posts, for although it was December, the air was freezing and everyone was rugged up, as if for a northern-hemisphere winter.

I stood on tip toes, straining to catch site of the display but couldn't see over all the heads. Suddenly the crowd heaved and I was thrust forward to confront the window. Rather than Santa's reindeer and a sled overflowing with beautifully wrapped gifts, all was grey. Sitting in the bare expanse was an oversized fish tank and in the freezing water, a dolphin. Everyone was goggling excitedly and as I watched, she sank slowly to the bottom, her eyes rolling up in misery.

The day I turned 31 an ant bit my bum and woke me up. It really hurt. Inexplicably, I was sitting on the carpet in the lounge room, rather than the sofa where I always sat. Utterly sick of feeling miserable, I decided I would 'get over' my past.

Just like that, I would magically turn into a different person, a happy, carefree one whose mind wasn't constantly drawn back to childhood. 'Enough is enough', I had said to the room at large, when the tiny insect who had made its way laboriously across the great expanse of carpet, reminded me I had a job to do. Who had sent it? I wondered.

Soon after the 'ant incident' I felt drawn to sing again and auditioned for and was accepted into the Melbourne Chorale. It was during my first Sunday afternoon practice session that I serendipitously sat next to the woman who introduced me to Binnie the Kinesiologist and 'inner child' work.

The woman also told me about the gentle, healing art of Reiki and as soon as her hands touched my shoulders, I knew I must learn it too. The process of becoming a Reiki channel is very mysterious and spiritual although not religious. It involves a series of physical 'attunements' to open the third eye to the flow of universal lifeforce energy, creating a pathway from forehead, through the body to the hands, where it flows out to wherever it is needed for physical, emotional, and/or spiritual healing. It was after the first attunement I dreamed of the miserable dolphin behind the Christmas window and knew she somehow represented me.

With the sudden influx of energy, the depression and dam of suppressed emotion began to crack and I felt a new sensation, a pressure in my chest that made it difficult to breathe deeply, or perhaps my lungs were trying to breathe properly for the first time in my life. Although I was still socially anxious, hypervigilant, deeply tired and now carried a boulder around in my chest, the Reiki gave me a feeling of hope and I began to enjoy singing. The Melbourne Chorale accompanied the Melbourne Symphony Orchestra and we performed great choral works: the Mozart

Requiem, Bach's Mass in B minor and Matthew Passion and Beethoven's sublime choral symphony. In the anonymity of the choir I could sing freely and lose myself joyfully in the act of creative self-expression.

I greatly enjoyed practicing Reiki I, but was impatient to complete Reiki II, which I felt very drawn to. To practice Reiki I, hands are placed on the subject—person, animal or plant—whereas the advanced level, Reiki II, enables the practitioner to send energy over distance and can enhance psychic abilities. I found Reiki II awe inspiring as I could send 'light' to dark places. Healing energy could be sent to friends anywhere in the world, to animals, to victims of natural disasters and wars, as well as problematic relationships; in short to anything and anyone in need, including myself. I felt I was fulfilling my spiritual destiny.

After the completion of the Reiki courses, life took another turn for the better—I enrolled in a weekly version of the inner child workshop and met Matilda. I had not expected to find my life partner, in fact I had decided it would be simpler and more productive if I dedicated my life to healing and steered clear of intimate relationships, which I found scary and perplexingly difficult.

I arrived ten minutes late to the first session and knocked hurriedly on the heavy front door of the old terrace house in North Carlton. The facilitator led me into a shabby but cosy living room, with five participants already ensconced comfortably in bean bags on the floor. Matilda, a radiographer by trade, had hurt her back lifting a patient and was lying on her tummy on a bean bag, close to the fire. I remember she apologised for wasting the group's time, explaining that rather than suffering the effects of child abuse, her only issue was an inability to say 'no'.

"Matilda, can you make me a cup of tea please?" the facilitator asked briskly after we'd concluded our introductions.

She began to wriggle awkwardly out of the bean bag, saying, "Oh yes, of course," before the rest of us chimed in, "No, you're supposed to say 'NO'."

Matilda seemed drawn to me, my childish rabbit jumper, black leggings and painful shyness. At the end of the second session, she suggested we meet for a bowl of soup at Hydromeda in Brunswick Street. "Oh no, I couldn't face eating before a session, I'm too nervous," I told her but promised to come along to keep her company. At the end of the next session someone suggested we go for a drink in Brunswick Street and so we all strolled to Mario's, where now ravenous, I ordered a big plate of pasta and glass of red wine. Mario's closed at 11pm. Undaunted, Matilda and I found the Gipsy Bar was open until 1am. I felt uncharacteristically relaxed with Matilda and we chatted away happily, never running out of things to discuss or worrying about how tired we'd be the next day at work.

One night after 'group' Matilda asked if she could take me for an outing. I asked her where to, but she told me it was a surprise. The next Sunday morning she picked me up at the house I was minding while the owners were away (I'd put all my belongings into storage and was voluntarily homeless) and we drove through the quiet suburbs to a beach. This beach did not have the urbane, almost cosy air of a built-up Sydney one, with houses hugging every piece of land to the cliff's edge, vying for the best views; this one was wild and deserted. Waves pounded the steep shore, gulls dipped and rose on a roller coaster of lapis lazuli, weed was thrown up onto the beach in huge pungent drifts and the raw, salty wind beat our faces until they stung.

We hiked along the deserted beach, the water too rough to skim stones. Around lunch time the clouds parted to reveal the pale winter sun. We sat on the damp sand and Matilda produced a Boston Bun and thermos of Lady Grey tea. I smiled, forcibly reminded of The Famous Five with their delicious buns and lashings of ginger beer.

Matilda seemed to genuinely like my company although I couldn't understand how or why. At some point along the way of our increasing intimacy I realised she had seen inside me, as far as I could go in those days and hadn't run away screaming. That she didn't find me repulsive was enough to ditch my safety plan of staying single and immediately attached myself to her like one of the barnacles on the rocks over which we were hopping.

Unlike me, she had lots of friends, normal ones and suddenly my world was filled with dinner parties, winery tours and novel, adventurous weekends canoeing down the Murray River, cracking tinnies at midday while we drifted in idle bliss and camped on sandy beaches under the stars by night. We went cross country skiing in the Victorian Alps, eating local freshwater trout and apple crumble for dinner, sitting in front of a huge crackling fire, sipping a local white wine that tasted of minerals and alpine earth.

One memorable Sunday morning, as I doubled back to fill my water bottle, a huge brown snake slithered across the path. He or she was a magnificent animal, the largest snake I've ever seen, but I turned back, deciding I did have enough water to last the hike back to our cars. The usual group of us had walked to Little Waterloo Bay at Wilson's Prom (Promontory) the day before and camped overnight in our little tents at a campsite surrounded by pristine bush. Before bed, we had walked the short distance to the beach to await the full moon's appearance and sat on our Therm-a-Rests, sipping port and eating chocolate, joking and bantering to pass the time.

We had sat for over an hour, the sky still moonless and our

ration of port running low, when someone noticed the froth on the waves had become visible. They formed a series of mysterious lines, glowing a luminous, electric blue although the night was as black as pitch and we couldn't see our hands in front of our faces. Intrigued, we stood like curious children, then walked toward the water's edge. Tiny blue stars erupted around our feet and we each left a trail of twinkling footprints. Enchanted, we capered around looking back over our shoulders, weaving and laughing. It was bioluminescence.

A year after we fell in love, Matilda took me home with her to England to visit her family and friends. Arriving in the northern hemisphere was a revelation and I felt I had come home. As an Australian of European descent I made sense in England, more so than in Australia, which I realised with a sense of deep knowing was ancient beyond reckoning and still belonged to the Aborigines, the trappings of Western civilisation a thin, suffocating carapace under which nature sat patiently, waiting to burst free again. By comparison, the quaint little villages of southwest England appeared to have grown themselves cosily from the emerald countryside.

We began that first memorable trip in Oxford and I felt I'd been there before. Then we travelled to Exeter in beautiful Devon to stay with Matilda's family and spent an enchanting month exploring the city and surrounds. We wandered into town to explore Exeter Cathedral and sip tea in the Cathedral Close. We spent hours rummaging through the huge antique centre perched on the river Exe. Walking back up the hill, we passed through the remnants of the great city wall, still intact in places and incredibly, the Roman workmanship still visible. Further afield we wandered in the high Dartmoor National Park and climbed the ancient granite tors.

I felt inexplicably drawn to Cornwall and so we borrowed Matilda's brother's old camper van, which embarrassingly spewed black smoke from the exhaust each time we started it, and headed off to England's western-most tip, driving down narrow winding lanes, the bordering hedgerows bursting with flowers. We visited the mystical St Michael's Mount and found a beach worthy of The Famous Five called Kynance Cove, one of my all-time favourites, only accessible at low tide and rivalling any in Australia with its pristine, fine, white sand, clear, turquoise water and dramatic cliffs complete with tantalising nooks and crannies to explore.

Being with Matilda was like running away from school, running away from my real life, 12-year-old chums wagging school together.

But the first flush of love always wears off and when it did, depression and that empty feeling returned. Interspersed with the 'good times' were periods of acute distress and hypervigilance caused by loud, insensitive neighbours and narcissistic bosses, who triggered subconscious memories of Uncle Arthur's controlling behaviour and rage. Their 'noise' infiltrated my head and my home like a seeping poison from which there was no escape, no safety, no respite. In an attempt to cope, I often pushed Matilda away, only to creep back again when I felt better, only to push her away again a day, a week, or a month later.

Our good times, travelling and laughing together and sharing a love of animals and a passion for food kept us going through the difficult times. I haven't been easy to live with, with my undiagnosed C-PTSD, depression, anxiety, and quiet borderline. There have been a lot of eggshells to negotiate, some more akin to land mines yet she has stuck with me through the good times and the bad.

40

THE DISTANT SHORE

It has only been four days. How can it only be four days, four days since Ronnie left?

"I gotta go," she had cried and disappeared from the screen.

Before the session, blissfully unaware of impending catastrophe, I had been looking forward to the start of the new year of therapy, proud to have lasted the whole seven weeks without sending her a single text. The long break had built my resilience and I had known it would be easier to manage the desperate yearning for her between sessions.

Over the course of a single year, I had opened myself up completely and we had stepped together into the darkness. I did not need to even utter a word as she knew how I felt, more so than I. It was like finally coming home. We had uncovered the tormented fragments of traumatised, neglected children and the torture of living so compromised an existence. She had found 'me' and told all my fractured pieces they were beautiful and strong. She'd told me, with my trauma history, I should be on the streets using, but by some miracle, was still here and had done so remarkably well. But despite my resilience, the pain of the attachment wounding had intensified and my behaviour had deteriorated. Now she had gone and all that stood between me and a collection of dysfunctional, crying, raging, traumatised child parts, was my flim-flam, fledgling 'Self'.

Now it was Wednesday, four days since she'd gone. On the Monday I had taken sick leave but today I cajoled myself into tackling the back log of work emails. I managed OK for a couple of hours but after lunch I was suddenly ambushed with a feeling of dread so dire that I found myself researching Ronnie's horoscope, desperate to find clues that might point to her recovery. I knew her birthday from Facebook and I can't remember how, but I knew her age too.

The horoscope predicted her health outcomes for 2021 would be poor and that an old illness would return. No shit! Now panic took my breath away as I imagined she would die but I would not know.

On day five, I woke up crying again. I hate, hate, hate her! All that crap about how she was modelling good self-care by taking a long holiday but it had been too late for her, even then. Her heart had shown symptoms of dysfunction way back in the spring. As a result, rather than going to the doctor like any sensible person, she had self-medicated and this had damaged her kidneys too.

She had told me, told *us* many times during the previous year she was reliable and trustworthy. "Nothing you can ever do or say would make me leave you," and, "I've been doing this work now for almost 13 years". She had come back 11 times before. Why not this year, I'd screamed at the wall. Why hadn't I started seeing her three years before? I would have been so much better by now and it would not have been such a wrench. All those clients like me, who had been vulnerable and needy and she had not abandoned them. No, just me and that other borderline she'd alluded to.

Now it's Thursday, and another interminable day has passed in what feels like a lifetime of loss. Was it only last Saturday, five days ago? Today, I would have been thinking we were managing really well, after seven weeks without her. We'd think, only two more days to go and we'll see her again. I read her old texts to get me through, through to when, to where, perhaps just the next few minutes.

Finally, it's Saturday again and it's three o'clock. I would have been feeling impatient but also more at peace as we'd be seeing Ronnie again soon. One week ago I was up in the attic, make up and favourite shirt on, ready to see her again, for the first time in seven weeks. I feel quite sick today. I wonder if she will be thinking of us at 4.30? I wonder what she is doing right now? I wonder if the Reiki I have been sending is helping her to heal, to come to terms with what has happened to her, and how her past came back to trip her up.

After we'd moved to Melbourne when I was a child, I had lived in the past. I would constantly throw my thoughts back in time, saying to myself, "This time last week, I was with Daddy, and we were at the beach", or "This time yesterday, I was in the music room with Miss Hann and she had told me she had once been engaged."

I wandered outside into our little backyard to sit under the eucalyptus tree with the red flowers. It was a blustery day, the sky blue and dotted with clouds. The sun flashed and dimmed, like a lighthouse on a lonely shore. Pepper was snoozing in the long grass and a magpie was warbling plaintively to herself from the paling fence opposite.

I wonder if she is thinking of me right now, I thought. Normally she'd be looking over her notes from the previous session.

It's 4.20 and I think with an ache, last week I had felt happy and safe because our Lovely Lady was close.

It's 4.25, five minutes to go and I remembered that during the previous year I had been living in 'Borderland' again, with a 'parent' who was emotionally there one minute and gone the next. Each week, between sessions I had felt 'at sea'. There had been no safe place on which to 'beach' myself until a glorious window opened for two hours each Saturday and a welcoming little island reappeared and I would crawl gratefully onto her shore. All too soon, she'd leave me again, awash, as her island of safety sank below the waves, leaving me adrift again, untethered and alone.

It is now 4.31pm and we'd be saying hello and my kids would be speechless and blushing and in heaven. The actual therapy had been about rescuing and unburdening these fractured parts who were stuck in the past, reliving their trauma but our year together had become all about attachment. We couldn't seem to get past it, the push and pull of many parts, who all needed different things and were driven by conflicting emotions, needs and ways of communicating.

In lieu of our therapy session, I sat quietly under the tree and sent Reiki to Ronnie, to aid in the recovery of her precious heart and kidneys and as a way of finding some connection with her.

41

THE SCHOOL OF LIFE

I tap: "Even though, I have lost my beautiful guide and now don't know the way, and feel a pain in my chest, I deeply and completely love and accept myself."

When Ronnie had first experienced EFT, she was so impressed with the modality she became a practitioner and then a certified trainer. She would have been a wonderful teacher, encouraging, compassionate and fun.

Ronnie's inner children had healed inexorably with the steady application of EFT over the course of years. "They are happy kids now," she had told me once, encouragingly. In my mind's eye, I see Uncle Arthur ordering me to clean the kitchen floor because one morning I forgot myself and woke up feeling happy.

When Mum was in a black, self-pitying mood, she was intolerant of laughter and if I 'forgot myself' and didn't take on the aspect of a funeral guest she would chide me for being insensitive. I was Mum's audience and emotional support and it was a one-way street.

Now that Ronnie had gone, the moratorium on using EFT was ended and so I tapped in an attempt to manage the constant mood swings and feelings of overwhelm, "Even though we gave all our power to the Lady, for her to look after and heal us, and I feel a heaviness in my heart, I deeply and completely love and accept myself."

This morning I watched one of Ronnie's Havening videos. The kids want to watch one each day and they sit as little kids do in front of cartoons, mouth open, staring avidly at the screen. Today I don't bother with the Havening Touch as the children are so sensitive and empathic they can feel the effects of Ronnie's stroking of her arms and face on their arms and face. For a time, all have fallen gratefully into her eyes and are lulled by the warm contralto of her voice.

On the evening of the following Monday after work, it seems 6th February 2021 is a long time ago. I've covered so much ground, experienced such intense emotional pain and hope and despair and hope and despair again, that it could have been a month, not a week and two days, since she left.

Although my chest feels heavy with tears, I feel a tiny glimmer of hope as I have just received an email response from my eccentric friend Veronica, an 80-year-old retired nurse and a Reiki and spiritual healer living in England. I had described what had happened and she let me know she sent both Ronnie and me healing. I feel comforted and encouraged by her wise insights and advice and even dare to hope Ronnie might get better and resume our therapy sessions together one day.

With that thought I went to bed feeling more upbeat and prayed self-consciously (I had begun to pray in 2020): "Dear Divine, please can Ronnie and I meet again one day to have that promised Havening session? Please can we have that session when we are both better—physically and mentally—when my kids are happier and they can take it without falling into 'Borderland', please? Thank you, I love you. Amen."

Comforted, the little kids cling to this glorious dream as they fall into a deep sleep.

The next morning was day nine and we had sunk below the waves again into Borderland. It was enticingly peaceful outside, sunny and warm and so very quiet. Another lockdown had been enforced in Melbourne so there was no traffic noise, no sound of voices or building works. It was beautifully tranquil, but we didn't feel at peace, we felt empty and forlorn. Before rising for work, I did some tapping to try to shift the malaise.

I'd had no luck with either of the therapists Ronnie had recommended. I had called one after waiting in vain for a response but had received no reply. The other therapist had written back to inform me she was fully booked for the next 12 months, which set me to panic because I desperately wanted to start processing the trauma but didn't feel confident enough to tackle it on my own, especially not the trauma relating to Uncle Arthur. I'd wanted to cut myself when he had reared his ugly head in April of the previous year.

I decided that while I waited for a place to become available, I would tap on whatever washed to the surface and leave it at that. How long would I have to wait though? The kettle boiled as I stood staring out of the window, not really seeing the flashes of sunlight glinting off the wet eucalyptus leaves.

What a strange life, what a strange world I thought, as I strained to focus on filling my mug with boiling water. God, it was 9.45am already and I really needed to start work. Instead, I took my Earl Grey tea outside and stood on the grass in bare feet. It felt wet and cold and quite unpleasant but proved a little grounding. Wattle birds were showering the lawn with gum nuts as I stood deep in thought, only dimly aware of the racket above.

Everything happens for a reason, even Ronnie's leaving, as intolerable as this felt. I knew I needed to 'titrate' the reservoir of trauma from my body but with sudden insight, I realised this was easy compared with healing the attachment wounding.

The wounds were sustained in the first three years of my life, when everything that happens is stored in implicit memory. Implicit memories are 'emotional' in nature, rather than narrative. It is not always easy to interpret implicit memories, but I am gradually learning that if I become present to the feelings, I often gain intuitive insights into the events that caused them.

Loving connection is literally food for the developing brain and if it is not received, the brain suffers damage. Because my mother was incapable of loving unconditionally and because she struggled to make sense of and regulate her own emotions and because my developmental needs were threatening to her, she couldn't teach me to regulate mine. As I grew into a girl, I was shamed if I expressed emotions and learned the only safe option was suppression.

It was inevitable that Mum's own childhood trauma would rob her of the ability to raise an emotionally healthy daughter. She had passed on her legacy, the curse of trauma to me, which I have experienced in feelings of social isolation, perfectionism, confusion over my sexual identity, feelings of emptiness and an inability to trust others and myself, feelings of worthlessness and intense shame, feeling chronically empty and when 'love' does slip under my guard, fear of being both abandoned and smothered.

The next morning is Tuesday, day ten and I wake up calling her name, "Ronnie, Ronnie?" and wonder wildly what day it is. I grab the phone. Oh, it's only Wednesday. Then I remember she has gone and it doesn't matter what day it is, because there will be no more Saturdays when I limp gratefully into her sunny presence.

I remember Tuesday was usually the limit of the little kids' endurance and as the pressure built, I would try desperately to hold off for a little longer, texting her to tell her we missed her so dreadfully. She'd often reply with something comforting like, "I know Saturday seems such a long way off, when you are so small and so deeply in need . . . ", but no more texts, no more Ronnie. No fix, no 'heroin', no temporary relief to dull the ache, or to calm the panic, or to fill the emptiness. Instead, I re-read her texts and then watch a Havening video. Finally, I drag myself out of bed and log in to work.

By Wednesday of the following week, day 17, as evening draws in, I inexplicably feel a little better. It had been a warm autumn day and I had had a lovely time pottering around Tuala's paddock, pulling out weeds, cleaning out her water supply and feeding her carrots.

As the ABC News draws to an end, I automatically tune in to the weather forecast, looking ahead to Saturday, noting it will be a beautiful 27 degrees, a perfect day to see Ronnie. I smile inwardly but then we remember, yet again, that we won't be seeing her, the fourth one since she had gone.

A lifetime of Saturday's stretches ahead with no Lovely Lady. What a bleak, sad thought. Suddenly I have an intuitive insight: we had always felt this yearning feeling during the week, even when we were seeing her. "Ah, it's just the illness," my 'Self' reminds the eight-year-old and we feel a little more hopeful. The relative lightness lasts until I begin preparing dinner and wonder what Ronnie is doing. Panic rises in my chest and I reach for the bottle of 'mother's ruin'.

That night, I couldn't sleep. The night pressed me to the bed and I felt agitated and distraught and wondered how I could keep on going, keep enduring. As I began to drown in a tide of panic, my mind grabbed desperately at potential solutions. The sheet was twisting my legs out of their sockets and I wanted to scream. I could get in the car and drive to Beechworth and sit outside her house. I could cut myself or kill myself, I could have more gin, I thought wildly, searching for possible relief.

In sheer desperation, I began to pray, feeling self-conscious, even in my maddened state. I told the Divine I must have made a big mistake in asking to heal, because Ronnie had been taken away. My stomach contracted as I considered how bad a person I must have been in previous lives. I felt so worthless and angry. I told God in a rageful hiss that I wanted to heal but 'He' obviously took great delight in making it so hard. Even after her sudden departure, neither of the therapists Ronnie had recommended were available, "What am I supposed to do?", I entreated, scowling up at the ceiling.

Suddenly words formed in my head. They were not the sound of the voiced thoughts of my inner children but words spoken soothingly in a calm, deep voice, like vibrations coalescing into words: "This is the easiest way."

What!? I didn't expect a literal answer but surprised out of my raging I rushed on to confess that I felt sullied, bad and unworthy of being loved. The loving vibration spoke again: "I love you, no matter what," and then, after a pause, "You have lessons."

The tone conveyed such acceptance, such loving kindness and compassion, that I felt deeply reassured. I knew I could murder 100 people and the One Who Is All would still love me "...no matter what". And then I realised with absolute knowing that I had chosen the right path and my suffering was not in vain.

42

MOUNT SUGARLOAF

It is a day shy of three weeks since she left and since that day, I haven't been able to put any of my clothes away. They litter the floor and hang off the bedroom chair. Somehow, I cannot straighten my room. If I do, I will be tidying away the mess that is Ronnie's leaving, all neat and gone. Still, I've run out of clean undies and so grab the lot, throw it all into the washing machine and press 'start'. No going back now.

The next day is Sunday and I wake and note the leaves of the Liquid Amber tree outside my bedroom window are splashed with red and gold. The big higgledy-piggledy pile of shirts and undies and jeans no longer litters the floor and I feel sad about it. Something precious has been discarded along with the dirty pile. The world is moving on but I am not keeping pace. The time Ronnie and I spent together is receding. Time, like the gentle flow of water over immovable rock, is already dissolving the seams.

Matilda and I head off for a bush walk on Mt Sugarloaf, to the east of Melbourne. I hope a walk in nature might assuage the grief of the hurting tribe, or at least prove a small distraction, if only for a few hours. As I climb into the car, the kids are missing their safe mountain of clothes.

The connection we shared, the feeling of being seen and understood, I miss that almost as much as the children miss her reassuring smiles and loving looks. Ronnie had been full of maternal warmth. She was candid, vibrant, eccentric, energetic and guileless and had become my saviour. She was perfect.

The next day is Monday and I'm supposed to be working but find myself Googling Ronnie's partner. I used to be very focused at work, but I'm done by 3.30 and make a cup of tea and sit outside, watching a nest of ants scurrying about industriously, feeling guilty.

Another day has trickled away and I haven't done enough. Even when I had been a productive worker, I had rarely felt satisfied with my output. I'd fret and worry until whatever needed to be done was ticked off my list.

Perhaps I should call the Albert Road Clinic and enquire about their treatment for BPD? Ronnie had given me the name and I had intended to investigate the programs they run. I wonder if that is where Ronnie went after she tried to kill herself, all those years before. I want to go to the same place. I'd better wait until I stop crying.

Yesterday Matilda and I were having lunch after our walk on Mt Sugarloaf, and I was telling her about the pain of missing Ronnie and she said to me, "You mean, you still haven't gotten over it?"

"It was only three weeks ago," I spluttered.

This was why I missed Ronnie so desperately. She was the first and only person who could understand completely where I was coming from. I looked away, feeling alone, misunderstood and resentful.

Later that afternoon as I walked to Iona's for my fortnightly session, the sky was sagging, toying with the idea of tipping its load onto my head, my mind wandered to thoughts of the Divine. Surely the Divine wouldn't give me more than I could cope with in this lifetime? That was a comforting thought. I need to Reiki that girl, the one who makes me feel I am on the edge of reason, that I might 'lose it' spectacularly at any moment... Who is that girl? Am I that girl? I must be. Just breathe, my 'Self' says, just remember to breathe, no matter what happens.

Iona is an experienced trauma-informed, somatic psychotherapist, but she is not Ronnie and many parts resent her. They are suspicious and worry she is incompetent because she doesn't do EFT or Havening. To the very small children, it's like she doesn't exist. They don't register her presence, can't seem to see or hear her. Mind you, I'm not sure they recognise me either.

I had stopped seeing Iona ten years before because I had felt her brand of therapy was too slow. Then a psychologist friend had told me about EMDR (eye movement desensitisation and reprocessing) for processing trauma and I had wanted to try it, so I'd finished up with Iona and gone to John, the psychologist. I was full of desperate hope he might help reduce my anxiety, because he was experienced in treating PTSD in Vietnam Veterans.

I ended up having eight sessions with John and during the course of the treatment, he gave me the diagnosis of PTSD, citing Mum and Uncle Arthur as unfit caregivers, who would have been charged, perhaps even jailed. I would have been taken away and put into foster care. Acknowledgement of the abuse and neglect felt wonderfully validating and relieving.

On my first visit I was extremely agitated, overwhelmed with anxiety. It was as if my body knew help was at hand and it let the distress loose in anticipation of release. *I need EMDR! Give me EMDR!* it screamed but all we did was talk.

I remember John told me that recovering from PTSD involved regaining a sense of agency, of control over one's decisions and actions, no easy feat. One of his strategies was to coach me in internalising the power of another, a superhero, a fierce animal, or a great leader.

John's own favourite was the Clint Eastwood character Dirty Harry and I'm guessing it resonated with his exclusively male clientele of Vietnam Vets. At some point in each session, John would turn his lanky frame toward me, one corner of his mouth turned down in the semblance of a sneer, his eyes narrowed to slits and drawl, "Do you feel lucky, well do ya… pun-k?" He would look expectantly at me and I'd feel compelled to smile approvingly and say, "Good one" or "Yeah". I felt embarrassed for him but had been trained to approve of male behaviour, to fawn and stroke their little-boy egos and so reflexively, I did it with him too. He didn't notice and by the eighth session, when we still hadn't done any EMDR, I quit and took up horse riding lessons instead. Horses can be my therapy now, I thought sagely.

And now it was 2021 and I'd 'come full circle', sitting opposite Iona again. Was I destined to remain stuck in my horrible past until it killed me? Today was no different from all the sessions since Ronnie had gone and with great skill Iona listened with presence and compassion to the three-year olds who had dominated each session. I sat with a pile of soggy tissues on my lap as more grief and misery bled from their little hearts.

43

THE PIER

I drifted up from the groggy recesses of a fitful sleep and recognised the voice of Mario singing in my head about his great love, Floria Tosca. I can see him lying face down on the stone floor of his prison. What a great actor he is, cries Tosca, who is hiding in the shadows. She calls to him in a stage whisper, "Presto su, Mario, Mario." He doesn't respond, so the famed opera singer leaves her hiding place and dashes across no man's land to kneel beside him.

She touches his brow and calls his name but he has been shot through the heart. The lovers have been double crossed and in a fit of madness, Tosca screams a malediction at the man responsible for their ruin and throws herself off the battlement of the Castel Sant Angelo in Rome.

She cried, "I gotta go," and with a quick wave disappeared. What did Ronnie do then? Did she start crying as her screen went blank? Is that why she was suddenly in such a rush to leave? Was it because her façade was cracking, or was she just busting for a wee? Did she break down in anguish because she had just betrayed the tender, damaged little children she had promised never to leave? Did she get up and wander idly to the kitchen to make a cup of tea? Did she tell the fridge, "Well that's that, another one done?"

It is 9.30am and I must work, I tell myself sternly but am triggered by the dream. I sit down on the sofa intending to tap away the sadness but instead stare out the window, observing the silver branches of the next-door neighbour's Japanese Maple tree and remember.

When I was 22, completing my final year at the Conservatorium, Mac finally told his wife Hetty of our affair. The next week, Deb popped her head around my bedroom door after a cuppa with Mum. She expressed concern about my welfare, asking how I was coping with the whole Mac situation. It had come as a great relief to confide because I felt so isolated and alone—my uni friends were either virgins or going out with 'normal', 'respectable' boyfriends/girlfriends and came from relatively stable families.

"Michele thinks life's an opera," I heard from Mac a couple of days later. Deb had told all I had said to Hetty. Compelled to continue oversharing, I told Mum of Deb's duplicitous behaviour. Isn't a definition of madness repeating the same behaviour and expecting a different outcome? Mum heaped scorn on my naivety—"Hah," she spat, "What did you expect, she's Hetty's friend?" Even then I lived in Borderland, caught in its mirage of drama and treachery but had no idea.

An hour later as I worked through the tedious process of another contract variation, a fresh wave of grief struck, like a sudden bout of nausea. "God I hate you, we hate you, we hate you, we hate you," I chanted as I started to Haven myself through the feelings. "Please come back, we so miss you, we miss you, please come back..."

The next day I cried and cried between attempts to work. Finally, at 4pm I gave up and went for a walk, taking off my shoes. The grass felt soft under foot as I wandered over the playing fields alongside the Merri Creek.

On the way home as I walked across the Heidelberg Road bridge, I felt compelled to stop and look over the edge, noting the long fall to the creek and rocky bank, and the winding, concrete path below. A voice in my head considered, "Would it kill us? To make sure, it would be best to dive, head-first and aim for the concrete path."

I don't want to kill myself, do I? The resourceful, suicidal 'part' was on hand to help us all out of our misery. Oh God, I need Ronnie, she'd know what to say.

The next morning I woke up and immediately started to cry. The little ones wanted me to text Ronnie very badly and it took all my willpower not to. I lay in bed and told the little kids I loved them. It felt an insipid gesture and I couldn't tell if they could hear me.

For a while work proved a welcome distraction but by midday the urge to write to Ronnie had returned and was growing stronger. Inside me, the hearts of the younger kids are little black rocks, the little black rocks she abandoned. Now they sound like whiny little animals and I give in.

In the text, the little three-year-olds 'fawn', which is a trauma response (fight, flight, freeze and fawn) as they are afraid Ronnie might be angry with them for writing and tell her, "Ronnie, our lovely, beautiful kind lady who left us, we love you, we miss you, forever is such a long time without you." I take over and end the text, *I'm sorry, I don't have the willpower to resist this today. We love you so much and so do I. Thank you for everything, my lovely teacher.*

Immediately I feel a profound sense of peace and the little kids are quiet but alongside the relief is a small, hard seed. Someone is scowling and says, "Thank you for everything, are you kidding? She abandoned us, remember!? She lied. She couldn't look after herself. She was weak."

The next day as we walked along the Merri Creek path, under the bridge we'd walked over the day before, the 'suicidal' part spotted a patch of tall, thick grass and shrubs to the left of the path. "Why not sneak in there and take an overdose?" she thinks triumphantly. Someone else concurs, "It doesn't need to be a violent death."

The musing continues, "Hmmm, we'd have to find a doctor who would prescribe pills... not our GP, she's smart. A shrink then? Yes, that would be easy, they doll them out like lollies." In my mind's eye, I see a fat old man in a Santa's costume leering at ten-year-old me, while he hands over a script with six repeats.

The next morning I lay in bed feeling too despondent to get up and dressed for work. We are all waiting for a reply from Ronnie although I thought she probably wouldn't respond, as she hadn't when I'd sent her that desperate text the day after she had left. God, was I destined to drown in my trauma, slowly and inexorably, until I was dead?

It's funny, we all walk the path of our lives in our own unique way and at some point, some of us come to believe there is a purpose to our lives and we must surrender to the journey. I had been in that happy place when I'd booked my first appointment with Ronnie. Sometimes intuition and inspiration lead you to believe that the 'creator' is real. You follow all the signs and they lead somewhere you weren't expecting, like off the edge of a pier and suddenly you are in icy water with unknown dangers lurking just below. You flounder about until you learn that everything, including the pain, is your teacher, especially the pain.

I compared the grief of losing Ronnie with the experience of losing Mum to cancer in 2000. I had cried a few tears when I thought about Mum's life, about how unhappy and unfulfilled she had been but felt no grief or sense of loss. The overwhelming emotion I felt was relief. A few years after Mum's death, my beloved cat died and I grieved for many months and still think fondly of him eight years later but when I think about Mum, I just feel sick. She invested nothing of her 'Self' into our relationship, a black hole of need, she demanded and stole what did not belong to her.

It's now 10.30am on a workday. Suddenly I come back to my 'Self' and remember I am ill and have a sickness called borderline personality disorder. This is the cause of my obsession with Ronnie. It is a powerful curse and I am searching for redemption and a way out of the dark maze.

4 4

GUILTY

And Richard III in Shakespeare's play is tormented by the ghosts of his own making—the men and boys he murdered. I too am tormented in my dreams but don't remember... I don't think I have murdered anyone?

One afternoon five weeks after Ronnie's leaving, I unintentionally fell asleep after an unusually productive morning's work. I dreamed and dreamed and woke up laughing like a maniac. She had bewitched us and turned us into baby foxes, the witch called Ronnie.

I feel quite odd. She put a spell on us and I want to slit her throat, and laugh out loud at the thought. I feel unhinged. There is a 'part' who has risen with the dreams, and she thinks Ronnie is a sorceress who has stolen our soul and turned us into animals. There is a gaping hole where our heart should be, empty but for stones, hard and black and inside, a bloody pulp, scarlet and raw.

Gosh, Matilda will be home soon and I need to get the dinner on. I slip the mask back on.

Matilda arrives home and heads straight to her study and I am cutting up wild rabbits for the cats' dinner and the carving knife feels so warm and comfortable in my hand. I feel calm and angry and it is a blessed relief compared with the relentless yearning and feelings of grief and powerlessness.

As I bend down to place a plate of rabbit on the floor for Maisie, an intrusive, compelling thought flashes across my mind and I am possessed by a blinding rage and see myself whack Maisie. In my mind's eye, I slap her so violently she skids away from me, across the floorboards. She cries out and I feel a thrill of savage pleasure in my loins and deep anguish in my gut to see her so afraid of me but then her fear re-ignites the dreadful rage and I want to kill her. Shame wells. I understand how it must feel to be a 'wife beater', the savage compulsion, the blinding rage, the terror, the sick pleasure, then the guilt.

Oh God, I am going mad and start to cry. "But hang on..." I say, "...just hang on." I can muster enough 'Self' to talk to the fear. "It's OK," I say aloud, "...the feelings of rage are just wounded children, acting out Uncle Arthur's rage. It's OK to feel rage, I understand," I tell the 'part'.

I struggle to keep from being subsumed by the past, to maintain a sense of 'Self' and now watch from the sidelines rather than being directed from within and feel compassionate concern but still unhinged. What can I do to stop from going mad, I think desperately and suddenly remember Reiki. Forgetting dinner preparations, I retire to my room to send the children soothing, healing, universal lifeforce energy. It helps.

Since peering over the Heidelberg Road bridge, I love holding the carving knife and the fiery energy of rage. It fills my cold, empty insides where love should be. "Boy," I think,

"... who ever knew I was so fucked up?" and laugh, because it seems so funny to have housed a warring tribe of grief-stricken, angry, lonely parts of all ages inside me and have had no idea they existed until Ronnie came.

A sudden ping from my phone. Oh dear, I was enjoying the respite from grief but the spell is broken and I head back to the kitchen to the half-full bottle of wine in the fridge. Ronnie has responded and the rage is doused by the joy and relief of the little three-year-olds.

"Hi Michele, thank you for that lovely text. So good to know that you are getting through it all. I'm working hard on getting well. It helps my heart to know you're coping (smiley face and heart emojis)."

As I turn off my light at 11.30pm, I realise I feel 1000 per cent better. It's like I'm a different person, which I remind myself, I probably am!

45

THE HAPPY NUN

I woke way too early and feeling dreadfully anxious, took valerian and eventually went back to sleep. She was waiting for me, talking to me, beautiful, in her 30s, with her dark hair and white skin. She looks so anxious and vulnerable. I want to touch her cheek with my fingertips, but she is not there.

One day, seven weeks after Ronnie left, I was driving down the wide, tree-lined boulevard of Royal Parade in Parkville, the campus of Melbourne University to my left. I had completed my music degree there and 20 years later, a master's degree.

A feeling of bleakness settled in my gut as I remembered how dreadful I had felt as a young woman, so depressed, not realising there was something so wrong. I had tried to ignore and then outrun the 'inner demons', who I now know are merely fragments of personality, seeking equilibrium and freedom from pain.

It would take many years of struggle to learn how I felt was not 'normal'. After all, if you've lived in an intense silence, a frozen stillness that presses in from all sides and that is the way it has always been, then how do you know there are other, happier ways to live?

I felt separate from the world, worthless and terrified and my inner self-talk was scathing. I often looked 'spacy', the pupils of my eyes unnaturally dilated, and people thought I was 'on drugs'. Such was the dissociated state in which I survived, that I had no concept of 'Self'. I peered apprehensively at the world through the grubby windows of an empty, many-roomed house and what I could discern through the distorted prism of my mind appeared hostile and strange. I wasn't capable of recognising friend from foe and often mistook one for the other.

If I had been diagnosed with BPD in my 20s, I don't think I would have survived the 'mental health industry'. The pathologising labels would have added to my negative self-image and I would have felt even more disempowered and demeaned. There was no 'cure' for PTSD until around 2000, no EMDR, EFT, Havening or Somatic Experiencing, only drugs to dull the senses and ineffective (for trauma recovery) 'talk therapies' like cognitive behavioural therapy (CBT).

My head swivelled to catch a glimpse of the elegant white Conservatorium of Music building as it flashed past. A group of us, our gang, used to head to Naughtons Pub for a beer or rum and Coke each Tuesday lunchtime and drink it with our homemade sandwiches before returning for the 2.15 Music History lecture. Simon, the trumpet-playing rocker of the group, used to rest his head on his arms and snooze the afternoon away, I remembered smiling.

It was a day for time travel and I was driving to an appointment with a hypnotist after reading the book recommended by my English nursing friend Veronica called *Many Lives Many Masters*. I had booked in for a past-life regression, hoping to uncover patterns of trauma and dysfunction in past lives that had carried over into this one.

Forty-five minutes later I pulled up outside an ordinary 1950s, suburban, brick house, in an outer southern suburb of Melbourne. I walked into a large, hushed, open-plan living room, the sound of water tinkling sedately, the air carrying the scent of some or other soothing essential oil blend and sat down on the wide sofa to wait. A few minutes later a young woman, who looked around 12 years of age, appeared as if from thin air. I slopped my herbal tea onto my jumper. Pretending not to notice she smiled, introduced herself and asked me to follow her to a consulting room.

After I had sat where she'd indicated, she excused herself and left the room. I hoped it was to fetch the experienced, Earth mother-type who would lead me safely through the perils of time travel but a few minutes later the young woman reappeared and it became apparent she was to be my 'tour guide'.

I sat impatiently through the first stage, a long psychotherapy-esque session in which I was asked about my trauma and the work I'd been doing with Ronnie and her leaving. Finally, after 40 minutes we were ready to start and I eagerly lay down on a very comfortable reclining chair and was covered with a snuggly blanket. The lights were dimmed, a pied piper's tune floated into the air, and we began.

My young guide began the process of hypnosis and after a time my body began to feel pleasantly heavy and deeply relaxed. Still aware of my surroundings, we started to travel back in time. "Imagine before you, the most beautiful, fluffy white cloud. Climb in. You are the objective observer, or you can choose to participate. You are always in control and at any time you can return to your cloud and know you are safe."

I stepped onto my marshmallow cloud. "Your cloud has begun to drift back in time with your subconscious, taking you back to a time in your early childhood."

Immediately a distorted roar filled my ears. There was the sensation of prickle and tickle on my legs, as the wind cast a spray of gritty sand into the air, like confetti. I ran laughing as Daddy chased me into the shallows. Little fish scattered, fins flashing silver before my little, three-year-old feet.

"It's Manly beach, and it was happiest place in the whole world," I said.

"Anchor this memory... peace and flow and happiness," she advised me.

I re-boarded my cloud, so soft and comfortable and moved on again.

"You are preparing to come into this word. You are in the womb—is it light or dark?"

"It's light and comfortable. I am looking forward to being born... very excited and have all these things I want to do, play, be happy, be a flower, make people happy and be joyous and have light flow through me."

"Is that your purpose here?" she asked.

"I think so, yeah."

"Is there anything Spirit might want you to know?"

"They say I'm doing really well," I tell her. "They are with me. They can be with me more".

"And why are you coming into this family?"

Somehow, I know the answer. "To help the family... help them heal."

My guides tell me it's to help Ronnie to heal too. "But I don't know if I am just making that up," I tell her. "But that is what comes... they are telling me yes, that's right. They are saying we do have a connection."

"What is Mum experiencing?" she asks.

"She's a bit scared," I tell my guide. "Her face looks stressed... hopes things will go OK... she feels alone... also a bit excited... she's looking forward to holding me... she doesn't really like Dad, she wishes her mother loved her... her mother, my Nanna, was very unsupportive and is worried she won't get the help she will need..."

It is time to move on. I reboard my cloud. "Travel to another plane, time is no longer linear... to another lifetime, one that will be beneficial for you to know."

At last, I think and after a few moments my guide asks, "What are you wearing on your feet, are you wearing boots or...?"

"I see brown sandals, brown cloth... I think I am female, a nun. I'm 19 years old."

"Look at your hands, what colour is the skin?"

"They are light brown," I tell her, surprised. I sense green, green grass and my heart is filled with a great love for God. Faint images or impressions come—Europe, big blocks of stone, Switzerland?

"What time in history?" asks my guide and I tell her, without knowing how I know, it is the 18th century.

"What is your name?" she asks and I tell her—it is Jeanette and I am feeling a powerful force of love in my chest, and my heart is filled with gratitude.

"Go to another significant event in that life. Go there now," she instructs.

"I seem to be being kicked out of home," I tell her. "I am

ten... that might be my mother, upset and cowering in a dingy corner of a dark, dirty room. There is a very rickety, dark wooden door," I say and then continue, "I think we are very poor and a man is screaming at me to get out and I am dodging his fist. I see a clear path of escape, fling the dilapidated door open and run for it. I feel confused and shocked and hurt and don't understand why it's happening."

A sudden insight tells me I don't belong to them. "I think I was adopted. I think my mother gave me away or left me. That woman, the one cowering in the corner took me in but the man is sick of having an extra mouth to feed," I say to the room at large. "And that is why he's kicking me out."

"Now, go to another significant event: three, two, one. Be there NOW."

"I think I'm with my Mom in a city, starving, my real mother. We are destitute. She is devastated. She loves me but I'm going to die if I stay with her." I pause for a moment. "She knows she has to get rid of me even though it will break her heart... one year old," I murmur. "I am feeling very upset. I can feel her distress. Could it be Ronnie?" I can't believe it and gasp.

"You think it's Ronnie?"

"It just came into my head," I tell her, feeling confused and hopeful and embarrassed.

"Just look into her eyes and see."

"I can't really see," I tell her but actually I am too afraid to look in case it is not her but say, "I'm more kinaesthetic, I can't see but I feel like it is her."

"Trust that feeling," my guide tells me confidently.

"I think she left me somewhere... in a better suburb, hoping someone would take me in. I can vaguely discern a high, pale stone wall with a big dark gate. My mother left me there and someone found me. She had had a child and it had died. She could breast feed me... Ha!" I laughed out loud, "I saw her in that dingy hovel, when the mean man kicked me out. She worked at the big house, with the high fence, she took me in . . . when the man threw me out, I wandered to a town and joined a gang of street urchins." I laughed again, "I loved it, I loved being wild and free with a bunch of other kids. Then when I was 12, a nun found me and took me to the convent and taught me to read. I lived a very long and happy life. I helped others by praying for them and I liked to be in nature and I was a very happy soul," I concluded.

"Now go to the last day of that life. Three, two, one. Be there NOW!"

"I am extremely old. I am in my bed at the convent and the breath is getting shallow and I'm gasping . . . I feel as if I'm being pulled up out of the bed, by my chest, by my heart . . . not a bad feeling. I had looked for my mother but had never found her. I had prayed for her. I had helped a lot of people by listening and caring for them and about them . . . I can see my nun-self, sitting close by a woman on a hard wooden bench. She has lost her husband and is grief-stricken. There are beads of pure light pulsing from my heart and connecting with hers. The beads touch her heart and melt into it."

46

THE PUPPY FARM

And she held out her hands to the children. The adult ghosts hung back, listless and fearful, but the children all came thronging forward. They had as much substance as fog, poor things, and Lyra's hands passed through and through them, as did Will's. They crammed forward, light and lifeless, to warm themselves at the flowing blood and the strong beating hearts of the two travellers and both Will and Lyra felt a succession of cold delicate brushing sensations as the ghosts passed through their bodies, warming themselves on the way."
(*The Amber Spyglass*, Philip Pullman, p296)

It has been eight weeks since Ronnie left. It might well have been eight years but the pain is fresh and raw and I miss her dreadfully. The two-year-olds are where the emptiness began, and I feel the ache of their desolation. They are little ghosts, not truly here, not real. They are snuffling in their hole, wounded and flawed, waiting to find the lost parts of themselves in Ronnie.

The little three-year olds still cry every single day, incredulous and bereft, aching to send Ronnie texts with flowers and ladybirds, hoping she will smile at them again. I'm working to resist the urge, which gets harder, not easier, as the time inches by.

All of us want to snuggle against her body, the toddlers, the little girls and even the teenagers. We imagine pressing our face into her neck and throwing our arms around her. She sweeps us into her arms, caresses our face and rubs our back. She kisses us and laughs into our hungry eyes.

I am still waiting impatiently for the therapists Ronnie recommended, to become available. The gratitude I felt for Iona when she agreed to see me again, even when her books were also full, has been replaced with feelings of impatience and resentment. Iona doesn't seem to exist for the inner children. Only 'I' can see her and while I appreciate her help, the children don't respond to her kindness or feel her empathy and compassion, don't recognise her expertise. All they want is Ronnie, their lovely, lovely Ronnie.

It's Monday, late afternoon and our fifth session progresses in the same way as the previous four. I am flooded by the little three-year olds and cry and cry for the loss of Ronnie. "Go inside . . . " Iona prompts gently, holding me energetically, so I feel safe enough to peer inside, " . . . and see what you might see."

I see a baby, tensing and cowering, her eyes closed tight, then black, pitch black. She is hiding or being hidden. Suddenly, I can't find my way out of the darkness and all at once can see the little me, taking the place of a poor dog, cowering in a cage, skeletal, short-haired and blond, from a picture I had seen of a puppy farm. I lead the dog out of the cage and take her to where the two-year-olds are at the farm, in the open grassy paddock, above their cave. She shakes uncontrollably. I stroke her and she slumps onto the grass.

Walking home, I feel angry. I've been flooded by a 'part' and automatically blend with her, so her feelings become mine and I lose perspective. I feel a sense of impatience and panic as a familiar feeling of fear that my life is running out rises again while I sit in the chair opposite Iona, to 'go inside'... so passive, so slow. Ah, I realise there are 'parts' who can see her. This one thinks Iona is stuck in the past, not appreciating there are now modalities that actually move the processing of trauma along much more quickly. Even though she left us, Ronnie knew this, she thinks contemptuously.

The 'part' wants to tell Iona to pull her finger out but someone else is afraid of rejection, that she will be kicked out of the therapy. But still, goes the internal conversation, I don't want it to take years and years of seeing her to finally feel better. Apparently, I'm already 57 years old. I don't want to be 85 before the rest of my life can finally begin.

'I' muse that Iona is more present than Ronnie, more emotionally stable, reliable and skilled in psychotherapy and this may be the reason the parts don't warm to her, they don't recognise clear boundaries as a sign of healthy caregiving. By comparison, Ronnie's personality during times of stress, even after her healing work, still displayed a level of fragmentation and her dissociation into child parts called to my inner children like a siren. Iona doesn't press my attachment button and so I know intuitively it is vital to continue working with her, as we have the potential to imprint a healthier model of attachment.

As I walk through the front door, I suddenly realise it is Ronnie's birthday and log in to Facebook, to see who has wished her a happy day. It's 6.30pm. Perhaps she is going out with friends to celebrate at a restaurant. I wonder if she's having a 'good day'. How much celebrating can she do in her compromised state? Can she drink wine? Is she still praying for us, like she said she would in the last session . . . ? Probably not. Does she ever think of us . . . ? I doubt it.

The feelings of relief and wonder I had felt after the past-life regression have faded and I feel quite unstable again. As I imagine Ronnie connecting with her friends and partner, it takes all my willpower not to whack myself in the head with my fist. The big carving knife calls and so I pick it up and trace the blue veins under delicate white skin with its tip.

I wonder why it was that Iona never told me I was sick, all those years before. I had spent most of my sessions offloading about the unhealthy dynamics at work, about how I was triggered by numerous bosses and a number of colleagues, about how I felt marginalised, my achievements unappreciated, about how unsafe I felt.

In the previous session with Iona, I had told her what the psychologist John had told me, all those years before, that I had PTSD. She had readily agreed. Why then, hadn't she told me herself? Again, I feel the panic of having to wait for one of Ronnie's picks.

The Lovely Lady might have been flaky at times, but she had taken John's diagnosis of PTSD a step further, telling me I suffered from 'developmental' or 'complex' post-traumatic stress disorder (C-PTSD). C-PTSD develops through prolonged and repeated abuse and/or neglect rather than a one-off traumatic experience, like a car accident, natural disaster, or sexual assault and shares many borderline traits.

Learning that my upbringing had been even more abusive and neglectful than I had appreciated felt deeply validating. No wonder I struggled to function effectively as an adult. The diagnosis of C-PTSD (and borderline) explained why I found navigating work and private relationships so difficult, excruciating at times and why I craved yet feared intimacy, became obsessed with kind women, felt empty, despairing, anxious and depressed and why I hated myself.

47

THE SHOPPING PLAZA

I would like to ask you all about obsession: I am obsessed with my ex-therapist. She got sick and had to stop seeing me in February.

I Google her all the time and found pictures of her when she was young. I imagine that I can step into the photos and kiss her, she is so beautiful.

And she had borderline herself and bipolar and I cry when I think of it and think there is something wrong with me because I managed better, I don't have bipolar and was never psychotic, like her. But sometimes I wish I was, so I can be like her.

She looks so beautiful in her madness, but I just have the urge to punch myself in the face. It's like I want to be her, like I could never be close enough to her and I yearn and yearn for her. I've just been sitting here looking at her photo, repeating over and over again that she is so beautiful, and crying.

And also, I don't feel good enough for her because I haven't suffered as much as she has, and my suffering will never be enough. I know it's not love but I keep saying, "I love you, I love you."

I am a 'high-functioning' borderline and so manage to hide my feelings of emptiness ... in fact I didn't know how I felt, just depressed and miserable and not good enough. And I feel so frustrated because I feel all these emotions bubbling up but can't even identify them, can't name them and a part of me wants to let it all out and fall apart but I never would because I am too afraid and too practiced at hiding my anguish, even from myself.

Post to an online borderline support group called 'Stuff That Works'.

A kind soul wrote back: "*Are you seeing another therapist, Michele? You need help with this. This is not healthy for you.*"

Thank God my latest work contract expires in seven weeks, as I am doing a really shit job and letting my very patient and understanding boss down. I should be clocking on, as it is 9.15am but I have that overwhelming, compulsive urge to write to Ronnie again today. The urge comes in waves. Writing to Ronnie calms the ones who need to connect but after a time the urge returns.

Today, I have the odd feeling I am living in two worlds simultaneously, one overlayed on top of the other and am not sure which one is real. Am I living with Matilda in the neighbourhood that has been our home for 24 years, or is the world happening 30 years ago, when I split with Mac and lived in North Carlton with Lee? This second one feels more alive today, more real.

I cave in and write to Ronnie telling her, *One day I will realise I haven't thought about you for a whole day but today is not that day.* I also send her a poem I wrote down on a napkin at a pub one evening in autumn and feel a warm blush of peace and contentment, a 'fix', as I imagine Ronnie opening the email and reading its contents. Now, I can begin work for the day.

Later that day, shamefaced, I tell Iona about my lapse of control. Without judgement, she smiles solicitously and then I close my eyes, to go inside. I am dimly aware I am lying in a largish cot, in a large open-plan living area. The space is dimly lit and get the sense, rather than see, my mother striding jerkily around the room, yelling, crying, moaning and talking incoherently. At some point she leans over me, her face terrifying, like a contorted monster's. What I see has been retrieved from implicit memory and I find it difficult to trust its veracity, as the images are very vague.

There is the hint of an emotion rising from my solar plexus but instinctively I push it down, too terrified to feel what is rising and too practiced at avoiding it. Iona, unlike Ronnie and other therapists I'd been to over the years, notes the sudden rush of questions as a diversionary tactic but listens patiently.

The next morning the alarm wakes me in the middle of a dream. I had driven past Ronnie's home in the desperate hope I might catch a glimpse of her. The feelings of yearning and desperation were intense and the landscape I drove through was so hilly it resembled a roller coaster.

I don't even bother trying to work and decide I need to take a couple of day's sick leave. It is only five weeks until my work contract expires and without discussing it with Matilda, I know I don't have it in me to secure another job. I am too destabilised, flooded, overtaken by mood swings. I am sick of attempting to work around my moods and am always so, so tired.

Today is no different and my feet walk the well-trodden path down by the Merri Creek, past Ronnie's old home. I'd found her address recently on a list of practitioners (which must have ended up there by mistake) and couldn't believe I'd been walking past the home she had lived in for 20 years without realising it. Today the little ones mutter the same refrain . . . if only they'd known she had lived there, they might have seen her bustling out of her front door. The pesky kids continue to tie themselves in knots of agony, thinking perhaps they had passed her at Northcote Plaza Shopping Centre, as one of her work venues until recently was on its doorstep.

I come to. Someone, probably a neighbour is giving me an unfriendly look. I'd stopped walking to stand and stare over the low fence for too long. We hurry away, over the little wooden footbridge along the winding concrete path, past our 'suicide' spot and up the steep incline, to the tree-lined path leading to the playing fields.

I take my shoes off and walk over the fragrant grass and it feels blissful. The children as always, imagine Ronnie is walking beside us, smiling indulgently at our innocent, childish ways. We'd written to her only three days earlier but relief has given way to impatience and is now turning to desperation again. I start to cry behind my sunglasses.

At home, I make a cup of my favourite chai tea and settle down on the bed. Pepper and Maisie wander in and lay down next to me. It is very cosy and the hot, spicy tea is fortifying.

An alert pings from my email page and I see it is from Ronnie. My heart starts to pound as I fumble to open it.

She wrote: *Beautiful work. I hope you are writing a lot. I've been thinking about our emails and I really think that for you to heal, it's better for you to share the contents of these emails with your therapist now, rather than with me. We've had a bit of a bridge transitioning to the new therapist and I feel that now is the time for you to work with them on the grief—and Haven on it. Hopefully you can 'collect' some Mum grief on the way.*

Michele, I wish you the very best with this next phase of therapy and will continue to keep you in my prayers.
All the best,
Ronnie

"... to work with them on the grief." Are you kidding me? What else have I been doing these past weeks? I scream. The cats streak from the bed. Burning with rage, I quickly fire back, OK then, send me the last Havening video and we'll call it quits.

And "... collect some Mum grief..." Fuck off, I have no grief for Mum. I feel as I always have, a yearning for the mother I never had and for you, you bitch, but never my real mother.

We had felt abandoned but now she had rejected us too. Talk about the gift that kept on giving!

48

THE HERMIT

As I walked past Ronnie's old home again, I was struck with a startling thought—she will recover and restart her trauma therapy practice. We passed over the footbridge, the Merri Creek bubbling cheerfully along beneath as we rehearsed a scene where she suddenly calls me. "Ah, but if I imagine it, it won't happen," I think. "But why not? It could, it might!"

The turf is vibrantly green and springy on the cricket pitch and I am the only one over the age of two without shoes. Feeling suddenly buoyed, almost elated, I stop walking and lie down on the sweet-smelling grass, warm and content in the autumn sunshine.

Since Ronnie left, I have been listening to book tapes about trauma, including classics such as *The Body Keeps the Score*, by Bessel Van Der Kolk, and *Waking the Tiger*, by Peter Levine. As I rise to walk home, I continue listening to the book *Understanding the Borderline Mother* by Christine Ann Lawson.

Lawson, a clinical social worker, discusses four types of borderline mothers as they were described to her by clients over many years: the Waif—Princess Diana; the Hermit—Silvia

Plath; and the Queen—Joan Crawford. Lawson doesn't give an example of the Witch although chillingly, she alludes to child murderers.

I recognise myself as the Hermit. The Hermit is likely to be introverted and doesn't mind time alone. It makes for uncomfortable reading though, as I relate to so many of the traits and realise the author is describing unhealthy behaviours I'd thought were 'normal', including excessive rumination, withering self-criticism and an identification with careers or hobbies for self-identity.

The Heidelberg Road bridge beckons and my mind wanders from the narration. The little 'helper' is activated and we stop to watch our body falling, imagining the terrible crunch of bones on concrete. I tear my eyes from the scene and we continue on our way.

Hermit types are exquisitely perceptive, which is a survival strategy in an unsafe world, hypervigilant and extremely lacking in trust. There is also a preference for relationships with animals and objects over people and this rings true. I can't remember playing with other children when I was a small girl. In my first years at primary school I spent most of my time alone in the playground, trying to avoid the bossy girls and crying. I was preoccupied with the absence of my mother, waiting on tenterhooks for her to 'see' me, bypassing my biologically driven programming to connect. How could I connect with children my own age, when I had never connected with my mother.

I did make a number of friends as puberty approached, a best friend called Laura, who was Italian and whose mother made delicious pasta dishes but we were separated when we went to different high schools. There were the twins with whom I went on trail rides, chased little blue moths in the long grass beside the creek, ate ice creams, rode my bike and swam for hours at the local swimming pool. We did fun stuff together but there was no 'confiding' or 'supporting'. I had friends at high school and university too but as soon as we'd graduated, I purposefully disappeared from circulation.

In the absence of any human intimacy, I did form attachments with animals, objects and pursuits. When I was six I became obsessed with learning to ride a push bike. The feeling of suddenly finding my balance and gliding along was intoxicating and I couldn't wait to do it again and again. Being invited on a trail ride with the twins to bounce painfully along, then to suddenly feel the pony canter for the first time had the same dream-like, utterly addictive effect. Mum and Dad wouldn't buy me a bike (let alone a pony) so I pretended to 'like' girls in the hope they would let me ride theirs, but they might as well have been made of cardboard, I felt no inclination to connect with them. Then, there was the tuba and the Chadstone High School band, opera, and coming full circle, the purchase of my own horse, when I was 52.

My inability to form meaningful friendships began at age two when according to Lawson, the young child begins to assert her individuality and independence. For a borderline (and narcissistic) mother, this can be extremely confronting. Mum's indifference and sometimes outright rejection kept me in a state of hypervigilant preoccupation with her. Her unpredictability left no room to explore or connect with other children and I have remained stuck in my search for maternal love all my life, finding temporary substitutes in other nurturing women.

The outcome of Mum's behaviour resulted in the creation of many fragmented two-year-old parts who are untrusting, fearful and difficult to reach during therapy. For some of these parts it is too dangerous to be seen and instead, present themselves as little fox cubs. By contrast, the three-year-old parts are loving, overly trusting, generous and sweet. How can this be?

I asked Iona about the odd dichotomy in my next therapy session and she suggested my two-year-old selves had been "completely fractured"—the two- and three-year olds are two groups of children who coexist, disconnected and unaware of each other's existence. This is disorganised attachment—the pushing away of and simultaneous yearning for love.

49

SURVIVOR GUILT

"She told us, she DID! Ronnie said we were amazing to have survived. But we're so unworthy and what if it's not enough?" the girl mused desperately. "And your noses and ears, your teeth and your tails. Oh, don't you see," she continued imploringly.

"Well, they are STUPID," bristled the cub. "They could have turned into fox cubs too, if they wanted, if they were clever like us", continued the little she-fox. "It's not hard, if you hurt."

"But it's CHEATING," cried the girl.

They snarled. One did a wee.

"Well, now we can't be loved. If you insist on being foxes and hiding in holes, then no one knows we are here either . . . and you get us all in trouble. Bloody little bastards," the girl added.

"Oh please come out and take your punishment, please," she pleaded with the cubs and continued for what felt like the 100th time, "We want to be like her. We need to be exactly the same or she won't like us."

"And you keep disappearing. Oh, we can't stand being empty," she continued and then added, "Can't you see our heart? Well, it's yours too stupid and it's fallen out and you're kicking it along the ground."

"We don't TRUST humans," snarled pointed milk teeth and fluffy bottle brush.

"But we want to be loved. We'll do anything, anything to be worthy... how can you survive anyway, without a mother, our Madonna, without love... without her?" she asked, suddenly curious.

"We don't know," replied the little fox.

Silvia Plath, a borderline 'Hermit', tragically attempted suicide when she was only ten years of age and her life ended in suicide. Research says 70 per cent of borderlines attempt suicide and 10 per cent succeed. Ronnie attempted suicide, I'm sure of it, although I haven't actually managed to find that out, it's only a hunch. My mother also attempted suicide. What is wrong with me then?

I have been agonising over the level of Ronnie's suffering compared with mine. Somehow, I take the thought of her trauma and pain very personally. But why do I feel so utterly ghastly, such a failure when I remember Ronnie had inferred I had coped better as an adult? I didn't have bipolar, wasn't ever psychotic, didn't end up in a psychiatric clinic, took the usual time to complete my music degree. Ronnie had said it had taken her 10 years to gain her degree and I feel so guilty that I can't breathe when I think of it.

I can't even explain the feeling, it's kind of crushing—yes, I feel crushed. If the shoe had been on the other foot though and it was I who had had Ronnie's adulthood and she mine, then I would still feel a complete and utter failure. I would then think, what's wrong with me that she did so well while I coped so badly? That I survived is so serious, so heinous a crime, it seems I will never be free of the guilt and shame.

I am supposed to be working as the hour had passed nine,

yet here I am again propped up in bed, feeling ill at ease and vulnerable, watching the last Havening video again, Ronnie telling us we are beautiful while she herself looks so ill. Someone gets upset and I start to Haven our arms but stop because I don't trust myself not to punch my face.

In the kitchen the previous night, while preparing dinner, I had held the carving knife to my stomach, pressing until I could feel the point making an indent in my flesh. For the past three weeks I have had the feeling there is someone lurking behind me, about to hit my head and I feel the urge to duck.

And now here I am, an hour later at the standing desk in my study, simultaneously reading emails and experiencing the feeling that someone is hitting me. My physiology is telling me to cower and duck but my pre-frontal cortex is making me work. The feeling of being hit is growing and I feel the urge to drink even though it's only 11am.

Sitting down, I attempt to soothe the parentified, eight-year-old part who is anxious we start work, saying to her, "I'll help you. I can do that for you. I love you. Do you need a hug?" She feels ashamed and weak and so vulnerable. She holds her breath waiting for it to be over, so I stop Havening but in a strange way despite the surfacing violence, I do feel my heart is opening up a little and connect it with our sessions with Iona. My thoughts are kinder and I feel more connected with people and my animals. I believe this shift has been precipitated by my attempts to genuinely communicate with and soothe the parts. They are starting to feel heard.

50

THE CHAMELEON

I had the most revolting dream last night. I was in bed and a bedraggled woman was standing over me, complaining. A long, crumpled tee shirt covered her skinny frame but could not hide two sagging breasts with protuberant nipples. Suddenly she grabbed one of the breasts and wrung it, while complaining bitterly. I looked and saw it had two nipples. She threw it aside and came and lay on top of me.

I was watching now from the corner of the room and saw a pale, yellow liquid gush out of both breasts as she continued to whinge. I lay frozen in disgust, unable to move. Then she climbed off and lay up close, propped on her elbow, her head resting on her hand as she continued to complain about her life. I lay there listening politely, covered in a thick, yellow, paint-like slick.

We are so different, Ronnie and Mum and I, but all sufferers of BPD. The Diagnostic and Statistical Manual of Mental Disorders (DSM), Fifth Edition, describes one of the nine borderline criteria as: "Frantic efforts to avoid real or imagined abandonment". Hitting the door behind which her boyfriend had retreated for an hour to escape her onslaught is how one borderline sufferer tells it.

I wouldn't be banging on any doors or climbing drainpipes or hanging onto moving vehicles, it would never occur to me. Sure, I will die when they leave but it is inevitable they will, because I am unlovable.

And when it does happen and they are gone, I sink back into the depths from which I had briefly emerged hungry and hopeful, tempted to the surface by the prospect of feeding, like one of those flaccid, ugly creatures from the deep, who rise to the surface in the dead of night so no one can see them. No wonder I have a strong urge to whack myself in the head or to pull my hair out when I Haven.

The seed of self-hatred was planted when I was two. In a session with Iona, I had experienced myself as too needy and Mum's terrifying face had scared the wits out of me. I had wanted comfort or connection or reassurance or a lolly, but this had been too much for her. To Mum, my need must have been as horrifying as the swarm of black beetles that crawled all over Tuala in the cave.

In our last session before Christmas, just after I had finally given myself a really good cut, I had told Ronnie of how, when I had turned up to see my GP and had shown her my weeping wounds, she had asked kindly if I would like to go to hospital. I had felt ashamed, mortified to be showing such weakness and had told her I didn't, but on the way home realised there was a part or parts who thought it would be a blessed relief to give up for a while. Ronnie had called it a "Ho, ho holiday in hospital" and I thought, "She must have had a few of those over the years."

"Yes, parts of me would like that," I had told Ronnie in the session.

Happily, I had imagined lying incognito in a hospital bed for days on end, with a faceless nurse bringing me food and tranquilisers. How wonderful! Then, there'd be the visit from a psychiatrist who would tell me patronisingly I didn't really have Quiet BPD, because "there is no such thing" and that I don't yell enough to have borderline and only cutting myself properly once doesn't count, even if it had been a particularly good one.

But then I supposed I would have had to meet genuinely 'crazy' people, because they run mandatory group therapy sessions at those places but I'm not actually mad, not like the ones who yell and have unsafe sex and swallow pills and climb drainpipes.

Madness is not feeling defective because you dreamed your therapist, the one who abandoned you, was raped and you haven't been, and you feel guilty and inadequate about it.

Madness is not being obsessively in love with your therapist even though realistically, you hardly know her. Nor is it the voice who whispers helpfully in your ear every time you walk across the bridge that you should jump off it and then one day the voice realises how stupid it has been, when pills would serve just as well, better in fact, than splatting on the concrete and everyone in your head agrees.

What about the times when you don't feel real but that doesn't stop an invisible person from hitting you, or punching you in the stomach or putting their finger in your two-year-old vagina?

Nor is it feeling damaged beyond redemption, fatally flawed and repulsive. No, this too is not 'madness'.

Gosh, I'm feeling better now because I've had two G&Ts, apple cake and chocolate and watched *Henry V Part I* on ABC.

It was very good but quite gory. Oh, and I was excited to see Joan of Arc in the play too. She gets around.

I love reading Kevin Redmayne's articles about BPD. In one, called *The Chameleon: The spirit animal of borderline personality disorder*, he says, "... through elaborate displays of mimicry and impersonation, the individual with BPD adapts to all environments."

One day, when Ronnie and I had been discussing BPD, she had said, "The miracle to me is that you don't have borderline because this is the sort of history I see with borderline clients ... and this is where, you know, you are the miracle."

Ronnie continued, surmising I really shouldn't have any 'framework of a self'. She told me that people with BPD come across as odd or perplexing because "with a therapist they'll be one person, with a friend they'll be another person, with a shopkeeper they'll be another person, with a person in authority they'll be another person. They don't have any stable identity."

"Well," I said, "I act differently with different people."

"Yes, but you know it's an act," Ronnie responded animatedly.

Well, apparently, I'd out-foxed even myself, because I had no idea that my functional self was an eight-year-old 'part', so wily, so expert and practiced at hiding all the other 'parts' and acting the 'grown up' that even I hadn't realised I wasn't the full ticket.

"... you see, the thing about the chameleon is that it is also a solitary animal," Kevin Redmayne continues in the same article. "It can spend a lifetime on one branch, just watching. A delectable morsel comes along—a tasty insect, a lovely locust—the chameleon will suck the life out of it. That's like the individual with BPD who sequester themselves off into intense exclusive relations too quickly. After spending so much time alone, the first sign of intimacy creates a desperate need to devour the object of affection. This is called 'Object hunger', and it doesn't build a sense of self, it again uses another person to shore up the ruins."

'Affect hunger' is my new favourite term—the need, the drive of the little ones to bask in their mother's loving gaze, to find comfort, not terror in her presence, to coregulate autonomic nervous system function, to mirror emotions, to sense the steady beat of her heart, to know she is always, will always be there with her light, just for you.

If you don't get it, the need never goes away and it is an ever-present yearning, craving, an emptiness in your soul, the roommate who never grows up to leave home, your shadow's shadow. Sometimes you can forget for minutes, sometimes for months as you distract yourself with food, alcohol, or try to outrun it with obsessions, ambition, workaholism or over thinking and with relentless, cutting rumination, but nothing ever fills the hole.

When the morning dawns along with the hangover, so comes the realisation with the sick intensity of a migraine that nothing has changed and you are still an empty vessel.

51

ON THE STREET WHERE YOU LIVE

It is now five months since Ronnie left but I still dream about her most nights, although often I can't remember the details. I have patches of missing her, or should I say, patches of not missing her, not many, but it's worth noting.

Yesterday I wanted to kiss her again. I still watch the Havening videos although occasionally there is a day when I don't. More recently, I find a spot where she is smiling her most radiant smile and pause the screen, so we can take in every lovely detail.

Just the other day I discovered via another EFT practitioner called Jenny, who I had started to see as an adjunct to my fortnightly appointments with Iona, that Ronnie was in 'semi-retirement'. It turns out Jenny was Ronnie's EFT teacher and they stay in touch.

I had had an intuitive knowing Ronnie would restart her therapy practice and the hope had kept the little kids going. We had all fantasised about that wonderful day but had never dreamed she would recover her health but not take us back.

"There is nothing you could ever do or say that would make us (my 'Self' and Ronnie) leave you, really, there is nothing," she had told us.

I wonder what Ronnie is doing now and imagine her, perhaps making a cup of tea and taking it to her study or talking to a friend on the phone. I wonder if she's seeing a client at this very moment, dipping her toe back in the water with straightforward clients, people she can help, not children with a bottomless pit of longing, a cesspit of despair. No, she will now refer those ones on, the ones who live in Borderland, who are now as she once was.

Last year Ronnie fell down what she called a 'mine shaft' but didn't realise she had slid so far until she bumped into something hard and intractable, the bottom. Now she is making good progress as she climbs back toward the sun. She is not looking back to see who she might have left behind, the collateral damage, the ones she took out when she crashed.

One day in mid-winter, four and a half months after Ronnie left, Matilda and I took the opportunity between Melbourne lockdowns to take a short holiday and headed to a little town called Walwa, near the Murray River and close to the Australian Alps. After enjoying the winter sun and warmer weather and sampling the regional delicacies, we set off to drive home to Melbourne.

"Let's go via Yackandandah," I suggested, and Matilda readily agreed. Yackandandah is an historic town in the northeastern Victorian goldfields.

After wandering along the crowded main street, rugged up ineffectually against the freezing chill of the foggy winter's afternoon, we clamoured into a warm, steamy café that smelled invitingly of coffee. We thawed over pots of hot, strong Earl Grey tea and toasties. As the afternoon closed in and we finally rose to leave, my heart started a staccato tattoo against my ribs. Pointing the car toward home, the highway took us to the Melbourne-bound freeway, via Beechworth.

"What's going on?" Matilda asked groggily, poking her head up as the car pulled to a sudden stop 15 minutes later.

"That's Ronnie's house," I replied sheepishly, pointing across the road.

I recognised it immediately from the picture on the satellite street view. She was in there, I could tell. A little, dark blue Hyundai was parked in the driveway, which I assumed to be hers. Another car was parked up on the wide, grassy nature strip, parallel to the low, blond brick fence. I assumed it belonged to the person who was sitting with their back to the wide, sunny, north-facing window, in the lounge room. I knew it was the lounge room because I had studied the marketing photos and house layout on Real Estate.com.

I reversed a bit so I could get a better view of the black head and perhaps a glimpse of who it was the person was talking to, Ronnie, I assumed.

"Aww, don't look, they'll see you," hissed Matilda.

"We've got tinted windows," I reminded her, without taking my eyes off the house. Matilda shuffled about like a disgruntled hen but made no reply.

Feeling annoyed because she had broken my concentration I said placatingly, "Look, we are miles away". I waved my hand to indicate the two-laned road, the nature strip and deep garden between us and the house.

"Come on, let's go," hissed Matilda again.

"Why whisper, no one can hear you?" I thought, as I continued to ignore her. My eyes glazed over and I said to myself, as if in a reverie, but that's where she is, she's in there, so close. That's where she spoke to us during our sessions, each Saturday.

I could just make out her dinky little laptop sitting on a desk, the surface of which rose a few inches above the windowsill in another of the north-facing rooms. There were objects in silhouette too, small things, little figurines and pens standing in a cup, her very own, small knickknacks. It crossed my mind that Ronnie might be prone to clutter, like Matilda. That would be an irony, I thought wryly.

"I wonder who that is?" I mused out loud, of the cropped, black-haired person.

"Look, come on, let's GO," cried Matilda, forgetting to whisper.

"Why?" I snapped, still staring avidly at the house.

"Because it's creepy, that's why!" she replied.

"Well, that's borderline for you, we do creepy things," I said, not caring what she thought. I'd waited too long and the moment was too important.

I could have sat there for hours but after another minute I reluctantly pulled away from the curb, away from Ronnie and her house, and her lucky visitor. She had been a mere 50 metres away. It was probably the closest I'd been to her since March of the previous year, when she'd Havened me with her very own hands.

She was inside there, in her home and I felt a lightness I hadn't expected at the sight of her car, her cosy house, chatting with a friend in the lounge, while her little computer sat patiently in her study.

She was still alive. She hadn't died of COVID or heart failure. Perhaps I would go back without Matilda one day, I thought. I could pretend to visit Tuala and then I might just sit outside her house for as long as I wished, or at least for as long as my bladder held out and perhaps I'd even get a glimpse of her.

As we drove down the tree-lined road and turned off to Melbourne, I didn't cry. Matilda had subsided into an uncharacteristically heavy silence, but before long had dozed off again. Happily, I was free to think and reminisce.

I felt buoyed. It was so good to know Ronnie was on the mend, seeing clients again... not like me but normal people, with perhaps a spider phobia or weight issue. Not borderlines or anyone too sick, too unstable, too needy, obsessive, manic, paranoid, no cutters or nutters, just normal people with a bit of a problem.

No really, I felt happy because there had been little parts who were terrified she might have died. To see a car in the drive, a visitor, her little laptop waiting patiently for her to sit down with a cuppa to read her emails, felt greatly relieving.

I wondered if this was what closure felt like. Perhaps now she would shrink to the size of a normal person, a human-sized woman, with strengths and weaknesses and foibles, just another (rather wonderful) human being?

We cruised down the freeway and approached Melbourne which was shrouded in low cloud. The highway snaked down to a great, flat expanse and in the distance, the skyscrapers of Melbourne's CBD rose to meet the pale, winter sky. The sun shone from behind us, from Beechworth and Ronnie's house. To the west, a blanket of heavy, black cloud floated slowly toward Melbourne, but straight ahead of us, the sky was a cheerful pastel pallet of powder blues and pinks and dove grey.

Perhaps finally, I could replace this dreadful obsession with a more wholesome regard for myself, I thought with renewed hope. We snaked down the long incline, Matilda snoozing while I continued to examine the memory of what I had seen.

The weather was imperceptibly changing as we drove through the suburbs near to home and by the time we had turned into our street, the Pollyanna sky had become a dreary, slate grey and the storm from the west was hovering just over the near trees.

As I opened the car door a draught of cold, damp air displaced the cosy little bubble in which I had been wrapped, with Ronnie and her home. Matilda and I unloaded the car as the rain started to fall, thick and sharp.

I hadn't noticed how dreary the hallway was, cold, all colour drained from the walls. The respite had ended as quickly as it had begun. I had reverted Cinderella-like into the empty, forlorn little ghost I was, incapable of generating any substance, or warmth of my own. Salvation lived 220 kilometres away, in a blond brick house, because she lived there.

52

THE CURSE

I constantly feel an invisible foe is hitting me on the right side of my head and when I lie down in bed my stomach feels vulnerable, as if someone is attacking it, or about to. I suppose it is a PTSD 'flashback', although I can't see anything, can only feel it, so I assume it must be an implicit memory.

As I drove to my second EFT session with Jenny I was feeling tired and generally unwell, as if succumbing to a virus. It was a familiar feeling that has come and gone since my teens.

In the session I am hoping to release whatever trauma it was that woke in me the urge to bash Tuala's head in, a couple of weeks back. I had been standing with her in her paddock, close enough to smell the comforting scent of her warm, red coat and she had looked at me with such loving trust that suddenly I was blinded by rage and wanted to smash her skull in.

Despite the urge to hurt Tuala, the violent intrusions are usually directed toward me and have become so regular, they interrupt the practice of self-soothing. I might put my arms around myself to comfort a distressed child but become aware of another child squeezing her, or see my kind face morph into a monster's. I might provide comfort through Havening or massage my ears to activate my vagus nerve but the urge to hit or squeeze will disconcertingly flash across my mind.

Feeling ashamed and deeply flawed, I told Jenny what had been happening and we began to tap. Almost immediately, I saw my 18-month-old self in a cot, while Mum ranted and screamed. She grabbed both my arms, just below my little shoulders and squeezed. Intuitively, I could tell she wanted to strangle me, she was beside herself.

We had started to tap on the sickening urge I'd felt toward Tuala. It had been triggered by her vulnerability, but a few rounds of tapping had transported me back 55 years to that cot, to my mother's distress and rage.

When we'd finished the tapping sequence and I had become calm, Jenny told me the violence I felt belonged to my mother. Ronnie had told me the violent urges implied I had suffered physical violence and I would have dissociated to contain the terror.

When we are very young, we don't realise we are separate entities, that we resonate like a tuning fork with our mother's emotions. I had internalised Mum's rage, believing it to be my own, had bathed in it, soaked it up like a sponge but now as an adult I knew I must own and resolve it, no matter the origin.

Mum's legacy was a poisonous, destructive heirloom, passed unconsciously down the generations, from mother to daughter. One day, I had told Ronnie I felt a terrible curse had been placed upon me at birth and as we had tapped together, she had said, "...perhaps it is time for that curse to just fuck off..." but then she had gone and I had to disagree.

53

PLAY SCHOOL

Last night I dreamed of a beautiful, wild fox. She was hiding out in an old, deserted school. She let me pick her up and I felt the softness of her pelt and the warmth of her body.

If you've never been in your body because you've been chased out of it as a very small child because you dissociated to cope, how do you know you are not in your body right now? You don't, you can't!

I am trying to 'sit' with the pain and discomfort of being 'in my body' and it feels horrible. Still, I need to get back in there, to be 'embodied' because perhaps being in my body will help me to feel 'real'.

I've been listening to *Sensorimotor Psychotherapy* by Pat Ogden and Janina Fisher and it's very triggering as it's all about holding trauma in 'the body'. I started to listen to it and felt very anxious, which is a 'hold all' for unexpressed emotions, like fear and anger.

I am with Iona and telling her I can't feel any emotion relating to the traumatic and neglectful experiences I had as a child.

To be 'embodied' involves feeling the painful and frightening emotions of those times. At present, I only feel them in nightmares when they leak out through fissures in the 'wall'.

Iona suggests we do some experimenting and I attempt to 'sit' with the anxious feeling. This is extremely challenging and suddenly from the depths of my memory comes a horrifying scene from the movie '*Psycho II*'. There is a dreadfully big carving knife and the mother's severed head resting in a pile of coke and then an image of being stabbed over and over in the stomach, as a little two-year-old.

"No wonder they don't want to go there," I murmur to Iona. Next comes the image of an enormous mountain, at the base of which is a swarming mass of slimy, black beetles, which represent the two-year-olds. The eight-year-old manager part is sitting safely on the lofty summit, feeling smug.

Iona asks how I feel about that and I tell her, at first I felt frustrated that the two-year-olds are in exile, their feelings locked away, unable to be processed but now I felt safe. I have merged with the eight-year-old and want to be as far away from those revolting beetles as possible.

"Is this happening inside or outside of your body?" Iona asks. I don't understand what she means but know the answer anyway. "It is all outside of me."

My homework for the week is to listen to the *Sensorimotor Psychotherapy* book tape and endure the feelings of anxiety or whatever else might arise just for a minute or two. The aim is to learn to tolerate the discomfort it evokes. One model of dissociation refers to this as 'widening the window of tolerance'.

"And tell the little protector part, it's OK, you are safe. I am with you," finishes Iona.

I wandered home in the cool evening air, feeling that although I was still a huge mess, I was at least achieving small wins, and very occasionally felt OK. I had also started to separate a little from Ronnie and the previous Saturday, for the first time since she had left, had felt relief that we weren't meeting, with all the drama and overwhelm it had entailed.

Feeling OK was great while it lasted but that night we found ourselves on another fishing expedition. At some point over the past year, Ronnie had hidden her list of friends from the public domain however I bypassed this hitch by clicking on one of her friends who had commented on a post. Then I'd searched Ronnie's name in her friends' Facebook page and was ecstatic to see a list of Ronnie's comments to various posts.

God, I feel so ashamed and embarrassed to admit this because it sounds so sick and creepy.

But I didn't feel sick and creepy, just triumphant and happy, like I'd discovered a lost bank account full of money. There was something about an art show, 'the' art show developed by Ronnie and a group of like-minded artists in 2018. My eyes popped like saucers, as I read it was scheduled to be re-launched in three weeks' time.

Immediately, I bought tickets for Matilda and myself, reasoning that I couldn't hide my going off without her. I did consider telling a lie, "Oh," I could have said airily, just as Matilda was heading out the door for work, "I'm going to catch up with work friends," but wasn't sure I could pull it off as I'm not a very convincing liar.

"Matilda, Ronnie's show is on in a few weeks. I've bought us two tickets," I ventured the next evening.

Matilda registered a look of mild shock.

"Well, you don't have to come," I said hopefully, in a reassuring tone, "but I thought you might be interested?"

She said nothing and so I blustered on, "You're more into art than I am." I had always saved my money for opera. I said it lightly, in a matter-of-a-fact tone, not wanting to appear too excited. Reluctantly, Matilda agreed she would come with me and as I started to prepare dinner, opened her laptop and began scrolling.

Along with the anticipation of seeing Ronnie again in the flesh after 18 long months, I was curious to see her work in a live venue but also felt relief and rage in equal measure—she was well enough to venture into the public domain again, thank God and... what was it, only six months since she'd abandoned us?

Ever since Jenny had relayed the message that Ronnie was 'semi-retired', I had been feeling more and more anger and now that she was obviously well enough to work again, the anger turned to rage.

As Matilda sat at the dining room table laughing at the antics of dogs on skateboards, my internal monologue ramped up a notch—how irresponsible Ronnie had been to take on clients who were really damaged and then to get sick herself, because she did not know how to look after her health. God, she'd had a nerve to tell me she was modelling 'good self-care'. My eight-year-old ran rings around her and her so-called 'self-care'. I'd always known that no one would ever pick me up out of the gutter had I fallen apart. I'd had to rely on myself all my life. She had dropped her most vulnerable clients and then, when she was well enough, had simply moved on, without any acknowledgement of the pain and damage she'd caused, like a hit and run driver... and curse her, she had not sent that final Havening video.

Early on in our therapeutic relationship, I had found out about the 'show' and had watched the promo on YouTube many times and trawled for photos and interviews. The show combines visual art with music and opens with Ronnie singing a song which I badly wanted to hear but was worried she might stumble upon me as she roved through the patrons. Still, nothing short of catastrophe would keep me away.

"When did you say it's on?" Matilda asked, a note of apprehension in her voice.

"Why, what's wrong?" I snapped, instantly on the defensive. A flash of insight gave me a clue and I continued evenly. "Look, it's OK, I don't want to talk to her, I don't want her to see me."

Matilda still looked unsure, so I said, "But I never make scenes anyway, you know that." I put my hand on her shoulder and squeezed it reassuringly, "You know that's not my style."

She nodded and I continued, "It's just that it's been ages and the little kids want to see her, feel her energy, that's all." I stood beside Matilda, silent for another moment and added, "I can take someone else, if you don't want to go?"

"Oh, if you want to take someone else, that's fine pet," Matilda told me solicitously.

"Matilda, I didn't mean that. I want you to come," I answered but in truth, wished I could just go on my own and not have to worry about my feelings leaking out in front of her. "I'm just saying, if you are worried then you don't have to put yourself through it." I could tell she was remembering our unexpected stop outside Ronnie's home the month before.

As it turned out due to COVID, Melbourne was in yet another lock down. Ticket holders were sent a link to a pre-recorded video of the work and there was to be a live Q&A afterwards, with the artists, so Matilda and I sat in the comfort of our lounge room to watch. Suddenly a woman's contralto voice was heard. As heads turned toward the sound, the camera found the form of Ronnie, sitting on a chair singing, as if to herself and my insides squeezed tight with acute embarrassment as I knew Matilda would recognise the song. I had taught myself to play it with my new guitar during the first lock down. Now, she would know why.

After the video replay came the live question session. There was a momentary pause and then six faces popped onto the screen. There finally, was Ronnie. At last our lives intersected in the 'now', not that she would know.

She was unaware I was watching her intensely, ignoring the others, even when they spoke, noting every tiny change in her appearance, from the wave of her hair, her curving lips that occasionally curled into a smile and the familiar dear, grey eyes. I sat very close to the TV, as little kids do when staring up at their favourite bear or cartoon character. The eyes of my inner children watched her hungrily through the 57-year-old pair.

Now it's over and I am in bed, to endure a sleepless night. She looked good sitting in her study, with the familiar backdrop. A thought flashes through my head, like a blinding picture arrow. I will go and sit outside her house without Matilda. I will go tomorrow and will see her and run up to her and hold onto her. She will engulf me in a full, tight hug and kiss the top of my head, like I'm her precious, little girl. She will cry and tell us all she is sorry.

54

THE JAILOR

But even that won't be enough, even if she ate me and took the flesh and bone that I am into her body. I know this. I've been consumed, swallowed before by a witch, who spat me out. She ate me, then spat me out, then ate me up and spat me out and washed her mouth out with vinegar, to rid herself of the cloying sweetness. But she was hungry again and ripped me to pieces even though I was distasteful to her.

All this eating and spitting happened, just the two of us, intimate, close together, close enough to smell each other, like animals. That's how closeness works, you are too close and you need to get away quick and then you are too far away and the night creatures encroach. You cry out, she hears, and you are dead.

It is the night after the show and I'm feeling very depressed and missing Ronnie dreadfully. When Matilda had gone to bed, I took a bottle of pinot noir and a block of chocolate and sat outside under the full moon and the silent eucalyptus tree, to think and to cry. I've seen her now, finally. She is better and I must 'move on'.

Iona had told me I must let her go. But how? The thought of never, ever seeing her again, of never speaking to her, is unimaginable. How can I go for the rest of my life and not ever see her? Life is too short. Life is too important and I can't imagine it.

The memory of our last face-to-face session in Brunswick Street came back to me in heart-wrenching detail, of how I had walked out into the street after she'd Havened my children and held my hands in hers, not knowing it would be the last time I would ever be close to her, be in her presence.

The following Monday, I told Iona sheepishly about watching Ronnie's art show. I also told her I was experiencing the physical sensation of someone putting their finger into my vagina. I had been experiencing this feeling, or perhaps it was a flashback, for the past month. I told her about my discovery that Mum was a witch, who slobbered all over my mouth as she was trying to eat me. Finally, I told Iona about an attempt to rescue a ten-year-old child in distress and how the two-year-olds didn't like what I was trying to do and wanted me to leave things as they were and how there was someone hitting all the kids.

"Do you want to go there now?" asks Iona and I nod, immediately closing my eyes.

"Sit quietly and go inside," she prompts and after a moment asks, "Can you see something?"

I can sense a lot of kids inside me somewhere. "It's like an underground dungeon or prison," I tell her. "The walls are dark brown. There is no light, except for a faint glow coming from the barred trapdoor I'm looking through." I can discern a whole lot of little kids and others who I can't see. "I can see some older ones now, perhaps age ten and there is someone in charge, their 'jailor'. She hits them, spits at them, beats them and screams if they make a noise or want to go outside and play, or escape, or cry, especially if they cry."

"Why do you do that?" Iona asks the jailor.

I tell Iona, "She doesn't like to but she says she has to keep them in line."

The 'jailor' speaks up, "They will do worse than me. I need to hit them to keep them quiet for their own good, or we'll get in worse trouble."

The ten-year-old sits quietly opposite Iona, tears pouring from my eyes. Her middle fingers are straight and rub against my thigh. Her toes curl up and the nails dig into the bottom of my shoes. She jiggles our feet and presses our knees tightly together. I can feel her deep shame and utter loneliness.

She gathers herself and continues. "They might like me if I hurt the children and keep them quiet. They don't like noise. They want me to look after them, so they don't have to. They get mad if they have to."

"You know it's 2021 and you live in a beautiful house, you have a beautiful life, with Pepper and Matilda and Maisie," Iona tells the ten-year-old.

I'm still blended and Iona's words don't make an impression, I just feel blank. With effort, I attempt to reach her myself and say, "I am here to look after the little ones now. You don't have to anymore and anyway, Mum the witch is dead and Uncle Arthur is dead too." She still looks confused so I tell her about the feel of the warm sun on our head and the beautiful scent of jasmine blooming now that it is spring. I tell her she can come out and experience all of this when she is ready, but still she looks uncertain and undecided.

Later that night as I prepare for bed, there is a fierce argument raging inside my head. "Look, not again. Can't you shut up about Ronnie!?" a child is saying. "Who cares about her anyway!? Ronnie, Ronnie, Ronnie! She can go fuck herself! She left us and she made a promise not to. She let us down, really, really badly. We already didn't trust anyone and now she's made it even harder. I used to like cuddles but not anymore, not from anyone."

"Well," someone else says, "Ronnie's the most dangerous, with her smiling eyes and warm, happy words."

I think it must be an older child because she goes on, "Even Uncle Arthur was better because he didn't pretend to be nice. Hate is easier to take than when love leaves. He was always mad at me but I deserved it because I kept forgetting things. I wanted him to love me."

"I wish Ronnie would come back," pipes up a little tot.

55

THE TEA PARTY

I dreamed I was speeding along a country road at twilight and my sight began to fail. The car started to veer off the road as a motorbike roared past. As the car slowly lost speed, it bumped over something and I heard a groan. The car finally stopped but I just sat there, as I couldn't wake up.

Through the dopy fug I became aware I was now in a huge, old mechanics workshop. The motorbike man I had run over was lying on the ground groaning and I could tell his legs were lacerated. With supreme effort, I managed to open the car door but fell out and landed next to him. I was hoping someone would call an ambulance because I was too sleepy to do it.

Suddenly, the injured man stood, picked me up and carried me toward the wall. Hanging on the wall was an axe and the man told me he was going to kill me with it. I could see he was planning to tap, tap, tap it on my head, to chop, chop, chop me up. I opened my mouth to scream but only a faint scratching could be heard. That was lucky I thought, as I must not draw attention to myself.

A month has passed since Ronnie's show and I can feel a little of the 'spell' of Ronnie wearing off. I put this down to all the EFT I've been doing and the therapy sessions with Iona.

There is some distance now and I am not quite so interested in her life. Strangely, I feel a bit sad about it, I miss missing her, as ridiculous as this sounds. In place of the yearning and wanting and needing, is the depressing emptiness, a feeling something is missing, that my life can't start until I find it.

The 'distance' only lasted a little time. The void began to pull me back and I found myself Googling Ronnie, yet again. On this latest expedition I found a photo of her when she was only 21, her hair jet black, her clear, grey eyes pensive. I had done well to climb out of the 'emptiness' hole but had inadvertently fallen back into the 'obsession' hole.

Staring at the photo, I wondered if it had been taken around the time of her first 'Ho, ho holiday in hospital'. Perhaps she had just been diagnosed with borderline or bipolar? The familiar feelings of yearning and the desire to find more of her, with the frustration that I couldn't, carried me further away from the hollow feeling.

Had Ronnie attempted to end her life? I shouldn't 'romanticise' it, I thought, as there had been nothing romantic about Mum's attempt but I couldn't help myself. Didn't she have a choice? I wondered. She was so young, she must had felt overwhelmed. Was she coming down from a manic episode? Did she realise she was about to crash again into crushing depression?

I, on the other hand feel I have a choice—I could actively stop working hard to hold myself together, let go of the railing and fall but I can't, the drive to survive is too ingrained. I was groomed to please my caregivers by enduring. They didn't do 'Ho ho holidays in hospital', and neither did I. Still, I feel a searing sense shame and failure, that my stoicism is a weakness and an act of disloyalty to Ronnie.

I am obsessing in the kitchen as I make a chai for the kids, for a tea party with the cats, outside in the spring sunshine. I am trying to pull us out again, but it's touch and go.

We've drunk our chai, and I've mown the lawn and done some washing but when I stop, I am overcome with agitation. I sit and go inside to find a little toddler, trapped in my head and railing against the bars of her cage (it takes a while for this scene to materialise). There are ten-year-olds around the outside of the bars telling her, "You are pathetic, you've bottled it all up. All that poison, it's going to kill us all." I see a soft, naked worm being squished underfoot. This is the pain they are suppressing—the toddler who screams in vain for Mum to rescue her and the toddler who freezes in fear of Mum.

I can see the child again in the place of the worm. The ten-year-olds are keeping her locked away, so she can't go on a rampage. They have staffs and look brutal. Suddenly I feel so very weary and hear the one in charge telling me she doesn't want to have to rescue them all, it is way too much for her, she hates them and is way too tired.

5 6

BRIAN

It is midnight and I am observing the children, unnoticed. They are still locked in their prison, afraid to make a sound. It is deathly dark and I can sense more than see the group of militant children, the controlling managers of the prison, lurking.

Suddenly, fine gossamer threads of light appear. The moon has risen and shines her silver tracery onto the black metal bars of the prison, transforming them into smooth, pale-barked trees. The light falls onto the jailors and they become young wolves and tumble about together, playing and cavorting in what is now a peaceful forest. They have forgotten all about their jobs.

A little way away in the centre of a grassy clearing, where the sound of running water tickles the star-studded sky, a little two-year-old stands looking about her in wonder and delight.

It is still a feral place inside my head and although the transformation of one little being is complete, there are many, many more children to find and rescue and heal. Will we ever become completely human? I wonder? I check inside and see a wolf licking the toddler.

I lay on the sofa feeling very tired and uncomfortable in the gut. I go to cut up Pepper's meat and feel the urge to put a piece of raw steak into my mouth. I want wine but am wary, as it makes cutting more likely although Matilda is home. The tapping work I've been doing about Uncle Arthur's abuse has been destabilising. We never got that far with Ronnie, the attachment trauma was always too activated.

I chat away to Pepper, crooning lovingly, "Ooooo, dat's yummy for your tummy, good booooy!" All the while, a separate part is calling out orders inside my head, "Go on, cut yourself… eat that raw meat… hit him… open a bottle of wine… stab your bloody eye out."

The voice is quite insistent and I decide to drink some wine, which is the least destructive option although it will lower my inhibitions. I worry I will text Ronnie or get into the car and drive to her home. Without realising what I am doing, I open the cupboard and reach for the gin and the voice says, "Smash your hand in the door."

The next day was a better day, the kids and I had a lovely picnic together at a picturesque spot near where Tuala lives. After eating our sandwich and oat slice we wandered along the quiet, tree-lined country road, and I felt much more stable. My 'Self' was fully present and I felt like a 'different person'. The previous night I had been in danger of acting on what the 'voice' instructed.

Since starting trauma therapy, I have been incessantly assailed by the 'voices' of many 'parts' and would like to explain I am not schizophrenic—the 'voices' I 'hear' are 'echoes' of past traumas, 'pieces' of my embryonic personality, activated in the present moment, rather than the 'voices' schizophrenics hear, which I believe are perceived as emanating from external entities. My 'voices' become activated when the 'parts' are 'triggered', that is reminded of some past trauma in the present moment and communicate through vague yet intrusive visual thoughts, ideas, bodily sensations and dreams.

As troubling as it is to live with fragmented/dissociated 'parts', it is comforting and affirming to understand the 'parts' are not monsters (sometimes referred to as the 'ego') but merely hurt children who respond, even after all they've been through, to loving kindness. If I had not learned of 'parts' and 'inner children' from Ronnie, I would fear I was insane.

I continued the work with Iona and one day a few weeks after the picnic, a strange child turned up in a session. This 'part' was different and I felt perplexed because he was a boy of approximately two years of age and completely black, as if he'd been incinerated. His coarse, straight hair stood up on end and he was mutilated. Iona spoke gently and with great kindness asking, "Does he need bandages?"

"No, cuts on inside," he told her, through me.

"Does he need to go to the hospital?" Iona asked very gently.

I told Iona he was too afraid to go. She then asked if he would like to see Tuala but I could tell he was afraid of her too; he was afraid of everything. Then I saw the little boy look into Tuala's feed bucket and could tell he was very impressed with the quality and variety of her feed and I knew he was starving.

The little boy knew I put a lot of time and research into optimising Tuala's health, feeding her nourishing things to help with her little ailments and to keep her strong. The little black waif continued to inspect the horse's bucket and as he did, I felt a pleasant flood of relaxation in my body in response to his feelings of hope and wonder.

On my walk home from the session I pondered his sudden arrival. Where had this 'part' come from? Why was he a 'he' when my other parts were all younger versions of me? The boy was so incongruous to my internal landscape I wondered if I might have a dissociative disorder like dissociative identity disorder (DID), formally called multiple personality disorder, along with Q-BPD? Was he an 'alter', that is, a more fully formed, unique identity that had been split off at a point of overwhelm, to develop a separate personality unbeknownst to me?

The next day I decided to tap on the little boy. Shyly, he told me his name was Brian and he was me from a previous lifetime. He had been abandoned and was filthy with grime, rather than charred, thank goodness. He had somehow found his way to this present life to be released from the pain and chaos of his horrible existence.

57

SURRENDER

It has been eight months since Ronnie left and I know I am healing, the intensive therapeutic work is paying off. Yesterday I had an epiphany while sitting under the eucalyptus tree in the back garden. I was present to the soothing nature sights and sounds and was reminded of the work I do with Iona, the mindful 'sitting' and 'breathing'. Suddenly, I knew healing could possibly be as straightforward as surrendering to the 'present moment'. Simple, but not easy.

The great secret to being present to pain, of enduring internal mayhem rather than running away through distraction or dissociation, is to breath into the hurt while feeling curious about it. Breathing 'through' the waves of emotional distress widens the window of tolerance and processes the pain of stuck trauma. As a small child, I had learned to do the opposite, which was to hold my breath. Holding intensifies rather than diminishes feelings.

Ronnie had told me she considered mindfulness the most important tool in healing trauma. The second was creativity, without which healing is almost impossible. I knew as soon as she had said it that this was true for me. Music has always been an outlet for my tumultuous emotions, my confidant and dearest friend. Listening to and making music feels profoundly soothing and its beauty carries me beyond pain to loving connection with our universe.

In understanding the importance of being in the 'now', I realised that obsessing about Ronnie was in part, a way of avoiding being mindful of the discomfort of being in my body, of feeling empty, grief-stricken and lost. Cutting, drinking, obsessing, ruminating, excessive researching, vicious self-talk, fantasising about a future in which I would finally feel safe and be happy, these all took away from sitting with painful, scary feelings and the opportunity to befriend and process them.

In her book *Healing the Fragmented Selves of Trauma Survivors*, Janina Fisher tells us the first stage of healing trauma is widening the window of tolerance. The survivor must learn to bear the once unendurable emotions and sensations as they arise from the subconscious and are perceived in the body.

Being present means actively listening to the concerns and feelings of the inner children, as they are the source of the pain and emotional dysregulation. All of my life I had sought to push intrusive, unwelcome feelings away, not realising they resided in disowned child 'parts'. The neglected, tortured children did not know how to manage distress, were not taught to ride the waves of emotion, and so became swamped and overwhelmed and quite naturally sought to avoid feeling.

Fisher instructs us that, when the survivor can tolerate the discomfort of feeling, then the process of discharging the trauma is less distressing and more effective.

During the year with Ronnie, Tapping and Havening to

process the encapsulated trauma had provided some down regulation of my nervous system but counter to this was the insurmountable obstacle of my attachment trauma, which she unintentionally triggered. The subsequent fear of abandonment was all consuming and excruciatingly painful and it exacerbated my propensity to dissociate and emotionally dysregulate.

To be fair to Ronnie, I was no easy client. I was what some therapists refer to as 'resistant' or 'untreatable'. At the start of our therapeutic relationship, I had appeared integrated, but this was a front, a mask I did not know I wore. As soon as Ronnie admitted she could 'see' the 'inner children', the needy parts 'attached' to her. From that moment, their fear of abandonment overwhelmed both 'me' and the process.

As the year progressed although she didn't admit it, I suspect Ronnie found the internal push and pull increasingly difficult to navigate and more and more frequently suggested 'I' 'let go'. "... if you could just let go of the pain," she'd say, as we Havened together, "... let go of the fear, because it belongs in the past, with Mum and Uncle Arthur." Unfortunately, the desperate little three-year-old 'parts' thought this meant they must let go of her.

To my adolescent parts, being told to 'let go of the pain' had the same ring as 'get over it' or 'just forgive him/her'. In my experience, people with unresolved trauma sometimes say these things to shift their own discomfort. Through the course of my life, so-called 'enlightened' people have told me to 'forgive'—forgive Mum, forgive Uncle Arthur, "for your sake," they'd say. A psychologist once suggested forgiveness was a choice—one simply made the decision to forgive and just like that, the barnacle-encrusted hull was scraped free of obstruction. I had felt quite inadequate and guilty because I couldn't find a way to release feelings of resentment, anger, hurt and need just by instructing my head to do it.

It might sound counter-intuitive, but I believe forgiveness happens when we forgive ourselves, that is when our wounded child 'parts' are healed and recouped. Listening to and meeting the unmet emotional needs of damaged inner children provides a profound sense of relief. This is because children have no filter for the damaging behaviour of their caregivers. Sick, traumatised or dangerous parents threaten the life of the child, the knowledge of which is intolerable. In the face of existential threat, the child takes on the mantle of the 'bad' child, while casting the damaging caregivers as the 'good' parent. I am 'bad' and that is why I am treated unfairly or hit or raped or ignored.

Taking on the parents' emotional dysfunction comes at a cost though, as the child carries a burden of debilitating shame into adulthood and quite probably passes it down to the next generation. Forgiving the selves inactivates toxic shame and this is possible when the young parts are listened to and nurtured. Letting them know 'it's not your fault' and 'you did nothing wrong', feels deeply, marvellously relieving and freeing. Self-love lifts the burden of guilt and renders the act of forgiveness to perpetrators irrelevant.

When I was 31, with the thought of forgiveness an impossibility, I cut all ties with Mum. A few years previous I had begun therapy with the express purpose of 'fixing' myself so we could build a healthy relationship, but another act of betrayal finally opened my eyes. I was forced to accept that I alone could not create a healthy relationship with Mum if she was not willing to also do the work. You can only build a bridge halfway across the divide. If you attempt to go beyond, the bridge will collapse.

I was crushed to understand we could never be close and worse than that, if I put myself in her path, she would continue to hurt me. So I didn't see her again for another five years. In the intervening period, Mum moved to live near her parents. She was still hoping Nanna would, after a lifetime of waiting, tell her she was loved. She waited in vain and was diagnosed with dementia and shortly after developed cancer.

A friend of hers phoned me one evening to tell me that Mum was in palliative care at Gosford hospital. I took leave from work and drove the 14 hours to see her for the last time. By the time I arrived, she was unconscious and did not regain consciousness. I called Luke home from his long overseas trip and he spent a final night with his beloved Mum in a little bed the nursing staff prepared for him.

On the following afternoon, after hours of sitting at her bedside, Luke, Dad and Grandad returned home. I stayed and settled down to send both Mum and Nanna some comforting Reiki. As the afternoon waned, a feeling of dreamy tranquillity settled over the room. There was the fragrant scent of jasmine, a wild tangle of the starry-flowered creeper laying at the foot of Mum's bed, while outside the window, crimson rosella's chattered and squeaked as they dangled from the weeping branches of a beautiful, red-flowered gum.

It was a strange situation because Nanna had been admitted to the same hospital a few days after Mum with a suspected obstructed bowel. I had asked Nanna if she would like me to organise a wheelchair so she could say goodbye to her daughter, but she told me in a quiet voice, "No, I don't think so." Nanna then passed on exactly one week after Mum.

Sometime later as evening approached and I stood watching the birds, the voice of Mum's lovely, gentle palliative care doctor said from behind, "How long has your mother been breathing erratically?" I turned to see Mum's breathing had lost its rhythm. We watched as she took another breath and then stopped. The doctor bent over, her face close to Mum's and placed a stethoscope on her chest. I was holding my breath. A sudden inhale, Mum's last breath, caused the doctor to jump and drop her stethoscope. Looking mortified she whispered, "So sorry" but incongruously, I thought it was funny, very slapstick, and stuffed down the urge to laugh.

I called the men back to say their farewells and sat close to 90-year-old Grandad, who had lost his daughter and in a week's time would lose his wife. Grandad could not bear to be hugged or kissed or touched but coped with the comfort of my thigh pressed against his for a little while.

Later, when they'd gone back to Nanna and Grandad's, staff came to take Mum's body to the morgue, and someone switched on the light. The face that had been cast in shadow revealed itself to be smiling softly. The eyes behind the closed lids had seen something, something or someone wonderful. I couldn't take my eyes off her face, as I had never seen her looking so wonderstruck and serene. We do go home then, I thought and from the look on her face, I knew that's where she'd gone.

I now understand complex trauma is a living legacy, a curse and is bigger than my own trauma. And the work I have done with both Ronnie and Iona has provided insight as well as some relief and I now feel a level of compassion for my mother, grandmother, for all my maternal forbears and for all the suffering in the world. It is caused by trauma, by a lack of love. This is the mature perspective of my 'Self' and I hold both the compassionate understanding of the bigger picture alongside the emotional hurt of my inner children.

To heal, the lost parts need us to bear witness to their pain, to validate their suffering, to see them in all their innocence and beauty. To 'see' and to love what we see, is to build a sense of trust. It is to envisage beyond the weary branches the eternally young sapling within. The inner children require the wise inner adult to bear compassionate witness to their rage and grief. Without this, 'forgiveness' is impossible.

58

VENUS AGAIN

Last night I dreamed I was in a stately house with a group of women and we were participating in some sort of alternative healing course. It was morning tea-time and the huge, light-filled Edwardian 'morning' room was full of the sound of enthusiastic chatter and the tinkle of fine bone China cups on saucers.

I mentioned my mother in passing to the group I was standing with, and a woman said enthusiastically, "Why, she's here too". I felt confused because I thought Mum was dead. Then someone else gushed, "Oh yes, she'd really love to see you."

I shrank back as another woman grabbed my arm and said, as if offering me a lovely treat, "I'll get her for you." I backed away, shaking off the hand and said, my voice unnaturally loud, "Oh no, please don't." But even as I spoke, I knew she was coming.

I ran desperately through the crowded room but was stopped by a fence, which I began to climb. Confused, I saw it was a balcony rail and as I straddled it, it broke, but rather than fall, I floated slowly toward a dark carpet of lawn that stretched into the distance. It was crossed with higgley-piggledy lines of big, dark trees, far, far below and in the distance, I could see the lawn was swallowed by a brooding, impenetrable forest. I landed lightly onto the soft grass at the edge of the woods, and night fell.

There was a gingerbread house all pretty and mosaiced with sweets. The door was open and light and the scent of caramel spilled over the threshold into the velvet blackness. Inside her dainty house I could hear the witch. She was speaking cheerfully to herself, saying "Yes, and pack those sweets too." I knew they were for the children. With a feeling of impending catastrophe, I stole away but the witch knew where I was, even as she talked cheerfully to herself and ambled after me.

A film came over my eyes and I was blinded. I could sense her as I fled, stumbling and careening over the rough ground. Then she was beside me, putting her arm around my shoulder, looking at me and smiling. I shuddered and pretending she wasn't there, stumbled blindly on.

All at once, I realised I was dreaming and began a desperate fight to wake up. I couldn't bear to go where the witch would take me. "Wake up, wake up!" I could not loosen the grip of irresistible drowsiness.

'Surrender', came the thought from somewhere outside the dream and the spell broke. All at once I became aware of two large, white birds nestling together cosily in a tree hollow to my left. Completely non-plussed, I watched the birds. They weren't moving. Cream walls materialised around the pair of cockatoos in their wooden frame and somewhere the wholesome sound of a magpie's warble, vibrated warmly in the air and my heart lifted. Bright and beautiful morning light spilled through the window. With relief, I realised I was home.

In December one year almost to the day of our final session before the long six-week Christmas break, I am taking the kids to see Ronnie give a talk in Beechworth, on using creativity to heal trauma. I found the advertisement on Ronnie's Facebook feed of course, although the organiser had posted it there, rather than Ronnie. Ronnie hasn't posted anything on her own feed since she got sick.

I can hardly believe a whole year will have elapsed since I left her shaky but resolute, with her promise we would reconvene the following February. Of course, that had not happened.

I can't wait and the parts are very excited as I write this. It's such an unknown though and I feel some trepidation. How are they/we all going to cope? It could be healing, could be a disaster! It might destroy the fantasy we built in our mind of our Lovely Lady.

How will she react if she sees me, sees us? Will she be hugging all her friends, who I imagine will turn up to support her? Will she acknowledge us, will she still recognise me? Will I be able to hide myself from her? What if it's cancelled again? It was supposed to take place in September but was rescheduled to early December because of COVID. What if there is another lockdown? What if she talks to me? What if she talks to us all? What if she doesn't talk to any of us? What will she look like? Will she smile? How will we feel seeing her again and being in her physical presence? Will we put her off her talk? Will we go back to feeling devastated?

As a way of justifying going, I decided it would be a test of sorts. If the parts got triggered, then I'd know we had more work to do and if they didn't, which was extremely unlikely, then I would be free to pursue the healing of my childhood traumas without crying every five minutes about Ronnie.

It's now one week before the gig and replacing some of the excitement is a feeling of anger. We are gutted in fact, because

Ronnie has taken the 'I am currently not taking on new clients' banner off her website. When she'd been sick, well who could blame her for putting her healing first? But the lack of signage is an announcement to the world she is 'open for business' again.

In our last ever session, she told me her doctor had "told her" to give up work and she implied it was for good. "I have to let you go Michele because my doctor told me to," is how it sounded to me. But then six months later in August, she had been well enough to do a public gig, even though it hadn't eventuated. Now, she was to give a presentation on healing trauma and was taking on new clients again. Such betrayal!

She could still have been true to her word and come back to explain, to give me closure, but she hadn't. She had crashed, taken us out and when she had recovered, had moved on without a backward glance. I feel so dreadfully let down all over again.

And I know people 'talk things up', but to read in her biographical notes she was *On a brief break from her trauma therapy practice... to deliver her art piece*, well really! On reading that, the kids feel erased.

There it is again, people don't want to work with borderlines, even 'quiet' ones apparently, because we are too needy, too much, too difficult, too draining. I'll bet she picked up some of her previous clients, just not me and that other borderline girl she was seeing. Ronnie had had borderline, so she knew about our terror of abandonment; it had been hers too once.

Perhaps the witch in the dream was Ronnie. For a time, she had been nice and kind and responsible, but in the end had been like all grown-ups, had run away to save herself, abandoning us in the dark forest. When she had recovered, rather than coming back in search of us she had moved on and had not even had the decency to apologise.

Perhaps the witch in the dream was kind? A 'white witch'? Was she perhaps Iona, guiding me down to Hell, to sit horrified with the mutilated children? The terror of the witch is the terror of the therapy hour. I want to flee, to leave them in their hole because I can't stand to feel their pain.

Was the witch my mother, after all? Laughing and charming those naïve, stupid women in that big, bright house, masquerading as one of them? Was that her gingerbread house? Was she the old hag, drawing us into her orbit with her delicious goodies, intent on eating us?

Perhaps it's me… in consuming me, have I become the witch, full of poisonous, black rage? Is that old woman with the sweeties, actually me?

Early on in our year together, witnessing my acute distress, Ronnie had told me that after we had cleared the big traumas, life would get easier. "You won't even want to come to a session because you'll be feeling so good," she'd said, but that had never happened. Instead, I had become subsumed in a painful tug of war, pulled apart by the competing needs and fears of the parts, which was caused not by 'big traumas' such as the abuse dished out by Uncle Arthur but by my damaged attachment system.

As we had battled on, Ronnie had told me on more than one occasion she needed to understand how my nervous system worked. "Every one's nervous system is different," she'd say but as the year progressed, the therapy had become more and more bogged down. The parts had become less trusting, not more; more afraid, not less.

Toward the end of the year, Ronnie sought to improve the therapeutic process by encouraging my 'Self' to communicate directly with the children while she supported 'me'. In the lead up to this point though, the sessions had become longer as the parts had demanded more attention via text and email between sessions. Counter intuitively, the more attention Ronnie paid to the little ones, the greater their need for her became, although I can imagine it would feel like the right thing to do.

Ronnie wasn't the first therapist to fall into this trap, nor will she be the last, seduced by the sweet, neediness of the little ones, wanting to erase their pain. Janina Fisher calls it "severe attachment wounding"—"These are often very high function individuals and what we don't see at first are the cracks in the foundations... and often I don't quite realise what I've gotten myself into until the quicksand starts to pull me down, and I start to feel stuck and I start to feel confused." Was this Ronnie's experience too?

Ronnie had known about polarised, warring 'parts' because she had had them too. She had told me they are a hallmark of borderline and although she had healed from her illness, still, when she was stressed, her parts took over and she fell into her own version of mental and physical dysfunction, "... down a 'mine shaft'..." as she referred to it.

It's late now for a change and I've been lying in bed, trying to puzzle out the strange episode in my life called 'Trauma Therapy with Ronnie'. I feel a little weird, as though I have lost something and then realise it is very quiet in my head. Where are the kids? They must have all gone to sleep? Ever since I found out they were there in that first session, they always seem to be with me, usually by way of a painful feeling in my abdomen or a sad mood, or the helpful voice that whispers of neat ways to end it all.

On the morning of Ronnie's talk, I woke in the stillness before the dawn and heard a little child singing to herself, like a small bird piping a sweet tune to greet the sun. As I listened, she became aware I was there and the song abruptly stopped. I haven't heard her again but wish she would come back. I hope she is OK.

It was 9.30pm when I finally drove away from Beechworth. Venus was bright and lovely, blinking benignly as the moon set on the western horizon. Three hours earlier I had been sitting at a little antique table writing on a scrap of paper I had scrounged from the bottom of my backpack. I was looking for a distraction to stop myself from crying. As she had been preparing her props for her talk, Ronnie had spotted me and smiling, had left her little stage to talk with me.

She had asked how I was going but I hadn't been able to speak and had just sat staring up at her in a parody of the start of our former Saturday sessions. There had been a quick, almost imperceptible twitch of her hand toward mine and an almost imperceptible response from my own, traitorous one. I hadn't stood up because my body was subsumed by a storm of competing urges.

She had looked down at me, smiling her very wide, dear smile, that crinkled up the sides of her nose. My mouth had smiled back but my eyes had stared. I really wanted to tell her that Iona thought I had DID, because that's the worst, the hardest one to live with, worse than borderline, Ronnie had once told me. I wanted to say, "She thought so, because when you left I was so fractured," but all I managed was, "I don't know what to say." Ronnie then said she didn't either.

After a few moments she must have remembered speaking with Jenny and asked how EFT was going. "OK," I shrugged. I didn't want her to think everything was now hunky dory and she was off the hook. We watched her, the little ones blushing, while the angry ones tried to maintain their cool, which was melting fast. Then she went back to her preparations and I started to cry. That's when I had done the rummaging and had written furiously about witches.

At the end of the talking and questions and applause, a woman in her 40s went up to Ronnie on the stage and they embraced. We watched avidly. Then infuriatingly, the man sitting in front got up and blocked our view as he stretched and messed around, slowly gathering his belongings. At long last he moved and I could see they were still hugging, arms wound around each other's ribs, hands clasping each other's backs like frogs on a lily pad. Eventually, they had broken apart and then another woman had introduced herself and they began to chat too.

Throughout the talk, I could feel a kid inside sneering at Ronnie. She kept up a fierce tirade though out most of the talk about how she'd been playing hide and seek with Ronnie but Ronnie had disappeared while she was 'it' counting down in a dark hole and how come Ronnie was playing with other kids now but she wasn't allowed to play, and supposedly it wasn't her fault! Eventually I had the presence of mind to attempt to come to the fore, which I managed, until the kids all saw her hugging that other, lucky woman and tears threatened again.

Still, on the way home in the car on the quiet, smooth freeway with another cloudbank to the west rumbling and flashing, a sense of peaceful satisfaction settled over them. The little ones had wrested back some semblance of control. Ronnie had gone but we had contrived to see her again, just to know we could, if we so wished.

Venus twinkled fitfully as she approached the luminous cloudbank and I shifted uncomfortably in my seat. I had forfeited the past two years of my life, yearning and obsessing over a fantasy, an ideal, birthed into existence by a tribe of emotionally abused and neglected children. Ronnie was a beautiful, unattainable construct, an illusion. I had visited that particular hell on numerous occasions in the past, obsessed with other kindly women who I hoped might replace my empty mother.

    It's now 2.30am. I didn't expect to sleep and the three-year-olds have endured another bout of crying, for the love and loss of their Ronnie. They always come with their grief. I tap and write and Haven and finally lie down and sleep.

59

DEAR MICHELES

And so, to the 'Dear Michelle' email, with the two Ls and the 'Kind regards'. After Ronnie's talk, I wrote explaining why I had taken the children to see her, and that we wouldn't make a habit of turning up to her gigs and hoped we hadn't put her off? She wrote back and assured me we hadn't. She also said she had, "Slowed right down with the practice and was just seeing people from Beechworth."

"Yeah well, her website says she is available for appointments online, 'all suburbs'," says the sneering one.

Where there was grief, now all is anger. Why won't she apologise? Then we could all move on. The sense of injustice is galling and the older kids who understand the meaning of betrayal are livid, while the three-year-olds can still only grasp she is not coming back. The night fades as the little kids take up my phone and write:

You didn't spell our name right in that email you sent last. You forgot is spelled Michele not Michelle. You didn't even care enough to get that right. You are better now but you could have said sorry now for leaving but you said you don't know what to say, just sorry and it would have made us all better, just sorry, I'm sorry that's all. You could have made amends. We understood when you were sick but you are not now but you are not sorry. This makes you like all the rest. One word would have changed the world.

It's not that you left, it that you didn't say sorry, you never said sorry.

To be fair to Ronnie, perhaps she was concerned she might destabilise me by making contact and thought it best I resolve the angry feelings with Iona, but I'll never know. The kids are deeply upset and I cast around for something to help and an idea pops into my head and I begin to write an imaginary letter from Ronnie to the kids:

Dear Micheles, little and big, ☺

Thank you so much for coming to see me the other night in Beechworth, it was so wonderful to see you again.

I am writing to you all to let you know I am so very sorry for the way I treated you. I made a big mistake in leaving so unexpectedly when I had promised I never would. I want you to know it was entirely my fault, not yours, you did absolutely nothing wrong and didn't deserve to be treated in such a bad way. I had a duty of care but instead I let you down. I know I hurt you terribly and added to your pain, rather than helping.

Do you know, I still love you and always will and I will never, ever forget you. I can see how beautiful you are and how deserving of love you are too. You are very special to me and will always hold a warm place in my heart.

One day if you still want to, we can meet and I will say sorry to you in person. Michele's Self will know when you are ready. We both want what's best for you and I'll be here waiting for you all. I will wait for you for as long as you need, even if that is forever.

I often think of you and wonder how you are getting on and pray to the Divine that you are feeling safe and happy with Michele and Pepper and Maisie and Matilda and Tuala.

Remember, I love you and always will.

Sending you all my love now.

Until we meet again,

Ronnie xxx

EPILOGUE

"What do they want to tell me?" asks Iona smiling curiously.

There's big trees and Tuala picks up her bowl. She throws it away. She wants carrots. We laugh. Birds eat her dinner. There's trees and cows. There's goats. Pepper is big. He loves us. Tuala runned and bucked. The vet said she is a good girl. She smelled nice. She is big. We love her.

Iona and I were discussing Ronnie for the first time in a while, as I had dreamed about seeing her again. It had started the kids fantasising about organising a coffee catch up. Would she finally apologise? We were exploring angles, emotions, the motivations of the parts and for the first time ever, one of the little tots got angry. This was real progress.

We were all following the blue tip of Iona's pen as we did EMDR and the little kids started to laugh, because it reminded them of a buzzy bee, making random detours back and forth, up, down and around. A little two-year-old suddenly put two and two together and thought it would be a good idea if the buzzy bee 'bit' Ronnie on the bum. "Mean Ronnie," for leaving us. She gave her arm a wide swing, as little ones do from the shoulder, as if hurling a discus, right at her bottom. I could feel her anger in my chest.

Then the related subject of abandonment came up:

"That's the borderline," said Iona.

"Mum, the borderline 'Waif'", I said.

"She wanted men to rescue her," said Iona.

"And I wanted kind women to rescue me."

Neither Mum nor I could conceive of saving ourselves, we were stuck at the helpless stage of development, relying on our mothers to save us from big, furry monsters with sharp teeth. I tried to explain the feeling to Iona, the absolute vulnerability: "It's like floating on the ocean at night, sensing the bottomless abyss below my dangling feet..." I lifted my legs off the floor.

"Unseen killers are circling below, waiting to rip you to pieces or worse, you sink and sink into impenetrable blackness, drowning, drowning but never dead."

We started another set of EMDR. Alone and abandoned, little fragments float like flotsam on the endless sea, the void calling them. We watch the progress of the pen's blue tip. "The sun is coming out," I whisper. This has never happened before, the scene is spontaneously transforming.

"We aren't alone, there are whales down there."

The biggest of the big, blue whales glide easily, flukes undulating hypnotically like a steady heartbeat, serene and comfortable in their world. Thick columns of sunlight dance their way into the depths. The whales will not let us sink and the ocean is not that deep after all. I can see a tiny plug in the sandy bed where the abyss should be.

When the whole 'Ronnie chapter' began in 2020, I wasn't sure what healing meant. When the 'parts' turned up in that first session and began to hurt like hell, I assumed healing meant they would disappear, I really hoped they would. That feeling has shifted 180 degrees and I have grown to love and appreciate all my 'parts', even the 'difficult' ones. All want to be free of their painful conditioning, to live joyfully, rather than

EPILOGUE

embodying loss, abandonment, shame, rage and fear. Together we create the complex jigsaw called Michele, each and every 'piece' integral to who 'I' am.

It is now late-2023, almost three years since Ronnie left so unexpectedly and my life is continuing to improve. In February 2022, I completed a clinical EFT course run by Dawson Church and EFT Universe and although I don't intend to practice professionally, I have been tapping with a fellow student once a week, working through the list of traumas and day-to-day issues. Each session has a soothing and grounding effect and I always feel calmer even when we don't process the big stuff.

Iona and I have continued our weekly somatic psychotherapy sessions. They are vitally important in helping me to heal the attachment wounds and to build relational skills and set boundaries. In addition, we also use EMDR to process trauma and integrate the experiences of the many child parts. The work can be slow and frustrating at times, as some 'parts' are still reluctant to be 'seen' and are very afraid of crying in front of Iona as their burden of shame is immense. They cannot be rushed though, nor should they be. There is a saying, 'go slow to go fast'.

Mindfulness and meditation provide further support to my trauma healing. The first mindfulness technique I learned was Transcendental Meditation (TM) when living with Lee in my mid-20s. It is a powerful tool for calming nervous system activation, managing stress and enhancing physical health.

In 2020, Ronnie introduced me to the Trust Technique to help calm Tuala's anxiety. The Technique is designed to build deep, harmonious relationships with animals. The method involves staying mindfully present to ambient sounds and bodily sensations in the presence of animals and it has a calming, regulatory effect on both animal and human. I began the online course in 2020 but the process was way too confronting for a bunch of dysregulated kids and I only returned to it a few months ago. I'm proud to say, I now have a strong enough 'Self' to practice this powerful yet gentle adjunct to EFT, EMDR and somatic psychotherapy.

Finally, there is Reiki, which I have been practicing for almost 30 years. I still use it regularly, sending Tuala energy when she is feeling anxious, to Pepper to manage his gut issues, to my inner children, to Matilda after a recent major operation, to the Middle East. Reiki has supported my passage through a difficult life and I wouldn't be here today without it.

In mid-2022, Matilda and I moved to the leafy outer suburbs of Melbourne, a semi 'tree change', close enough to Matilda's work but far away from the wearing chaos of inner-city living. When we lived in Northcote I was constantly reminded of the 'bad' years when I had struggled with depression, anxiety and PTSD, and had had the 'breakdown', and our Northcote home will always remain inextricably linked to Ronnie, in the familiar streets, the desperate walk I took during lockdowns to the All Nations Park, my suicide spot near her old home and the place we met for that first, fateful session.

By contrast, our new environment is fresh and green and novel. Sulphur crested cockatoos shriek, kookaburras laugh at dawn and dusk, red and green king parrots hang off the trees and bronze wing pigeons pick and coo in the grass outside the windows of our sunny, north-facing lounge room, causing much indignant consternation from Pepper and Maisie. Out the back, in our huge sloping rear garden, Matilda and I planted lemon scented and weeping snow gums, banksia and bottle brush, sticky wattles, and cherry and plum trees. The children are delighting in their rampant growth.

And what of Ronnie? The intense feelings of grief and guilt, of anger and longing have greatly reduced but yes, I do occasionally pop onto her Facebook page and wish I could just pick up the phone and call her to discuss the momentous year that was 2020.

Ultimately, it was I who attracted Ronnie into my life. I needed her help to dismantle the 'wall' and she arrived on-cue like a summer storm, intense and powerful but ultimately nourishing, soothing and healing when all was parched and dying. Her empathy, her insight broke me apart so I could weave the pieces into wholeness and know 'I' am enough.

In sharing with you my story of hurt and healing I hope, dear reader, to bring to light the sinister and lingering effects of childhood trauma and the hidden nature of mental illness. We are primed for loving connection but when we are hurt by the ones we love and become damaged ourselves, we inevitably hurt ourselves and others. We must break the cycle by holding the pain of our disowned parts with love.

If you enjoyed *A Hole Where My Heart Should Be: Lifting the Curse of Intergenerational Trauma* and have the time, please consider writing a review. ☺

REFERENCES AND RESOURCES

Books

Dissociation Made Simple: A Stigma-Free Guide to Embracing Your Dissociative Mind and Navigating Daily Life, Jamie Marich, PhD, North Atlantic Books

Healing the Fragmented Selves of Trauma Survivors: Overcoming Internal Self-Alienation, Janina Fisher, Taylor and Francis Ltd.

Internal Family Systems Therapy, Second Edition, Richard C. Schwartz and Martha Sweezy, Guilford Publications

Many Lives, Many Masters: The True Story of a Prominent Psychiatrist, His Young Patient, and The Past-Life Therapy That Changed Both Their Lives, Brian L. Weiss, MD, Touchstone

Mind to Matter: The Astonishing Science of How Your Brain Creates Material Reality, Dawson Church, Hay House

No Bad Parts: Healing Trauma and Restoring Wholeness with the Internal Family Systems Model, Richard C. Schwartz, PhD, Sounds True

Riding Between the Worlds: Expanding our Potential Through the Way of the Horse, Linda Kohanov, New World Library

Sensorimotor Psychotherapy: Interventions for Trauma and Attachment, Pat Ogden and Janina Fisher, WW Norton & Company

Tapping into Past Lives: Heal Soul Traumas and Claim Your Spiritual Gifts with Quantum EFT, Jenny Johnston

The Body Keeps the Score: Brain, Mind, and Body in the Healing of Trauma, Bessel van der Kolk MD, Penguin Books

The EFT Manual, Dawson Church, Energy Psychology Press

The Emotionally Absent Mother: How to Recognize and Heal the Invisible Effects of Childhood Emotional Neglect, Jasmin Lee Cori, Expertelligence

The Highly Sensitive Person: How to Thrive When the World Overwhelms You, Elaine N. Aron, Element. An imprint of Harper Collins

The Power of Attachment: How to Create Deep and Lasting Intimate Relationships, Diane Poole Heller, PhD, Sounds True

The Toa of Equus: A Woman's Journey of Healing and Transformation Through the Way of the Horse, Linda Kohavov, New World Library

Transforming the Living Legacy of Trauma: A Workbook for Survivors and Therapists, Janina Fisher, PESI Publishing & Media

Trauma and Memory: Brain and Body in a Search for the Living Past: A Practical Guide for Understanding and Working with Traumatic Memory, Peter A. Levine, North Atlantic Books

Understanding the Borderline Mother: Helping Her Children Transcend the Intense, Unpredictable, and Volatile Relationship, Christine Ann Lawson, Jason Aronson Inc.

Waking the Tiger: Healing Trauma, Peter A. Levine, Random House US

When Things Fall Apart: Heart Advice for Difficult Times, Pema Chodron, Shambhala

Will I Ever Be Good Enough: Healing the Daughters of Narcissistic Mothers, Karyl McBride, PhD, Atria. A Division of Simon and Schuster, Inc.

Your Thyroid Problems Solved: Holistic Solutions to improve your thyroid, Sandra Cabot MD, Margaret Jasinska ND, WHAS Pty Ltd

Links

ENERGY MEDICINE
Usui Reiki network
https://Reiki.com.au/

MINDFULNESS AND MEDITATION
Transcendental Meditation Australia
https://tm.org.au/
The Trust Technique
https://trust-technique.com/

PSYCHOSENSORY THERAPIES
EFT Universe
https://eftuniverse.com/
EMDR Association of Australia
https://emdraa.org/

HAVENING TECHNIQUES
https://havening.org

PSYCHOTHERAPY
Somatic Psychotherapy Australia
https://somaticpsychotherapy.asn.au/

INTEGRATIVE MEDICINE
Australasian Integrative Medicine Association
https://www.aima.net.au/
The Thyroid Pharmacist, Izabella Wentz
https://thyroidpharmacist.com/

Made in United States
Orlando, FL
28 October 2024